Gretel's

March 2, 2017

Meredith Wayne Price

For Barbara,

Enjoy & cherish life's
adventure and love those
who share your journey.

Meredith Wayne Price

Uberauen Publishers
Ormond Beach, Florida

Publisher's Note: Most of the action in this novel takes places in the fictional
town of Uberauen during the first half of the 20th century. The story is a work
of fiction based on family oral history. Liberties have been taken with names,
places, and dates. The story is based in part on actual events and actual people;
but most of the characters have been invented, and those that are portrayed
as occupying certain official positions bear no resemblance whatever to the
persons that actually held those positions at the time described in the novel.

Book design by Frances Keiser of Sagaponack Books & Design
Cover design by Hubert Forner

ISBN: 978-0-9971097-0-2 (softcover)
978-0-9971097-2-6 (hard cover)
978-0-9971097-1-9 (e-book)

Library of Congress Catalog Card Number: 2016902490

Summary: Gretel and the men and women of her family confront
upheaval as the 20th Century unfolds and world wars erupt.
Based on historic times and true family events of forbidden
romance and love affairs, gossip, suicide and deaths, life plays out
in the surroundings of their medieval walled village.

FIC014000   Fiction / Historical / Germany / 1914-1945
FIC041000   Fiction / Biographical / Cultural Heritage
FIC066000   Fiction / Small Town & Rural

www.uberauen.com

Uberauen Publishers
Ormond Beach, Florida

Printed and bound in USA
First Edition

Gretel's Cross is dedicated to my spouse, Hubert Forner,
and to the memory of his delightful mother, Gretel.

Hubert D. Forner, 1991

Family Tree of Gretel Geyer 1904 - 1990

*(The names and dates of Gretel Geyer, her husband Otto Forner, and their sons
are accurate. Names and dates of many family members have been fictionalized.)*

First marriage of Barbara Schmitt

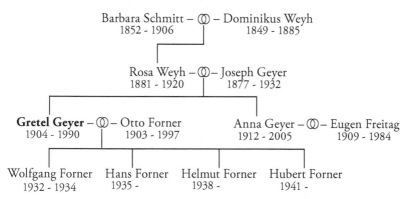

Barbara Schmitt – ⓪ – Dominikus Weyh
1852 - 1906   1849 - 1885

Rosa Weyh – ⓪ – Joseph Geyer
1881 - 1920   1877 - 1932

Gretel Geyer – ⓪ – Otto Forner   Anna Geyer – ⓪ – Eugen Freitag
1904 - 1990   1903 - 1997   1912 - 2005   1909 - 1984

Wolfgang Forner   Hans Forner   Helmut Forner   Hubert Forner
1932 - 1934   1935 -   1938 -   1941 -

Second marriage of Barbara Schmitt

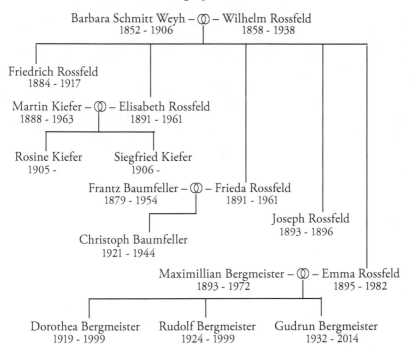

Barbara Schmitt Weyh – ⓪ – Wilhelm Rossfeld
1852 - 1906   1858 - 1938

Friedrich Rossfeld
1884 - 1917

Martin Kiefer – ⓪ – Elisabeth Rossfeld
1888 - 1963   1891 - 1961

Rosine Kiefer   Siegfried Kiefer
1905 -   1906 -

Frantz Baumfeller – ⓪ – Frieda Rossfeld
1879 - 1954   1891 - 1961

Joseph Rossfeld
1893 - 1896

Christoph Baumfeller
1921 - 1944

Maximillian Bergmeister – ⓪ – Emma Rossfeld
1893 - 1972   1895 - 1982

Dorothea Bergmeister   Rudolf Bergmeister   Gudrun Bergmeister
1919 - 1999   1924 - 1999   1932 - 2014

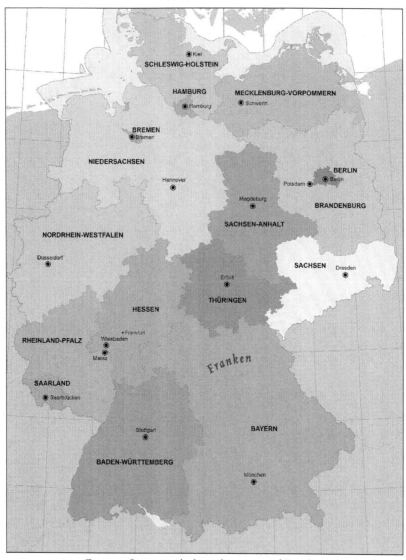

German States, including the region of Franken
where fictitious Uberauen is located

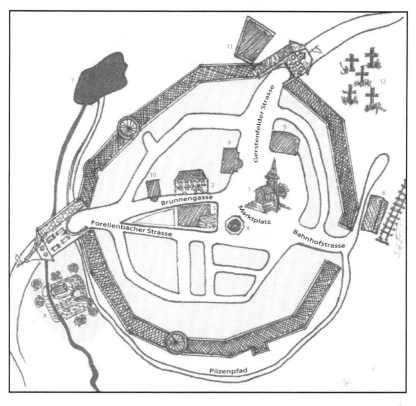

1. St. Severinus Church/St. Severinus Kirche
2. Golden Knight/Goldener Ritter
3. City Hall/Rathaus
4. Fountain/Brunnen
5. School/Schule
6. Train station/Bahnhof
7. Ice pond/Eis Teich
8. Garden/Garten
9. Blumentritt's Store/Blumentritt's Laden
10. Steinhauer's Bakery/Steinhauer's Bäckerei
11. Dance Hall/Tanzsaal
12. Cemetery/Friedhof

Contents

Acknowledgments

The author extends special thanks to Dr. Helmut Forner, Gretel's son and Hubert's brother, for his long and arduous effort in completing the wonderful translation into German. In addition, Dr. Forner has collaborated tirelessly to provide historical contributions, business advice, and most importantly, friendship.

Otto Forner and Gretel Geyer, 1926

PART ONE: TIME OF INNOCENCE

Gretel Geyer, 1907

1. GIRLHOOD

"Gretel," Rosa Geyer called from the kitchen window, "you and Fritz go out the big gate and scoop up that horse manure that is right where the guests have to walk when they come in to eat dinner."

"Yes, Mama," answered Gretel dutifully. "Fritz," she bellowed, "come and help me scoop up the horse apples."

"Aw, man, do we have to?" moaned Fritz Rossfeld. "Why do we always have to clean up the horse poop?"

Rosa Geyer overheard the discussion that was taking place under the big arched door to the courtyard at the Golden Knight. "Get busy and clean it up. We're working in here too, you know. And be sure to put the horse apples where we can use them to fertilize the garden later on this week."

"Okay, okay," Fritz answered under his breath. "I'll go get the shovel from the dung heap, and you can bring the manure basket, Gretel."

Wirtshaus zum Goldenen Ritter (Inn of the Golden Knight)

So Fritz and Gretel giggled as they busily rolled and scraped the horse manure into the shovel and then dumped it into the basket, while neighbors walked and drove past them on the Brunnen Gasse.[1] People working at city hall about twenty feet away and across the street pointed and chuckled. Of course everyone had seen horse manure before, but it was funny nonetheless.

Just when Gretel and Fritz were finishing the cleanup job, Edith Luder, whose mother worked at city hall, came strolling by with a couple of her friends from school.

"Well," Edith said, "look what we have here at the Golden Knight. It's Princess Gretel and her knight, the Prince of Horse Poop." Edith Luder laughed and pretended to gag. Her friends followed suit, holding their noses.

Gretel and Fritz caught a quick glance at each other and smiled devilishly. Then they plunged their gloved hands into the basket of horse manure and each came up with a horse apple.

Fritz yelled, "The Knight of Horse Apples is having a jousting contest today. He's looking to see how fast some big-mouthed damsels can run."

And he threw one of the horse apples, which whizzed by Edith's head. She and the other girls started screaming and running away toward the marketplace as fast as their nice long dresses would allow.

People continued looking out the windows of city hall to see what was going on. Frau[2] Luder, Edith's mother, frowned and tapped on the glass. Seeing that it was only some kids playing, the other office workers went back to their boring jobs of recording numbers.

After the excitement with the horse manure, ten-year-old Gretel Geyer rushed into the laundry room of the Golden Knight, washed with soap and water, and slipped into a freshly starched white apron. There were so many people with the same first names in Uberauen that people sometimes called her "Geyer's Gretel" because that's how everyone could tell them apart.

"Okay, Mama, I'm ready to help serve lunches," Gretel said as she looked over her mother's shoulder and inhaled the delicious aroma of wild boar roast with brown gravy.

Rosa handed the hot plate of appetizing food to Gretel. "Here, take this lunch and a beer to Herr Waldberger."

When she placed the steaming plate of wild boar in front of Herr Waldberger, he said, "Thank you, Gretel."

---

1   Brunnen Gasse – Fountain Lane
2   Frau – Mrs.; Herr – Mr.

Somehow Herr Waldberger was related but she wasn't exactly sure how.

Gretel returned to the kitchen to wait for Rosa's orders. While standing at the kitchen window and squirming to a tune in her head, Gretel noticed her step-grandfather, Wilhelm Rossfeld, resting in the Franconian sunshine. He was sitting on a weathered bench under the grapevine that twisted and twined above the kitchen window and guest entrance of the Golden Knight. Wilhelm dug around in the pockets of his bloody butcher's apron for some matches to light his pipe.

Gretel watched Grandfather with interest but she couldn't guess his private thoughts.

It had been a long, tiring and dirty morning of butchering a steer. Even though he had done it hundreds of times, it was not pleasant. He struck the matches one by one until he was able to light his pipe. Then he leaned back in the warm sunshine to watch the smoke rise.

"Thank you, dear Lord," Wilhelm prayed aloud, "for a few minutes of rest and peace. Amen."

Keeping his eyes closed, he daydreamed of his deceased wife. *Was I responsible for your death, Barbara? If I was, please forgive me. How am I going to live the rest of my life without you? I will always remember the wonderful romantic marriage we shared. Life is so lonely without you. All I do is work and worry about family problems. I miss you.*

Wilhelm opened his eyes and blinked at the sun's brightness. He blew smoke rings and watched them drift away across the courtyard like private holy incense. Finally he pushed himself up and reluctantly went back into the slaughter shed to work with his son, Friedrich.

Barbara's first husband, Dominikus Weyh

I guess Grandfather just needs a few minutes to smoke, Gretel imagined. She would find out as time went by that Wilhelm kept the large family, with all of its branches, loved, employed, clothed, fed, protected and as happy as possible. Right now, to Gretel, he was just a sweet, sometimes gruff, man with a really big, bushy mustache.

The whole family tree was so confusing! Gretel's grandmother, Barbara, had been married twice. At age ten, to Gretel, marriage sounded exciting but mysterious. She knew that Wilhelm was her grandmother's second husband and that Barbara drowned in the ice pond, under "mysterious circumstances,"[3] in 1906.

Barbara's daughter, Rosa, and Joseph Geyer, who baked pastries down the street at Steinhauer's Bakery, were Gretel's parents.

Rosa and Joseph Geyer on their wedding day, 1900

Today, as always, Gretel really enjoyed watching everyone rush around in the kitchen at the Golden Knight. Sixteen-year-old Aunt

---

3   "mysterious circumstances" – Gretel did not yet know the story of her grandmother's death. … Continued in Notes, page 240.

Emma Rossfeld, Rosa's step-aunt, was a great cook, but she needed help to get the onions, carrots and celery root sliced for the gravy.

Emma gave her brother, Fritz Rossfeld, and niece, Rosine Kiefer, instructions. "Okay, for the gravy and red cabbage I'll need chopped onions, carrots and shredded cabbage. Fritz, you and Rosine can decide who does what, but please hurry."

Gretel especially admired her twenty-year-old step-uncle, Friedrich Rossfeld. *He always works so hard and he's so funny,* she thinks as she looks out onto the courtyard and watches him move slabs of beef to the smokehouse. She tapped on the window and shouted, "Move a lot faster down there!"

Friedrich smiled up at her and shook his fist, making Gretel laugh.

"Gretel," Rosa said, "you can help too, instead of pestering Friedrich. Fritz and Rosine are busy chopping, so you can sweep the hallway before people start coming for supper."

"Yes, Mama," Gretel said as she went off to get the broom.

The meat from Wilhelm and Friedrich's butcher shop was used as the food for the Golden Knight dining room, and shoppers also came in to buy the meat. There were lots of yummy delicatessen items for sale, such as *Leberwurst, Würstchen, Frikadellen and Kartoffelsalat.*[4]

About once a week the rabbi would come over and check the meat at Wilhelm Rossfeld's butcher shop to be sure there were meats prepared for sale as kosher. Wilhelm was always happy to be sure there was kosher meat because the Jews in Uberauen were neighbors and good customers.

It was fun to work at the Golden Knight and the butcher shop, but sometimes Gretel, Rosine and Fritz got a few minutes to play in the courtyard.

One day Fastnacht's Betti stopped by after school to visit, and suggested, "I've got an idea. Let's play hide-and-seek."

While the child who was *it* was counting and pretending not to peek, the other kids spread out in the courtyard of the Golden Knight to hide behind a wagon, a chicken coop and Hasso's dog kennel. They knew not to get too close to Hasso because he was the watchdog.

After a few minutes Rosine Kiefer was bored. "I know, let's play hide-and-seek in the cellar."

Nobody told them they couldn't play down there, but they didn't ask, either. The rounded, low entrance door to the cellar was just outside the gate in the Brunnen Gasse.

---

4   *Leberwurst* – liverwurst; *Würstchen* – little weiners; *Frikadellen* – hamburger patties; and *Katoffelsalat* – potato salad

The stairs were narrow and the steps high and steep. There were no electric lights so the kids had to light an oil lamp or candle.

Gretel whispered, "It's so dark and spooky down here!"

"I can light the oil lamp," said Fritz while digging in a pants pocket for his matchbox.

Gretel and her playmates always looked around the cellar with wide eyes. They saw great big beer casks, hanging meat, dusty baskets of turnips, cabbages, eggs and ice packed with sawdust.

Gretel and Rosa had brought the fruit and vegetables from the garden and stored them down there. The ceiling was vaulted like a church and dusty spider webs and spiders hung all over the place. On one wall there was a chute where coal, wood, ice or bags of potatoes could be slid right down into the cellar from the courtyard.

"Wait right there," screamed Fritz. "Catch me when I slide down the chute."

"No, no, it's too dirty!" shouted the other kids.

Fritz ran up the stairs and out around, into the courtyard. He flung the little metal door open and it clanked loudly against the stone wall. He climbed inside, and slid down the chute. "Wheeeee!" he shrieked.

Gretel and the cousins caught Fritz when he reached the bottom.

"You look like a chimney sweep," Rosine said. She laughed. "You're gonna be in so much trouble!"

The kids scurried up the steep, narrow stairs and back out into the sun on the Brunnen Gasse.

"Gretel, time to set the table," Rosa called, and then she noticed Fritz. "Oh my God, what have you been doing," she said with a gasp. "Get upstairs and take a bath before Grandfather Wilhelm sees you." Rosa smiled as she rumpled the hair of the soot-covered little imp.

But it was too late. Grandfather came out of the slaughter shed carrying a cowhide dripping blood. His tired blue eyes were suddenly on Fritz and the other children.

"What's this all about?" he asked with a keen, steady gaze. "Come in and talk to me while I'm eating supper this evening."

Gretel, Fritz, Rosine and Fastnacht's Betti all stood like statues. Wilhelm Rossfeld's command was like the voice of God.

Later that evening after Grandfather had bathed, changed clothes and enjoyed a beer with his friends at the Regulars' Table, Rosa presented the sinners before the court of judgment—Wilhelm Rossfeld. Wilhelm didn't smile, and being the family disciplinarian was not his favorite task. Like most parents and grandparents, he would much rather have given each child a hug and a kiss, but he knew he had to maintain order in the house.

"Did you go into the cellar without asking me or Rosa?" asked Wilhelm. His blue eyes were not cold, but his face showed resolve.

"Yes, Grandfather," answered all the children in unison.

"Then tell me you're sorry," Wilhelm said in a stern voice.

"I'm sorry, Grandfather," answered Gretel, Fritz, Rosine and Fastnacht's Betti, more or less at the same time. The children felt genuinely ashamed and embarrassed in front of the other guests in the dining room.

After a meaningful moment of silence for effect, Wilhelm said softly, "Then I forgive you. Come and give me a hug." Wilhelm hugged and kissed each child and they eagerly hugged and kissed him back.

Dining room with Regulars' Table to the right

Wilhelm sent the children back to the kitchen, and turned his attention to his friends. The men drinking beer at the Regulars' Table were busy smoking, arguing politics, swearing, singing, lying and playing cards. The table was next to the piano because Herr Jorg, the organist from St. Severinus Church, knew how to play. They met at the same table every evening, at the same time. Everyone knew not to let anybody else sit at "their" table. The other guests just smiled and enjoyed the bawdy songs the men sang. The most favorite was from Franconia, "Cheer Up, the Air Is Fresh and Pure." Everyone in the dining room knew the words, so they joined in as Wilhelm and his buddies belted out the song with volume and gusto.

After a nice long drink of beer, Herr Jorg said, "I keep hearing that we're going to have a war. Have any of you heard anything about that?"

"There are all kinds of war rumors, but Kaiser Wilhelm will handle everything," said Herr Meyer with conviction.

Then the men at the Regulars' Table went right back to telling stories about their wild youth.

In the kitchen everyone rushed around to finish and serve the evening meals. "So, this is Princess Gretel von Uberauen, who will be clearing the dirty dishes from the dining room tables this evening," teased Friedrich. "Where are her white gloves?"

Gretel loved it when Uncle Friedrich teased her. She chased him and tried to whack him with her table-washing cloth.

"Maybe Gretel will balance the tray on her head," Fritz said, laughing. "Her head is flat on top, with those braids wrapped around it."

Gretel switched quickly from trying to flip Friedrich with the wet rag, to swinging wildly at Fritz.

"Back to work, Gretel," ordered Rosa.

"I'll get even with you two." Gretel laughed as she headed off to gather dirty dishes from the dining room.

Working in the dining room wasn't her only job. On laundry day, Fritz, Rosa and Gretel washed aprons, tablecloths and bed linens in a big washtub with a wood fire under it that heated the soapy water. Gretel's two-year-old sister, Anna, played nearby. The brew bubbled and foamed as Fritz stirred the fabric around in the hot water with a strong, well-worn wooden pole. When all the linens were washed and rinsed, Gretel put the cloths through a hand-cranked wringer to press the water out.

Ladder wagon from Humprechshausen

Today Rosa, Gretel and Anna put the laundry basket in a wagon that had slatted sides and wood-spoke wheels. The steel rims scratched and clunked loudly on the cobblestone streets as they rolled the wagon to the garden. They turned right, down the Brunnen Gasse, toward the Forellenbacher Gate.[5]

Gretel and Rosa cheerfully exchanged greetings of "Good morning" with Frau Steinhauer.

Since Gretel's father, Joseph Geyer, worked at Steinhauer's Bakery, he noticed Rosa and the children walking by. "Oh, yes," he grumbled to himself, "go ahead and pretend to be the perfect little *Hausfrau*, Rosa. I don't know why I ever married you." Then Joseph went back to mixing cake batter and worrying about his marriage.

As they passed the bakery, Gretel noticed a farmer who was watering his horse at the fountain. She immediately recognized him as one of the farmers who sold steers and hogs to Wilhelm Rossfeld. "May I pet your horse while it's drinking, Herr Brüchner?" Gretel asked politely.

While Gretel petted the horse, Rosa looked around uneasily at the people walking by. *I wonder if they all know and if they're just pretending to be friendly?*

Gretel noticed that some passersby continued to look at Rosa and whisper. "That's Rosa Geyer that I told you about," whispered Frau Luder to Frau Pucher, and then both women stared at Rosa, Anna and Gretel.

Rosa stole a glance at little Anna, who was now riding on the laundry bags.

Gretel wondered why Frau Luder was pointing at Mama.

Feeling nervous and threatened, Rosa thought, *If I wasn't such a coward I'd go back there and confront Frau Luder. But I don't want to draw attention to myself.*

Gretel, Rosa and Anna walked on down to Forellenbacher Gate. Uberauen still had two ancient city gates and some of the old city walls standing.

Gretel looked up as they went through the gate. She pictured herself posing with a bow and holding arrows to defend Uberauen. The gate opening was wide enough for a pair of horses and maybe someone on horseback to pass each other under the tower, but it wasn't very wide.

Rosa pulled the ladder wagon until they reached their family's garden plot outside the old city walls. When they pulled the wagon into the garden, Anna hopped right down to play in the dirt while Rosa and Gretel got busy with the clean laundry.

---

5   Forellenbacher Gate – Trout Stream town gate

They carried the laundry over to the area of the garden that had knee-high green grass, and spread out the clean white sheets to be dried and bleached by the sun. Gretel held the hem of the sheets on one side while Mama held the opposite edge and they lowered the sheets down onto the grass together.

"There, that looks good," said Rosa proudly.

Rosa turned to Gretel, saying, "You and Fritz can come back later in the day to gather up the sheets, tablecloths and aprons to bring back to the Golden Knight for starching and ironing."

"Yes, Mama," Gretel answered. She thought to herself, *Maybe I can run faster than Fritz when we come back here this afternoon.*

The family depended on their garden fruit and vegetables for meals at the Golden Knight. Today, some of the vegetables were ready to be harvested, so Rosa, Gretel and Anna put some bags with carrots, head lettuce, peas and beets onto the wagon. When it was loaded, Gretel and Rosa pulled the wagon, with Anna perched on top, back toward the inn.

Rosa dreaded another encounter with Frau Luder. "You know what? Let's go on up the *Pilzenpfad,*[6] to the small city door today, Gretel. That way we can visit with some different people."

"Okay," said Gretel as she pulled the wagon along the path that followed the old city wall up to the pedestrian city door.

When they got back to the Golden Knight, Gretel and Rosa stopped pulling their wagon at the little door and chute where Fritz had slid down and gotten dirty a couple of weeks before.

"Gretel, you go down into the cellar and catch the vegetables when I slide them down the chute," ordered Rosa.

"Yes, Mama." Gretel ran out into the Brunnen Gasse, opened the low, rounded door and stepped inside. She lit a candle and started down the steps into the cellar where she could see the bags coming down the chute.

We had so much fun the day Fritz slid down this chute, Gretel remembered with a private giggle. Grandfather really got after us!

Later in the afternoon Gretel and Rosa finished storing the vegetables in the cellar. They washed their hands, combed their hair and tried to make themselves look presentable. It was time for evening prayers at St. Severinus Church. They would have just enough time for Mass before serving the evening meal. Sometimes the men said they were "too busy" to go to church. After all, the women were expected to take care of children, church and cooking. That evening, Grandfather Wilhelm, Aunt Emma, Rosine Kiefer and a couple of other cousins walked to

---

6 *Pilzenpfad* – mushroom or toadstool path

church together for a short service. On Sundays the church service was longer and more formal.

St. Severinus Church was right on the marketplace and close to the Golden Knight. Rosa and Joseph had brought Gretel and Anna here to be christened when they were babies. Gretel was actually christened Eva Margarethe Geyer on August 12, 1904, but everyone called her Gretel. There were plenty of other Gretels in Uberauen, so those who shared the same first name were distinguished from each other by saying the family name first, as in Geyer's Gretel.

Gretel joined her family for Mass

I love the way everything in church looks, sounds and smells, Gretel thought as she sat in her usual pew in the middle left, facing the altar. The air in church was filled with the pungent smell of burning incense. Gretel loved to gaze at the little white-skinned cupids and gold-covered crosses. The Holy Mother's white statue was trimmed in shiny gold. She was depicted holding baby Jesus. The windows were high, narrow and come to arched peaks in a style named Gothic, after an ancient Germanic tribe.

While Gretel knelt to say her prayers, the choir came in, singing, "Praise Ye the Lord." Gretel had to admit that she kind of daydreamed during church. All she could think about was how much she wanted to chase the boys that she knew from town and school. She could see some of them sitting with Fritz Rossfeld and Ernst Waldberger a couple of rows away and toward the back of the church. The boys noticed her looking at them, so they quickly stuck out their tongues at her.

Of all the nerve, Gretel thought. She smiled and immediately stuck out her tongue at them too, but Frau Meyer, who was sitting behind her, wagged her finger and Gretel had to stop.

Gretel looked left and right to locate her friends while the priest gave the sermon, but she kept seeing the boys. Now they were pushing up their noses and pulling down their lower eyelids to make pig faces. Gretel was absolutely bursting with the desire to make faces back at them, but she knew that Frau Meyer would tell Mama. Frau Meyer was a regular shopper at the butcher shop and she expected Gretel to behave properly in church.

When it was time for young Father Weible to finish speaking, the organist, Herr Jorg from the Golden Knight Regulars' Table, got himself seated at the massive organ. The beautiful silver organ pipes reached to the high ceiling. Gretel didn't always know what the music was, but she loved the music by Brahms, Bach and Mozart because the whole church vibrated with the heavenly organ sounds.

The curly-haired altar boy held up his hands to extinguish the altar candles and his draping robe made him look like an angel, except that he was still wearing the dirty boots he had worn to feed the cows that morning in the barn. Everybody noticed what was on his boots. All thoughts of angels and heaven vanished in the muffled giggles and whispers from the congregation. Rosa glared at Gretel and squeezed her hand, while stifling her own urge to laugh.

Since he didn't know why everyone was murmuring, the altar boy kept waiting for the organ to start this part of the service ... but it didn't start! Everyone looked around and started getting fidgety. They whispered to each other and wondered what could be wrong. Finally, Father Weible sent the altar boy with the smelly boots, down the main aisle and up the stairs to the space on the balcony where the organ air pump was located.

"What's wrong?" Frau Kübler asked her husband.

"I don't know," he answered as he craned his neck to look up at the balcony.

When the altar boy got back behind the wall, he found the air pump operator, young Reinhold Haferstroh, asleep in a chair that he had leaned up against the back wall of the organ.

"Reinhold, wake up," the altar boy said in a loud whisper, and the pump operator woke with a snort. He had been dreaming of his wild night of drinking and flirting last night under the trees of the marketplace. "Start pumping," urged the boy. Finally the teenager began pumping the long wooden arm up and down that worked the air bellows of the complex organ mechanism, and it sprang to life. Herr Jorg played and beautiful music flowed like a heavenly wave that filled the church.

The parishioners sang heartily as the organ music swelled and their voices soared. Gretel and Rosa were enjoying the hymn when they heard a god-awful voice from behind them. Every congregation has a singer like Frau Meyer.

Oh no, Gretel suddenly realized, *we forgot that Frau Meyer is a terrible singer and she sings really loud! I'd love to turn around and wag my finger at her for her awful singing.*

It was as if Rosa was a mind reader. She reached over and squeezed Gretel's hand while giving her a knowing smile. Gretel turned and grinned at Mama.

When the church service was over, the Geyer-Rossfeld family greeted friends and neighbors as they left the church and headed the short distance back to the Golden Knight to serve dinner.

"Holy Mary, Mother of God, please forgive me for not going to confession," prayed Rosa. "I feel so ashamed, but I don't know who to talk to or what to do." Rosa walked along, immersed in her own thoughts as the family moved down the Brunnen Gasse to the Golden Knight.

2. COURTING

Every day, twenty-one-year-old Friedrich Rossfeld was busy helping his father, Wilhelm, with the butchering. It was heavy, bloody, smelly work but the meat they prepared and sold was a steady source of income for the whole large family.

Friedrich was cleaning the slaughter shed, washing the floor and moving the slabs of beef around. He daydreamed while working on this July day in 1914. *Maybe when Papa and I are finished butchering and chilling the meat, I can bathe and then go to see if my friends are at the marketplace.* Friedrich had to admit that when it came to friends, he was much more interested in seeing which girls were sitting on the church steps.

Wilhelm was observing his handsome young son. The father knew what he was thinking about and it wasn't beef filet or stomachs. He smiled to himself, thinking that young people always thought their generation invented love and sex, but he and his generation had experienced them too. Wilhelm grinned knowingly.

Sometime after 6:00 p.m. both Wilhelm and Friedrich were worn out from butchering the steer and the job was finished. Wilhelm left to get cleaned up before going into his dining room at the Golden Knight where Rosa, Emma or Gretel would bring his dinner and a beer.

"Papa, I'll take my bath and then go and see who is at the marketplace," Friedrich mentioned casually.

Wilhelm had long since figured that out. He answered, "Have fun."

As Friedrich walked onto the marketplace he already knew there were plenty of unwritten rules about when and how to flirt in Uberauen. It was okay to meet and visit with friends or flirt, as long as the girls' parents knew the boy. Sometimes families still insisted on girls only going out with family members or girlfriends that the family trusted. Friedrich didn't mind having a little sister or brother, aunt, grandma or cousin with the girls his age when he talked to them. The families just wanted their daughters to find a nice boy. Of course, it wasn't bad that everyone in Uberauen knew everyone else and everyone else's business. Everyone also knew that Wilhelm Rossfeld owned two prosperous businesses. Friedrich was not only handsome, he was a catch.

Fountain and church steps

On the marketplace Friedrich met his buddies who were sitting around the edge of the fountain. It was the usual crowd: Ralf Aachener, Markus Schöneberger and Wolfram Diehl. The boys pretended to ignore the girls who were gathered on the church steps visiting. The girls likewise pretended to ignore the boys who were laughing and teasing at the fountain. Markus was trying to bum a cigarette while Ralf Aachener was swinging to knock off Markus's cap. Wolfram splashed water on the back of one guy's pants as he sat on the fountain, so it would look like he peed in his pants. The friends posed, strutted and showed off for the girls. The girls continued to pretend that the boys did not exist.

Before the boys could even get started with flirting today, Wolfram tried to get the guys to be serious for a moment. "Have any of you read about war with France?" he asked with unusual seriousness.

Markus held up his hands in a *stop* gesture. "I hope that whatever happens, they will leave me out of it."

"Do you think we'll have to go? All I think about is finding a wife," said Friedrich honestly.

The other boys laughed and made it clear they didn't want to discuss anything serious. They were already looking over at the girls on the church steps.

The girls knew how to break the ice and start conversation. Sometimes they would send a little sister to ask one of the guys how his mother was doing. That was always a good excuse for the boy to walk over and report that his mother was fine, and thanks for asking.

Today, the boys used another good plan that everyone understood. Friedrich walked with his friend Wolfram over to the group of girls so he could pretend to ask his sister what time they needed to go home for dinner. That way, Friedrich could safely cross the dangerous empty space between the fountain and the church and talk to Wilhelm's sister, Frieda.

Fortunately, once some talking and flirting began, then the other boys came over to see the girls. Of course no one could prevent a girl from looking across the wasteland of the marketplace and smiling broadly at the boys sitting on the fountain. That was permitted.

Today, the maiden aunt of Fräulein[7] Blumentritt was the chaperone for the girls. Friedrich visited and flirted with Fräuleins Diehl, Haferstroh, Brüchner and plenty of others. He didn't yet have a serious girlfriend, but he did sort of prefer Frieda Diehl.

Later on, Friedrich thought as he went back to the Golden Knight, *I really need to find a wife. I'm not getting any younger!*

Gretel was well aware that Friedrich flirted with the girls from church and on the marketplace. A few days later when Frau Brüchner came into the butcher shop with Luise, Gretel rushed across the courtyard to tell Friedrich.

"Friedrich, I know you're not interested, but Luise Brüchner is in the butcher shop buying meat with her mother. Just thought you might want to know." Gretel giggled.

Friedrich, covered with blood and animal feces, as usual, glanced cautiously at Wilhelm.

With a devilish twinkle in his eye, Wilhelm said, "Oh, I think you should take that tray of smoked *Wurst* to the butcher shop while we have some customers over there."

Friedrich snatched the filthy butcher's apron off with a sweep of his arm, hurried in to wash, grabbed the tray of cold cuts and rushed across the courtyard to the butcher shop. Gretel and Rosa pretended not to notice anything unusual about Friedrich delivering the meat instead of Gretel.

---

7   Fräulein/s – miss/es

"Good day, Frau Brüchner. Good day, Luise," Friedrich said bashfully. "Good day, Herr Rossfeld," the Brüchners answered politely.

Friedrich glanced shyly at Luise while slowly and carefully placing the *Wurst* in the display case, which he normally never did. Luise occasionally looked modestly in his direction while her mother chatted with Rosa. Both adult women were fully aware of the need to visit a little longer so Luise and Friedrich could look each other over.

Friedrich finally forced himself to speak. "Oh, by the way, Luise, will you be going to the Church Blessing Festival?"

Luise looked at her mother for permission to speak to Friedrich, and then answered. "Why, yes. Will you be there too?"

"Yes," answered Friedrich, but then he couldn't think of anything else to say.

Rosa jumped in to save the stumbling Romeo. "Oh, Luise, Friedrich will be there for sure, and so will we. Please save us a spot at your table."

Both Friedrich and Luise continued to steal glances and smile, happy that somebody had helped them make a date.

Friedrich rushed back to the slaughter shed and put on the dirty apron to help Papa with the butchering and cleaning. He was deep in thought but smiling all over!

"So, did you get the *Wurst* delivered to the butcher shop?" Wilhelm asked calmly.

"Yes, Papa," answered Friedrich.

"Did I see that attractive Fräulein Brüchner going in there with her mother?" he asked innocently.

"Yes, Papa," Friedrich answered again.

"Well, I hope you made arrangements to see her someplace other than the butcher shop." His father smiled.

"Thanks to Rosa, I'll meet Luise at the church festival." Friedrich grinned in triumph.

As the weeks and months passed, Friedrich continued to flirt with eligible girls and dream of his romantic future. Little did he suspect that big changes were coming to Uberauen and the world, with devastating consequences.

3. CHRISTMAS

Time rushed by and 1914 was quickly running down. Gretel's school was ready to be out for Christmas break. Her father, Joseph, was baking special Christmas cookies at Steinhauer's Bakery for those *Hausfrauen*[8] who weren't good at baking. Rosa and Aunt Emma decorated the dining room at the Golden Knight with the help of Gretel, Anna, Fritz and Rosine Kiefer. Most of the decorations were spruce sprigs, wood carvings or stars made of straw. Rosa and Emma had unpacked some embroidered decorative Christmas tablemats that women in their family had made in years past.

In the evening after everything was cleaned up at the Golden Knight, Rosa and Joseph celebrated Advent in their room with Gretel and Anna. On the three Sundays before Christmas, Rosa and Joseph's family gathered together at a little table with the Advent wreath. Joseph lit one candle each week, until all the candles were lit and it was time for baby Jesus to be born.

"Mama, let me light a candle too," suggested Gretel.

Anna insisted on lighting a candle because Gretel got to light one, so Joseph held Anna's little hands to help her light a candle.

Joseph is being so agreeable this evening. I wonder what's gotten into him? Rosa thought as she watched him helping the girls light candles. *I wish we could be in love like we were when we first got married. Now I know he isn't interested in me.*

Joseph saw her sitting there like a little Mama Madonna while thinking he knew what she was really like. He clenched his lips as he pretended to be festive for the children.

Gretel and Anna watched the shadows of their family moving on the walls of the room. Mama and Papa had wallpapered the room a couple of weeks before and now their Advent was celebrated in a room with yellow wallpaper that had little pink roses and green leaves.

---

8 *Hausfrauen* – housewives

While enjoying the Advent candles, Gretel was thinking that Christmas would be here soon and she wondered when the Christmas Market would start. She wouldn't have long to wait.

A few days later Grandfather invited Gretel and Friedrich to sit with him at breakfast.

Wilhelm sipped his freshly brewed coffee at the kitchen table. He said, "I've arranged for the family to have a booth to sell *Wurst* from the Golden Knight, and some homemade cookies at the Christmas Market this year. You two will be in charge."

"That sounds like fun," Friedrich said quickly. After all, it would be the perfect chance to talk to all the girls that went by.

Gretel wasn't sure what the job would be like. "What will I do, Grandfather?"

Wilhelm dunked some bread into his coffee and took a nice loud slurp. "Rosa and Emma can get some tips from Joseph and then bake Christmas cookies here for a couple of days. I'll go ahead and butcher as usual. Friedrich, you and Gretel can roast *Wurst* and also sell baked goods at our stand," Wilhelm explained.

"Sure, Gretel and I make a great team. We can do that," said Friedrich, jumping up from his chair.

Gretel was nodding her head in agreement, anticipating the fun of working with Uncle Friedrich.

With Joseph's suggestions, Rosa and Emma began baking goodies to sell at the Christmas Market. They baked Christmas *stollen*, little hazelnut breads, *springerle*, wasp nests, cinnamon stars and lots more.

Early on the first morning of the Christmas Market, Friedrich, Gretel and Fritz set up tables for guests to use as well as their covered booth with a table for the baked goods. Fritz started a charcoal fire to roast the Thüringer bratwurst, pork wurst and red wurst.

Here I am again, all alone in the slaughter shed, trying to wallow this damn hog around, Wilhelm complained to himself. *I wish Fritz would get his ass back over here to help me! He's probably farting around with his friends at the marketplace while I have to do everything by myself. But I guess if I were honest I'd have to admit that life would not be such drudgery if I just had my Barbara to go home to every night.*

"Okay, Fritz, I think we're all ready to go," said Friedrich, with his hands on his hips. "You go on back to butcher with Papa. Gretel, you can stand in the booth and sell the baked goods and I'll grill the *Wurst*. They can all pay you, Gretel, okay?"

"Oh, good, I get to handle the money," Gretel said, rubbing her hands together. She went into her booth to get squared away for the first customers. It soon became clear, however, that she was far too short to reach over the table and serve anyone, so she rushed back to the Golden Knight and got a crate that was used for carrying wood, potatoes or cabbages.

Out of breath from rushing, she jumped up on the crate for her first customer. "Good morning, Frau Haferstroh. What would you like?"

It was fun to see everyone she knew, and the baked goods were selling quickly. Friedrich was kept busy grilling the *Wurst* that were served on a paper shell with a homemade roll and some mustard. Wilhelm Rossfeld's meats were famous all over Uberauen and everyone came over to buy something. Of course the guests also usually wanted a beer or Uberauen's flavored mineral water. The neighbors sat at the tables to visit and gossip. It was cold outside, so they all ate their *Wurst* quickly before it got cold.

After an hour or so of having fun, Gretel noticed Edith Luder and a couple of her friends passing by.

"Well," Edith said, "who do we have here? It's the girl with the strange family. They'll let almost anybody sell food in this town." She sniffed while looking coldly at Gretel.

What is that girl's problem, thought Gretel, *and what in the world is she talking about? I'm sure glad I don't care what she thinks. I have a great family and nice friends. Who needs her!*

Gretel wisely turned her attention to the next customer, as if Edith did not exist. "Good morning, Frau Schreiner. Would you like some cookies?" Gretel asked sweetly.

Gretel watched Edith and her friends with Georg Pucher as they continued to gossip, point and make snide remarks about her and Friedrich.

"Oh, Georg, I'm so glad to see you. Did you notice that Gretel Geyer and her trashy uncle Friedrich are selling food here? It's a disgrace," Edith said as she looked down her nose at Gretel and Friedrich.

Thankfully, the obnoxious group finally walked away.

Back at the Golden Knight, Emma grumbled privately as she worked. *Oh yes, 'bake cookies when we have a few extra minutes.' That's just what I need when the Christmas crowds are coming in to eat lunch and I have to prepare all the meals! Normally it wouldn't bother me, but I'd like to go to the Christmas Market too and see if there are any nice men there.*

" 'You girls just bake some cookies in the afternoon that we can sell at the Christmas Market,' " Rosa said, sarcastically quoting Wilhelm.

After she finished chopping the onions for Emma's gravy, she flopped onto the nearest chair, thinking that her life seemed so cramped that she felt unable to breathe. She wished she could break out from everything and really live.

Christmas Market

At the Christmas Market[9], business was brisk for a few hours, until after lunchtime, and then there was a natural lull with slower sales until about 2:00 p.m. Then, while Gretel was busy selling some cookies to Frau Kübler, Waldberger's Ernst and Fritz Rossfeld snuck up behind her and put snow down the neck of her coat.

"Fritz, you're supposed to be helping Grandpa! Okay, that's it, Ernst!" she shrieked. Grabbing the arm of her friend, Fastnacht's Betti, Gretel charged after the loudly laughing boys.

Friedrich was left to wrap the cookies for Frieda and Frau Diehl, who chuckled and watched Gretel and Fastnacht's Betti charging after the boys.

"Oh, let her go and have some fun," Friedrich said. He smiled. "She's still a little girl."

---

9 *Deggendorfer Christkindlmarkt* – Christmas Market in the town of Deggendorf. Photo courtsy of the friendly city of Deggendorf, Germany.

The chase was on as the boys laughed and ran across the marketplace. The faster the girls ran, the farther the boys were getting away. Slushy, dirty, watery snow scattered in all directions. Fritz turned and stuck out his tongue at Gretel and Fastnacht's Betti.

"Oh, I'll show those guys," Gretel yelled to Betti as the two girls giggled and kept running.

Ernst and Fritz doubled back from the fountain and ran toward city hall. They stopped on the front walkway of the building to tease the girls.

"You can't catch us. You can't catch us," they shouted in a sing-songy chant.

Gretel thought quickly. "That's what you think. Come on," she whispered to her friend. They turned and ran around the old half-timbered building and garden in front of city hall, where they stopped for a second at the snow-filled garden.

"Stay low behind the garden fence," Fastnacht's Betti whispered.

Between the city hall entry door and the marketplace the boys were still shouting, "Na-na, na-na, na-na," but they were looking in the opposite direction. Gretel and Betti formed deliciously large snowballs to launch their sneak attack.

"Let's rub the snow on the back of their heads," suggested Gretel.

The girls darted onto the sidewalk with their armaments held high. At the last second, Ernst heard them and turned to fend off the attackers.

"No way, girlie." He laughed as he smashed the snowball on the front of her coat. Then Ernst chased Gretel and Fritz chased Betti, with each child trying to stop and gather snow for weaponry. They ran up and down the aisles of the Christmas Market, sometimes joined by other kids.

Getting tired, Gretel stumbled and fell face-first on the slushy paving stones.

"Mama is going to kill me when she sees that I ripped my stockings," Gretel admitted to Betti.

Gretel finally slid back under the tarp in the back of her booth. Friedrich was still patiently handling the workload for both of them.

"Well, did you have fun chasing the boys?" Friedrich asked.

Smiling, covered with wet snow, and with two ripped stockings, red-faced Gretel answered, "That Ernst Waldberger makes me so mad!"

"Ha-ha-ha!" Friedrich's laugh was loud, and he kept smiling to himself. He knew so well that love for an eleven-year-old consists of girls chasing boys and boys chasing girls.

4. A JANUARY DAY IN 1915

On a cold January morning Gretel woke up in the bedroom she shared with Anna above the dining room in the Golden Knight. It was still cold in the room, even though Mama had started a fire in the little coal stove in the corner next to the chimney. It was fun to stay cuddled under her warm, thick feather bed and look around the room.

In the dim morning light, Gretel admired the new pale-yellow wallpaper with the pink roses and green leaves. The spring flowers looked especially good on such a cold morning. She rolled onto her side, and her gaze fell upon the coal bucket and shovel. *Um, I'll have to remember to bring up more coal from the cellar and clean the ashes out of the stove when I get home after school.* She pictured herself scattering the ashes on the icy street and front steps of the Golden Knight. Someone in the family always kept the steps clean and washed, but ashes prevented customers from slipping on the icy pavement. Finally, she made herself jump out of bed.

Gretel smiled as she quickly wrapped herself in her warm housecoat. *I remember when Papa and I went shopping for this,* she recalled fondly. The Blumentritt sisters had a clothing store around the corner, next to the church on the marketplace. The Blumentritt sisters were great salespeople, Gretel remembered.

"Good morning, Frau Blumentritt," Joseph and Gretel said together.

"Good morning, Herr Geyer," the sisters answered politely. The two ladies who owned the store had a reputation of not buying new stock until their older things were sold, no matter how long items had been on the shelf. Nevertheless, Gretel picked out her nice, warm, dark red, flannel robe with some pictures of ladies from the emperor's court. Gretel thought she had never seen anything so elegant!

"Oh, for heaven's sake, that looks just wonderful on you, Gretel!" gushed the younger Frau Blumentritt.

"Thank you," answered Gretel while smiling to herself. *Frau Blumentritt would have said I looked wonderful even if I looked awful.*

Memories of shopping with Papa were still on her mind as Gretel hopped around the bedroom and tried to get her house slippers on. *Oh, do I love these warm slippers,* she thought. Then she rushed down the hall to the toilet. She knew that the toilet was always clean because she or another family member cleaned it on a regular basis. Everyone took baths down the hall in the bathroom next to the toilet. Water was heated in a wood-fired boiler that towered in the corner.

Gretel scurried back to the bedroom through the unheated hallway that had windows all along it.

Hallway Windows

From the windows, you could look down at the activity in the courtyard. This morning, Grandfather Wilhelm was hitching up the horses to his livestock wagon.

Farm wagon

I wish I could go with him and ride on the wagon out to a farm in Gerstenfeld,[10] Gretel thought. *School is fun, but riding with Grandfather would be even better!*

Once she was back in the bedroom Gretel got Anna up, down the hall to the toilet and then into her clothes. Both Anna and Gretel wore white cotton underwear and underskirts. Then they put on long, warm, woolen dresses and long stockings in the winter. Today Gretel picked out a school dress that had embroidered flowers, lace around the collar and big mother-of-pearl buttons down to her waist. When she came home from school, she would put on a starched white apron over her dress to keep it nice and clean while she worked in the butcher shop or the dining room of the Golden Knight. It took a while to get her long stockings on, and then Gretel began to put stockings on Anna too.

Anna kicked her legs, saying, "I want blue stockings!"

"Today you get to wear your pretty gray ones because your blue stockings are in the dirty clothes basket," Gretel explained. Anna pouted for only a second.

Before taking Anna downstairs for breakfast, Gretel went over to gaze out the bedroom window that looked down on the Brunnen Gasse. The street was only about twenty feet wide. People were already bustling past the Golden Knight to go shopping, attend Mass at St. Severinus or try not to be late for work. City hall across the street was already open for customers.

Gretel rubbed the pretty frost feathers and flowers on the window. She kept an eye on Anna, who was warming her hands next to the heating stove. Gretel breathed on the cold windowpane and made a melted spot. Just then she saw Edith's mother, Frau Luder, looking at her from her city hall window. She was only a short distance away. Gretel impishly stuck out her tongue at Frau Luder while she pretended to lick the melted circle on the frosty glass. It was obvious that Frau Luder had seen her, because she made her usual snippy, fussy face and backed away from her window. Gretel smiled naughtily. She knew she was supposed to be polite to her elders, but she didn't like the arrogant way that Frau Luder whispered about her mother, Rosa. Besides, every time Aunt Emma went to pay the licensing fees at city hall, Frau Luder treated her poorly and sometimes accused the Rossfelds of not paying their taxes.

That is a stupid cow, thought Gretel of Frau Luder, using a typical rural expression.

"Gretel," shouted Rosa from the bottom of the stairs, "you and Anna

---

10 *Gerstenfeld* – town of Barley Field

get down here right now or you'll be late for school." The order drifted up the stairs and down the hall to the bedroom.

Gretel finally realized that she had to hurry. She rushed Anna down to the kitchen and their bowls of oatmeal with cream.

"So, Gretel, time for school," said Joseph as he tugged on her pigtails.

Gretel turned and smiled at her Papa because she loved when he teased her.

Mama was already supervising the cooking for the day's lunch special: Rossfeld's famous homemade pork roast with potato dumplings, red cabbage and gravy.

While Gretel and Anna eagerly ate their oatmeal, Rosa absentmindedly peeled potatoes for potato dumplings. She had done it so often that it was second nature.

She wondered if that was all there was to life … hack, hack, stir and mix. When she was a girl she had imagined her life would be much different from the way it was now.

Emma was also daydreaming while she prepared the yummy beef stock. She pressed the boiled vegetable mush through a metal sieve and allowed herself to think again about being twenty-one and unmarried. 'I don't even have a boyfriend. Pretty soon I'll be an old maid working in the kitchen and nobody will want me!'

Both Rosa and Emma suddenly realized that it was getting late. Gretel looked up to check the cuckoo clock on the kitchen wall and saw that she had only eight minutes to get to school. She grabbed her knit cap, coat, gloves and scarf, and then bolted out the kitchen door.

Gretel ran up to the marketplace, past the church and turned left to the beautiful stone schoolhouse. She entered the school just as the teacher, Herr Bästlein, was clanging the handbell. All the kids hung up their coats quickly in the cloak hall and took their seats.

Herr Bästlein came in and got the older students in one room busy on their assignments, and then he went into the room where the lower grades were seated. The teacher was so strict that all the children were afraid of him. Just the same, every time that Herr Bästlein turned his back to write on the chalkboard, Waldberger's Ernst pushed Gretel's elbow and tried to make her put wild ink blobs on her assignment sheet. Gretel knew that Ernst and his family were related because of Grandma Barbara's family tree, but that was all she knew. Her cousin, Fritz Rossfeld, was also in the classroom and he was so naughty—but funny.

Gretel smiled as she tried to write. *Oh, I get so mad at Ernst! At playtime I'll chase him all around the playground.*

As long as they didn't whisper, Gretel got to sit with her best friend, Fastnacht's Betti.

Gretel with white bow in kindergarten

Again today during playtime, Gretel and her friend chased Fritz and Ernst. It was always fun until Georg Pucher, the playground bully, tried to hit, kick or trip one of them.

"Hey, Georg," screamed Fritz at him, "quit punching Alois! He's half your size!"

Fritz turned to Gretel and Fastnacht's Betti. "I'd really like to punch Georg Pucher right in his piggy face!" he boasted loudly.

"The next time he kicks me when Herr Bästlein is teaching, I'm going to tell on him," Fastnacht's Betti promised.

The sad truth was that, like all bullies, Georg Pucher had everyone buffaloed into being afraid of him.

But life didn't really revolve around Georg. Soon it was time to get back to their schoolwork. Herr Bästlein rang his handbell, and the kids marched dutifully back to their seats.

When the students were seated after recess, Herr Bästlein went immediately into his lesson about German nouns and articles. Suddenly Fritz Rossfeld waved his hand. All the students were shocked because nobody ever dared to interrupt the teacher.

"You're interrupting the lesson," Herr Bästlein said. "What do you want?"

"May I be excused to go to the toilet, Herr Bästlein?" asked Fritz.

There was a muffled gasp in the classroom. What was he thinking?

Everyone knew they had to plan their toilet breaks for recess time.

Herr Bästlein answered coldly, "Yes, you may go, but you'll have to sit in your seat when everyone else goes out for recess."

Fritz quickly left the classroom and ran straight to the toilet that was down the hall. He was glad Herr Bästlein had let him leave because he couldn't wait until recess and, besides, he was tired of the boring lesson. *Who cares about those constantly changing articles: der, die, das, den, dem, masculine, feminine and neuter ... blah, blah, blah,* thought Fritz.

After he finished his business and was on the way back to the classroom, Fritz began to think about how unfair it was for him to be held prisoner in his seat while the other students got a break. *I had to pee,* reasoned Fritz. *Just because I forgot to go after the last break, now Herr Bästlein wants to make me stay in!* With each step he took back to the classroom, the gears in his head turned more and more toward mischief. Visions of a plan flickered in his young brain until he had thought of the perfect revenge against Herr Bästlein.

He felt around in the pockets of his knee-length *Lederhosen.*[11] Aha! His homemade spider was still there! Fritz gleefully pulled the fuzzy toy spider out of his pocket and began to fluff it up. The legs were made of twine that was used to tie meat to a drying pole in the family's smokehouse. The yucky body was made from some leftover hairy cowhide that was wrapped into a ball with thread. The finishing touch: the big, glassy, beaded eyes that Fritz had stuck on with envelope glue.

Fritz thought back to when he glued the eyes on the spider. *Did I close the glue bottle? Aunt Rosa will get mad when she discovers that I was digging in her drawer again and snitched these beads!*

As he reached the stairs to the second floor, Fritz remembered that there was a warm air vent in the classroom ceiling that allowed heat from the classroom coal stove to heat the storage room upstairs.

Oh, man, he thought, *I'll get even with Herr Bästlein!* He bolted up the wooden stairs, taking two steps at a time. When he reached the cluttered storage room, he cautiously opened the door and slipped inside. *There must be some string in here someplace,* he figured. Finally he found a spool of thread that the teacher had left in the supply room in case someone ripped their clothes. Fritz could hardly wait to continue with his delicious plan!

He crawled over to the vent in the center of the floor, peered down at all the kids' heads and stifled a giggle. *This is going to be so much fun!*

Herr Bästlein droned on with the lesson about German masculine

---

11 *Lederhosen* – leather pants or knickerbockers

nouns. The young scholars sat perfectly still and daydreamed while pretending to hang on every word.

Fritz carefully squeezed the fuzzy spider down through the air vent. As it began to appear in their line of vision, some students were surprised and shocked. They wanted to say something to Herr Bästlein, but didn't want to interrupt him and get in trouble. The fluffy, fuzzy spider continued its slow, jiggling descent. By now all the kids had seen the spider and some muffled giggles began to be heard, even though the children were afraid to draw attention to themselves.

The playground bully, Georg Pucher, was thinking that he'd love to tell old Bästlein what Fritz Rossfeld was doing. It would be fun to get him into trouble and then he'd get spanked. On the other hand, it would be fun to see Fritz get spanked after all the fun was over, so he decided to wait and watch.

As Herr Bästlein turned back to the class, ZIP the spider was yanked back up and out of sight. All the students gasped.

The teacher asked the students coldly, "What *is* the problem today?" He turned back to the lesson on the chalkboard and the fuzzy spider jiggled slowly down from the vent, accompanied by muffled giggles from the children.

Herr Bästlein snapped back around and was startled by the fuzzy spider right in front of his eyes! "Eeeeek!" he shouted spontaneously.

The classroom dissolved into hysterical laughter as the students lost all control of their schoolroom manners.

For Fritz it was only a momentary triumph. Of course, Herr Bästlein spanked him. Georg Pucher loved watching him cry. After that, Fritz knew the teacher would tell his father, Wilhelm Rossfeld, about his shameful and disruptive behavior.

The teacher called out, "We must keep order!"

Everyone agreed.

Fritz was required to sit inside during playtime that day and for another four days. He also had to write an apology to Herr Bästlein, explaining why such behavior could not be tolerated. Worst of all, he had to get his father's signature! Fritz wrote in his best German, but he secretly had to admit that it really had been a great trick! It was a moment of boyhood glory.

On her way back home from school with her cousin Rosine Kiefer, that day, Gretel walked past St. Severinus Church, with the marketplace in front of her. The Blumentritt sisters' store was after that, on the corner of the Brunnen Gasse. City hall was farther down, on her left.

Everything always stays the same in Uberauen, she thought, *and everyone knows everyone else and everyone else's business.* Before she even opened the door to the Golden Knight, she expected that Grandfather would already know what Fritz had done at school.

"He's gonna be in troooouble," Gretel said, and she giggled with Rosine.

5. FIRST COMMUNION

At Easter time in 1915 Gretel was ready for her First Communion at St. Severinus Church. Along with some other young people, she had studied Catholic Church theology and history. Finally it was time for her, the extended family, and the parishioners from the church to have a First Communion celebration.

All the Communion candidates were having a great time laughing, flirting and teasing each other at the school, but then a dark cloud in the form of Edith Luder suddenly appeared, to dampen the mood. She brushed past Gretel from behind and viciously pinched her on the arm.

"Ouch! What are you doing?" screamed Gretel in shock and genuine pain.

"Oh, don't be such a big baby," Edith snipped. "You're just a little nobody, as far as I'm concerned. Move out of the way with your ignorant friends, and let me pass."

"Yes, I'll move, but just to get far away from you," Gretel said. "You're lucky that I'm saving my nice new dress for the ceremony, or I'd mop the street with you!"

Everyone else laughed spontaneously at the mental vision of Gretel flopping Edith up and down on the cobblestones.

Then Edith answered Gretel and everyone watching, with an icy threat: "Oh my, I'm so scared of you." She feigned fright and held her hands to her face. "I can't be bothered with children, but don't worry, I'll get even with you someday." She glared at the young teenagers while she walked past them to chat sweetly with the lady chaperones.

Fritz blurted out, "I can't believe the grown-ups don't see what a bitch that Edith Luder can be!"

Everyone was happy to laugh and leave the tension with Edith behind them.

To lighten the mood, Gretel teased Ernst. "Well, look at Ernst. He does have something else to wear besides knickers!"

Ernst turned slowly around and modeled his new clothes for everyone. "Wait till you see my *good* stuff," he said, and laughed with the others.

Gretel's First Communion

As each boy and girl tried to look pious and grown up, they walked gracefully down the nave of St. Severinus Church. Herr Jorg's organ played and the building shivered.

At the altar railing, each candidate knelt to receive the bread and wine representing the body and blood of Jesus Christ. After each new candidate lit a special Communion candle, Father Weible blessed them all, and the procession made the return march up the main aisle. Music and emotion filled the space inside the church.

Joseph and Rosa sat, thinking about how grown-up their little Gretel had become as she piously marched past them.

Oh, it won't be long until she'll be coming down this same aisle on her wedding day, Rosa imagined, and she wept just thinking about how quickly time passes. *I wonder what my own life will be like then?* Rosa was so moved by the thoughts of life rushing by that she continued crying long after the procession has passed.

Joseph, too, pondered life, finding it hard to believe that his little Gretel was getting so grown up. Life could certainly throw some difficult problems at them. He prayed that her life would go better than his.

Outside the church door, on the marketplace, all the young people greeted the parishioners. Everyone was smiling and happily shaking hands. It was really emotional and all the kids knew that they had reached an important milestone in life. They were now almost grown up and members of St. Severinus Parish.

As the big Rossfeld-Geyer family walked together, back to the Golden Knight for a Communion celebration, Joseph and Rosa were again deep in their own private thoughts.

Rosa worried how she would ever set things right and wondered what would become of her.

Joseph puzzled, as he walked along looking down at the cobblestone street, about how life went on, but when would it get better for him? He didn't know what to do.

6. MARCHING OFF TO WAR

Uberauen remained an island unto itself, but life in the new twentieth century was changing rapidly. Despite all the attempts to prevent it, war began in 1914 and continued for several months. The year 1915 came and went without Friedrich being drafted.

At the Regulars' Table one evening, Herr Meyer said, "I've read in the newspaper that the war is really going well for Germany and we should win soon. Is that what you guys think?"

Wilhelm was terrified that Friedrich would be inducted, but tried to speak with a nationalist tone. He wouldn't want anybody to think that they were not patriotic. So Wilhelm Rossfeld said, "You can hear all kinds of rumors. Some of the boys who come back alive from the front say the trenches are muddy, the men are infested with cooties and the slaughter goes on unabated."

Herr Jorg shook his head. "I still don't understand what we're hoping to gain in this war. Does anybody really know why we're sending thousands of young men to their deaths?"

Friedrich served a couple of beers to the men at the Regulars' Table and overheard the conversation. "Well," he told the older men, "I don't know what it's about and I really don't want to go, but I guess I'll do it if I have to."

Herr Meyer said, "You know, a real man would have volunteered by now, instead of waiting to be drafted." He frowned at Friedrich.

"Oh, in that case maybe *you* should volunteer tomorrow," Wilhelm said in reply.

There was no response and no further discussion in Friedrich's presence.

Emma came cautiously to the dining room and said, "If you ask me, there are too many people who like to sell weapons or march their young men around in uniform. Then they go off to be killed. It's crazy!"

Herr Meyer said, "Nobody asked what you think, girlie. You had better get back to your cookstove, where you belong."

Wilhelm and the other men at the table secretly believed that Emma was correct in part of her assessment.

Then, in the spring of 1916, the dreaded imperial induction letter arrived for Friedrich. It wasn't a surprise for anyone, but the threat of death was real and they all knew it.

Early the next morning Wilhelm, Rosa, Joseph and Emma drank coffee together at the kitchen table. Gretel and Anna were still upstairs and Friedrich had not yet come down from his room. At first everyone sat silently ... except for the sound of spoons scraping the bottoms of the coffee cups.

Finally, Wilhelm had to share his thoughts. "I am so scared that Friedrich will be killed. Here I sit, his father, and I can't do anything to save him."

"I know, Papa," Emma said. "We've lost Mama and baby Josef, and now Friedrich's life is in danger. It just isn't right."

Silence and coffee sipping continued for a minute, and then Rosa said, "I've been so worried about my own life and my own marriage, as you both know."

Joseph was so embarrassed by his wife's comment that he just stared into his cup.

Rosa continued. "Now I'm terrified that Friedrich will be horribly wounded or killed. I feel so helpless and unable to change anything." She took out her handkerchief and caught her tears.

Soon Emma and Rosa were both crying. Wilhelm wanted to give in and join them, but realized that he had to stay strong for Friedrich.

Upstairs in his sparsely furnished room, Friedrich held his head with both hands and sat on the edge of his bed to think. He continued to inspect the details of his room. His Sunday suit was still hanging over there on the hook. *Dear God,* he thought, *will they use that to bury me? I'm trying to make sense of what's happening to me but it's going so fast!*

He walked over to look out the window, at the foggy courtyard below. *I wonder if I could leave on the horse or maybe the train, without anybody noticing?*

Hasso looked up and started barking and wagging his tail.

Maybe I could get to Coburg and catch a train to Switzerland. No, I can't just leave like that and shame my family. Besides, everyone in Uberauen would think that I'm a coward and I'm not a coward. I can fight, but I'd sure like to know what the hell we're really fighting about. What if I get killed? Damn, I haven't even been in love yet, and now I have to go to war!

For a few more minutes Friedrich continued looking around his room and then down onto the courtyard while possible alternatives to leaving for the front were nixed one by one. He finally gave up and went down to breakfast with Papa and his family.

A couple of weeks later, all the young men from Uberauen who were being inducted into the army were ordered to meet at city hall. Frau Luder and Herr Meyer bustled around and tried to look officious as they prepared the young inductees for a march in rough formation to the train station.

While watching arrogant Frau Luder get the young men into lines, Gretel cried softly. *I can't believe they're sending Friedrich off to war. Is this really happening? There must be something we can do.* But Gretel searched in vain for answers. Then she tried to straighten herself up to be brave for Friedrich. She knew he must be terrified but wanted to stay looking tough. *I'll bet he would rather rush into the safety of Wilhelm's strong arms,* Gretel thought, *but instead he is expected to act like a brave soldier.*

Friedrich was prepared to be a brave soldier. He stood proudly so that he would not disgrace himself and his family with tears and whimpering. The other young men from Uberauen were trying to make light of the terrifying situation too. Friedrich was glad to see his friends: Ralf Aachener, Markus Schöneberger and Wolfram Diehl. All the young men who had flirted with girls together on the marketplace were glad to share this scary and thrilling moment with close friends.

Finally Herr Meyer told the young men to begin marching. With a proud military march step that he had actually never practiced, he led the men out along the sidewalk in front of city hall and then up the cobblestone streets to the train station. Family members and girlfriends accompanied their young men to spend as much time with them as possible. Emma held Friedrich's right arm and Wilhelm walked on his left. Gretel walked arm in arm with Emma and Friedrich's sister, Frieda. Everyone tried to be in a festive mood. Some people even waved the German flag, while others scattered flower petals on the street. The Uberauen brass band played martial music to accompany the young men marching.

After the otherworldly parade to the station, the new soldiers were relieved to finally be seated inside the train cars. Friedrich leaned across his friend, Wolfram Diehl, so he could wave at his family members who were waving at him from the platform.

Courtesy of Eisenbahnmuseum Lehmann

Train Station, 1902

"Take care of yourself," shouted Wilhelm above all the noise of the puffing steam engine and the shouts of other families and friends.

Slowly the steam engine began its measured puffs, and the train moved gradually out of the station. All the families, neighbors, friends, and girlfriends watched as the train carrying their loved ones became smaller, ever smaller, until it finally disappeared.

Gretel and the crowd walked solemnly back to the marketplace. She then joined Rosa and Emma, who filed into the pews of St. Severinus Church to pray for Friedrich's safe return.

Gretel's prayer was probably much like everyone else's: "Holy Saint Nepomuk, please guard and protect Friedrich during this war. Bring him back safely to us soon. Amen." *I wish I could think of something good to pray that would really protect Friedrich, but I don't know what it would be,* Gretel thought sadly.

Little did Gretel suspect that the same tragic prayers were being repeated all over Europe by loved ones of soldiers who were being sent to fight in the same horrible and senseless war.

Gretel walked alone, deep in thought, out of church and into the warm, peaceful sunshine on the marketplace. *Surely the world must still be in order. There is city hall, Blumentritt's store, Golden Knight and St. Severinus Church.* As she started the short walk down the Brunnen Gasse to the Golden Knight, Gretel couldn't imagine that her world would not stay exactly as she had always known it. But in fact, her girlhood was rapidly ending and horrible international changes were already under way that would affect all the rest of her life.

7. THE GREAT WAR

The cuckoo clock in Emma's kitchen ticked rhythmically while Friedrich was away at the front. Even so, it seemed like Gretel had hardly flipped the calendar, before it was already autumn. Life continued very much the same in Uberauen, except for the terrible war news that the men talked about at the Regulars' Table.

Then, before Rosa and Emma began to put out the Christmas decorations, a letter came from Friedrich.

"Before you even open it, I can tell you that it's been censored. We'll read only mild things in Friedrich's letter, but at least he's alive to write it," Wilhelm said, shaking his head.

The Western Front
December 9, 1916

Dear Papa and Family,

I'm writing to you again, as best I can, from the trenches we've been living in for an eternity. It is really cold, wet, muddy, and I'm miserable. Memories of home keep me going. Thanks so much for the package of meat, canned food, warm gloves and socks! As usual, I shared some of the goodies with the other guys.

We would all really like to spend the night in a nice clean bed where we could cover up with a warm feather bedspread. Sometimes I think about the fun and work I shared with you at the Golden Knight. Of course I think about the pretty girls that I can't talk to, but I brought along a couple of their pictures. Some of the nurses at the front look pretty good, but they're too frazzled to flirt.

Here in the front lines we face the horrible new war machines that are being used. Since we are in muddy trenches, now both sides are using poisonous gases. We have to have practice drills to get masks on before the gas chokes us! Then we have our Zeppelins, and both sides have airplanes that can fly over to take pictures for reconnaissance or to drop bombs. This is truly hell on earth!

When we get the order to go "over the top," we know that many of us will be killed or wounded. Right now everything is relatively calm, but the past couple of weeks have been horrible! We had uninterrupted artillery fire, night and day for four days so that we couldn't even get out of the trenches. We lay there in the cold mud as our rations were used up and just had to keep our heads down when we heard the screaming of the grenades. At least we finally got the new steel helmets to replace the spike dress helmets that we had before.

Just lately it got even worse because the machine gun fire from the enemy lines stopped, and masses of French troops left their trenches and charged toward us! It was unimaginable carnage! I had to keep loading and reloading my machine gun as my fire mowed down the French guys like mowing hay. I just can't allow myself to really think about what I'm doing!

The horror continued as the frozen dead bodies of our buddies and those of the enemy soldiers were gathered up and stacked in mass graves on the battlefield. Thank God, you really can't imagine the heartbreaking sight of so many young lives cut short. Their stiff bodies were ceremoniously laid to rest for Kaiser and fatherland. The priest mumbled a few words as the bugler played "Ich hatt' einen Kameraden." I can't stand even listening to the bugler playing this sound from hell!

I'm sorry. I don't want to worry you. It's not the Golden Knight, but most of the time we've had pretty good food, some beer and cigarettes, but we have also gone days at a time with nothing to eat.

(Censored: When we're out of food we sometimes have to eat the rats that are everywhere in this filth. They have even eaten our fallen comrades!) The worst of it is the cold and mud. It's like an evil meat grinder and every day more guys are getting wounded and killed. It's horrible! The slaughter reminds me of the butchering that Papa and I do, but these are our friends getting blown up and shot! I try not to think about it happening to me, but I've been here so long that I worry about my luck running out.

Something strange but wonderful did happen the other night. We are all homesick, so we started singing Christmas carols. When we sang "Stille Nacht, Hilige Nacht," the Americans and English joined in and sang it in English and the French sang it in French. I kept wondering why we're shooting and killing each other. They have never done anything to me, and I sure as hell have never done anything to them!

I keep asking myself, what's the point in all this slaughter? Oh, I get insanely angry at them when they shoot one of our guys and I curse them for all eternity. Later on when it's dark and quiet, I'm sitting in cold mud, urine and blood. I just want this insanity to end!

I have all of you in my prayers, and I'm so glad to know that you're all praying for me. When all goes well, maybe I'll be back to hug all of you again soon!

With the hope of seeing you all soon,
Your brave soldier boy,

Friedrich

Another blink of the eye and it was 1917, with Friedrich still fighting in France and the family living in constant fear that he would be killed. At every Mass, Gretel, Rosa, Wilhelm and Emma joined other family members at St. Severinus Church to pray for Friedrich and the other brave young men from Uberauen.

As often as possible, between serving lunch and then cooking and serving dinner, one of the family members wrote a letter to Friedrich. There really was no news in Uberauen except about the war, so everyone tried to write something comforting. Then in early April of 1917, it was Gretel's turn to write.

Uberauen
April 5, 1917

Dear Friedrich,

All is well in Uberauen. It's finally starting to get warm and some of the daffodils are ready to bloom in the garden. Mama says we'll have to dig up the soil and start planting our vegetables. We've been saving the wrinkled potatoes to cut into pieces and plant for this year. We'll really have to hurry and get the lettuce planted because all the lunch guests are asking for it.

A couple of days ago, Grandfather and Rosine Kiefer rode with the horse and wagon over to Gerstenfeld to buy a hog and some chickens from that guy that lives across from the church. As you well know, you can't make a hog go where you want it to go. Grandfather, Rosine and the farmer all used gates and canes to guide the hog up into the big wooden wagon. Rosine said that it squealed and lurched all the way back to Uberauen and kept trying to jump up and get out!

Tonight, Mama and Emma will be cooking your favorite dinner: pork roast with bread dumplings and green beans. For afternoon coffee you get, Apfelküchlein mit vanille sosse! Yum! The men at the Regulars' Table will all be asking when dinner will be ready!

Over the weekend, Frieda, your sister, not Fritz's Frieda, came to visit for a couple of days and sends you her love. She's been working as a telephone operator in Nurnberg.

Papa made some good private money this week when there was a wedding at church. Flour is hard to come by, but he got to bake the wedding cake and they even ordered some of those little French finger cakes. Papa says that some people are sneaking sawdust into their bread, but we haven't come to that yet.

You know about our "sweet" Frau Luder. She and other officials are constantly checking to see if Grandfather is using the rationed amount of meat for the butcher shop. Of course she'd like nothing better than to file charges against him if she could—bitch!

Last night the bride's family reserved the extra room at the Golden Knight for their wedding rehearsal dinner. Grandfather was smiling about the big money he made on that!

Speaking of food and rationing, you've probably heard about everybody using turnips because there's so little to eat. The newspaper even has recipes for making turnip soup, turnip stew, etc. It would be funny if things weren't desperate for so many of our neighbors.

Well, it's getting close to time for the men to come to the Regulars' Table and enjoy their beer, so I'd better close for now. We all REALLY miss you and pray for you every day.

Keep your head down and stay well!

With all of our love,

Gretel

Each day there were war bulletins posted at the train station in Uberauen and city hall, with news of battles and, worst of all, the names of those young men who had been killed. When Ralf Aachener and Markus Schöneberger were killed, nobody wrote to tell Friedrich because they knew he himself was worried enough about surviving the war.

Then on April 13, 1917, Frau Meyer from city hall came into the kitchen at the Golden Knight, sobbing uncontrollably. Everyone froze.

"Friedrich is dead," she whispered through her tears. "It was on this morning's news bulletin that came over the telegraph. He was killed in France."

"No!" gasped Gretel. "That's impossible. There must be some mistake. Friedrich can't be dead!" Memories of her wonderful young uncle zipped through Gretel's mind. In milliseconds she remembered him smiling, selling Christmas cookies, butchering meat, and always laughing. "Friedrich is such a handsome, funny, sweet man. Surely, God has not taken him away from us," Gretel cried as she held on to Rosa.

Emma felt faint as she walked over to hug Frau Meyer, Rosa and Gretel. "I've been afraid we'd get this horrible news and now it's happened. Friedrich, poor boy, he was just getting started in life and now he's swept away. My heart is breaking!"

Rosa, Fritz and Emma hugged and cried together, including normally aloof Frau Meyer. Although he dreaded having to share such awful news, Fritz went out to tell his father.

"Father," Fritz began softly, "it breaks my heart to tell you, but Friedrich has been killed."

Wilhelm bent suddenly forward, "No! No, it can't be!" Even though he was still covered in animal blood and feces, Wilhelm grabbed his living son, Fritz, and hugged him tightly. "Fritz, how will I ever live through this?" Wilhelm kept his head bowed and held onto Fritz as the two of them went back into the kitchen.

"This is more sorrow than I can bear," whispered Wilhelm as he joined his family in the kitchen.

He hugged Emma and remembered all the death and mourning in his life. "Barbara is dead, baby Josef ... and now Friedrich too. Why? It's not fair! My God, what have I done to deserve such punishment?" He held the telegram in his twitching hands and read a couple of words: "for Emperor and country," "heroic sacrifice."

"You idiotic *Schweine!*[12] You have my son's death on your conscience for all eternity! I curse you all to hell!" Then Wilhelm sank into a chair and held his head in his hands while he sobbed.

Finally, Gretel was the only family member who dared to stand next to Wilhelm and hold him around the shoulders and console him.

Friedrich Rossfeld from Uberauen died a hero's death for Kaiser and fatherland, and now lies in a mass grave that is frozen over. His name

---

12 *Schwein/e* – pig, pigs – a serious epithet in German

joins that of countless others on a little cross in rows that stretch to the horizon.

The loving family of Friedrich Rossfeld, logically, did not think beyond their own extreme sorrow at losing him. The awful truth was that families from around the world were mourning the deaths of their own wonderful sons in the Great War. The suffering in France, Germany, Belgium and England was catastrophic. It was so horrible that people called it "the war to end all wars." That, unfortunately, was also not to be the case.

A few days later a funeral Mass was held to celebrate the life of Friedrich Rossfeld. Gretel and all the extended family walked together to the funeral service at St. Severinus Church. Just a couple of weeks before, she had been there for the funeral of Friedrich's other friends. That sad event didn't begin to prepare her for Friedrich's death and funeral.

"Mother Mary, please take the soul of my wonderful Friedrich and hold it gently to your Sacred Heart," Gretel prayed while sobbing softly.

Similar prayers were being repeated by every friend, neighbor and family member.

Father Weible gave a comforting sermon and someone read the 23rd Psalm. When the reader came to the part about "Yea, though I walk through the valley of the shadow of death, I will fear no evil," you could hear quiet sobbing all over the church. Up and down the rows of pews and up into the high ceiling of St. Severinus Church, the space filled with empathetic sorrow, sobbing and prayers for Friedrich's soul. His horrible death and funeral struck those parish families especially hard whose own wonderful sons had been slaughtered on the front.

After what seemed like a very long time of weeping and praying, Herr Jorg began to play, through his own tears, "Mozart's Requiem." The beautiful organ music flowed over the families and friends as they sadly moved down the main aisle and out onto the marketplace. Everyone walked out arm in arm while trying to comfort each other in this time of grief.

When Gretel reached the marketplace outside the church door, she could see the Golden Knight, city hall and the Brunnen Gasse. *Is this a dream world?* She held Mama and Papa's arms and walked on down to the Golden Knight. *How can Uberauen look as if nothing has happened? Friedrich is never coming back to us, and yet everything looks just the same.*

Everyone knows everyone else and everyone else's business in Uberauen, but today at least, it feels like one large grieving family.

Joseph held Gretel's arm and wished he had something to say that would relieve her pain, but he had no words to comfort her.

Wilhelm walked with Rosine Kiefer and Emma. "I don't know how I'll ever live through this," Wilhelm said simply. "The anguish of losing Friedrich consumes my whole being!"

Friedrich and his friend, Wolfram Diehl, were killed just two days apart. Most young victims of the Great War were buried in mass graves on or near the battlefields where they fell. A famous poem by John McCrae that was written in May of 1915 conveys a bit of the anguish of seeing young men's lives so horribly cut short.

Here is the first verse from *In Flanders Fields*.

> In Flanders fields the poppies blow
> Between the crosses, row on row,
> That mark our place; and in the sky
> The larks, still bravely singing, fly
> Scarce heard amid the guns below.

8. MAXIMILIAN BERGMEISTER

For several months, Gretel and her extended family grieved for Friedrich and missed him terribly. But life has its euphoric ups and tragic downs. Just when it seems as if life is too bitter to go on, hope for a new beginning comes along.

Wilhelm spent hours each day mourning Friedrich's death, but he, also, was forced to face the future. His days were full of worries: *How am I going to live in my old age? How will we ever get by without Friedrich to inherit the business? Who will be here to raise this family and find good wives and husbands for everyone? I still can't believe that Friedrich is gone. I could cry all day if I didn't stop myself. It's just too much pain! But I must move on, for my sake and for the family.*

While he was methodically slicing up a hog by himself, Wilhelm made an important decision. In the late winter of 1918, he began to read through the "help wanted" and apprenticeship notices in the newspaper, but none of the young men sounded like the perfect choice. Wilhelm had already mentally sorted through all the young men in the area who had survived the war, but none of them were butchers who might also be a good prospect for Emma. A whole generation of men had been decimated by the war. Would anybody be left to work? So he decided to place an ad in the newspaper himself and see if there were any young butchers looking for a job.

So, how should I word this? Wilhelm pondered. He finally wrote the ad: "Well-established butcher shop and delicatessen seeks fully qualified partner." *That should do it,* he decided confidently, and then posted the letter.

Now, if the young butcher turns out to be a good match for Emma, that would be even better. Wilhelm smiled at the idea.

After only a few days Wilhelm received a letter from a young man named Maximilian Bergmeister, who said he was interested in the job. Wilhelm wrote back and invited him to come for a visit to see if they were a good working match.

Wilhelm was still worrying. Would Maximilian Bergmeister really show up for the interview? Maybe he would be incapable of taking on such a job.

—❧❦—

Before she heard about Wilhelm interviewing a new butcher's assistant, Emma was again brooding over her own life. Friedrich's death had touched her and all the family deeply.

I'm twentyfour years old and still unmarried, thought Emma as she professionally prepared a delicious dinner for the guests at the Golden Knight. *If this keeps up, I'll be an old maid working in the family kitchen while other girls fall in love. Men don't know that I'm in here cooking. Nobody even knows I exist!* She felt angry and frustrated, but there were few people she could talk to and there seemed to be no way out of her predicament. Emma did not yet know that the winds of change were bringing good news.

As he drank his beer at the Regulars' Table that evening, Wilhelm told his family that Maximilian Bergmeister had been invited for a job interview.

Fritz raised his eyebrows and asked, "What will a new butcher do that we aren't doing?"

"You've never wanted to be a butcher," Wilhelm answered honestly. "The sight of blood and guts is disgusting to you. I have to find a man who likes butchering."

"I know that Emma wants to ask if he's goodlooking," Gretel said, and then laughed.

Everyone in the family circle willingly joined in the laughter—including Emma.

"How would I know how he looks?" answered Wilhelm with fake disinterest.

"He's probably got a greasy mustache and pimples," suggested Rosine Kiefer, while stroking her bare upper lip. Everyone laughed.

It was so nice to laugh again, Rosine thought to herself. They had all cried over Friedrich's death for so long. She loved being able to laugh and have fun.

Gretel asked, "What if he turns out to be really stupid and he can't even help out?"

"Don't worry. If he's too stupid, I'll know it right away," Wilhelm asserted with conviction. Just you let me handle this."

"I don't know," Emma said. "I'm excited about the idea of a young man in the house"—more laughter—"but we don't even know if he's a hard worker."

Wilhelm shared his thoughts aloud: "Well, he's coming here for a few days. You're all welcome to ask him questions after I finish mine. Maybe that will help us all make up our minds. However, I'll make the final decision."

"Yes, Grandfather," everyone replied.

After the family discussion, Wilhelm returned to work. He sat for a few moments in the courtyard, under the grapevine, to smoke his pipe and reflect. *While I'm looking for a new butcher to learn this job, the most important thing is to find a man who knows what he's doing. Of course, the perfect choice might also marry Emma.* Wilhelm blew smoke rings and smiled to himself about his clever matchmaker plan.

Of course there are no secrets in Uberauen because everyone knows everyone else and everyone else's business. When Maximilian Bergmeister stepped off the train from Wurzburg, everyone peeped cautiously out their windows or from their buggy or car to see what he looked like.

Gretel's friend Edeltraudt, from the telegraph office, sent her little brother to run and tell Gretel.

"Fräulein Geyer, Edeltraudt says to tell you that a young man got off the train from Wurzburg," recited the little brother.

"Did you see him? Is he handsome, or does he look awful?" Gretel asked eagerly.

The young boy looked puzzled. "Well … if the guy I saw but didn't know, is the butcher … I guess he looks okay," answered the boy cautiously.

"Oh, that's wonderful! Please tell Edeltraudt thanks," Gretel said as she gave the boy a cookie.

When Edeltraudt's brother had gone, she shouted to everyone in the family, "Edeltraudt said that the new man is here! Meet me upstairs." Gretel's announcement echoed in the house as an immodest screech.

"Gretel, Emma," Rosa said, "don't carry on like a couple of fishwives! Don't you dare stare out the windows," Rosa said as she rushed into the dining room so she herself could spy out the window.

While part of the Rossfeld clan was jostling up the stairs to stare shamelessly out the windows, Maximilian Bergmeister strode up the Bahnhofstrasse from the train station, to the marketplace.

Conniving Edith Luder had heard that Maximilian was coming for a job interview with Wilhelm Rossfeld. She skillfully held back the living room drapes and secretly watched Maximilian walking confidently up the street. *Um,* Edith thought, *too bad he's just a working-class butcher. He's nice-looking.*

———❊❊❊———

Maximilian reached the marketplace and noticed the fountain, St. Severinus Church and city hall as he searched for the Brunnen Gasse. A few more steps took him to the Golden Knight. There he paused for a second, in front of the short, rounded door to the cellar, where Gretel and the kids had played hideandseek.

What a greatlooking place, Maximilian thought as he surveyed the buildings facing the street. *There is the butcher shop and this is the inn.*

Of course Gretel, Emma, Fritz and everyone else were peeping clumsily out the windows for the best view of Maximilian. In the slaughter shed, Wilhelm was dying to look too, but he had to be professional.

Fritz shouted, "Here he comes!"

"He's sooo handsome," Gretel said, and giggled as she and Emma watched boldly from upstairs. "Do you think he's married?"

Gretel, Rosine and Emma speculated and squirmed at the prospect of a handsome single man in the house.

While everyone was occupied, eightyearold Anna Geyer slipped behind the curtain, where she stood in plain sight from the street. Maximilian looked up and saw her. Anna waved haltingly, but Maximilian thought it would be better to pretend he didn't notice her.

"I'll hurry downstairs to meet him," Emma shouted over her shoulder. She ran along the windowlined hall to the stairs.

Everyone else continued to peep from behind the curtained windows.

In the meantime Maximilian moved past the cellar door, under the large entry gate and approached the front door with the grapevine hanging above it. Since it was a business, he walked hesitantly through the door and into the hallway of the Golden Knight.

There, Emma calmly greeted him like the young businesswoman that she had become.

I wonder how I look, Emma wondered. *I've been cooking all day. My hair is a mess. My apron is dirty and I've been running down the stairs.*

There was nothing for her to worry about. Maximilian was a hardworking and down-to-earth young man and, besides, he was worried about his job interview.

Maximilian surveyed Emma from top to bottom with unobtrusive precision: pretty … nice smile, shapely breasts, curved hips. He wondered if she was married.

He smiled at her and said, "Good day."

"Good day," answered Emma. "Just wait here in the dining room, Herr Bergmeister, and I'll call my father." Emma directed Maximilian to the dining room. "Would you like a beer while you're waiting?"

"Yes, thank you," Maximilian replied politely as his eyes followed her every movement.

Emma left Maximilian in the dining room and rushed back to her familiar kitchen. *Oh, I hope my face isn't red,* Emma worried as she brought Maximilian the beer.

"To your health," Emma said, as servers always did when serving food or drink to patrons in Franconia.

"Thank you," Maximilian answered. "I can really use a beer after that long trip on the train."

"I can certainly understand that," Emma replied, pretending to calmly make business small talk. "I'll go tell Papa that you're here."

Emma left the dining room and walked with the air of a skilled actress past the bench under the grapevine where her Papa smoked his pipe, and out to the slaughter shed to get Wilhelm.

I would die of embarrassment if that young man sees me with a red face! But he is nice-looking. She chuckled and smiled with anticipation.

"Papa, the young man is here about the job," Emma told Wilhelm calmly.

"Oh, good, I hope he's the right one. I could sure use some help around here—besides you, of course." Wilhelm smiled at Emma and gave her a quick forehead kiss. "I'll go wash a little bit in the laundry room and slip on a clean apron. Then I'll meet you in the dining room. Bring me a beer," Wilhelm said as he moved off to get cleaned up.

His hope was that this young guy would turn out to be somebody dependable. He considered himself too old for the work. Wilhelm's thoughts dwelled painfully for a second on memories of Friedrich. However, he could not allow himself to grieve for his son just then. He had to stay focused on the present.

The job interview went well. Maximilian had kept a professional journal of his employers and their assessment of his skills and reliability. He had all perfect grades and notations from previous employers. While Wilhelm and Maximilian held a businesslike interview, Fritz, Gretel, Anna and Rosine continued to eavesdrop from the top of the stairs.

Occasionally the floorboards creaked, but Wilhelm and Maximilian tactfully pretended not to hear the sounds.

I'm very impressed with this young man. I'll hire him, Wilhelm decided spontaneously.

Wilhelm was so confident that he invited Maximilian to move right into one of the rooms above the smokehouse. The members of Wilhelm's extended family at the Golden Knight watched and wondered what would happen next.

Maximilian's arrival at the Golden Knight brought on lots of changes. Emma finally had a new romantic prospect. Wilhelm had a hardworking butcher by his side to help in the butcher shop, even as thoughts of Friedrich still preoccupied his mind. For Rosa, however, overwhelming old concerns remained unresolved.

One autumn morning Rosa was peeling potatoes and chopping vegetables as usual. Emma brought Max (Maximilian) a morning break snack of boiled beef, homemade bread and salt. Rosa smiled to herself. *I'm so happy for Emma. She certainly deserves a chance at having a good life. My own life is ruined and I don't know how to put everything right again. Right now I'm just exhausted from grief and worry.*

Without knowing that Franz Baumfeller was having similar thoughts, Rosa tried to reasonably reevaluate her life while trying to concentrate on her work at the same time.

Rosa Geyer, 1900

This potato looks too rotten for me to even save, she thought as she dropped the potato into the slop bucket and reached for another.

Welcoming the chance to be alone, Rosa indulged in her puzzling considerations: *Joseph and I just maintain the appearance of a marriage. He has no interest in me and actually loathes me! We haven't had a sexual relationship for years and I have no idea how he gets sexual satisfaction. I guess it's not surprising that I seek affection from Franz. But do we really love each other, or are we just 'playing around,' the way the vicious gossip describes us? The bullying, shunning and gossip is weighing me down to the point that I live in constant fear and dread. I'm at my wit's end. What can I do?*

Rosa continued to search for answers while she mixed the batter for her potato dumplings. *I'm a devoted Catholic, so we can forget about getting a divorce. Joseph can't leave me and I can't leave him. On the other hand, I suffer unrelenting guilt about bringing Anna into the world, even though I love her deeply. I'm afraid to go to confession, and Father Weible has been after me for years!*

Everyone in the family already knows about us, but they love me and want to find solutions. Wilhelm has endured Mama's death and baby Josef's. Losing Friedrich in that awful war was almost more than he can bear. They've been reluctantly patient with me while hoping for a resolution, but there is no time left to wait. I've got to act!

So Rosa wrote a short letter to Franz and then dropped it in the post box in front of city hall. It simply read: "Meet me at 2:00 next Tuesday at the vegetable garden."

The next day, Franz Baumfeller received Rosa's fateful letter.

Oh my God, why is she taking the risk of writing to me? Franz wondered as he ripped the letter open. *She wants to meet me in broad daylight! On the other hand, I guess it's actually better, so nobody is suspicious. I don't know what kind of rendezvous Rosa has in mind, but it's probably a good chance for us to clear the air and for me to let her know that we have to stop seeing each other.*

On Tuesday it was time for the fateful meeting.

"Emma, I'm going out to get some carrots from the garden and I'll be right back," Rosa said casually. She maneuvered her basket out the entrance door of the Golden Knight, and then strode across the courtyard.

Max was looking up at the kitchen window as Emma was smiling down at him.

That is so sweet, Rosa thought. But although she was happy for Emma, it was also a painful reminder that her own chances for an acceptable relationship seemed to be over forever.

Always aware that someone might be watching her, Rosa walked up to the marketplace. At city hall she turned onto the Forellenbacher Strasse so Joseph was less likely to see her walking past Steinhauer's Bakery.

As she neared the Forellenbacher Gate, she thought, *I have to admit that I'm still really attracted to Franz. Maybe in another world we could have had a life together. Right now I'm scared to death of being found out!* She glanced up at the window of Steinhauer's Bakery and then continued walking through the city gate and on out to the garden.

Oh, no, there's Frau Steinhauer working in her garden. This is not going to be easy. "Good morning, Frau Steinhauer," Rosa said as she passed her neighbor. "So, are we getting a fresh head of cabbage or a bouquet of flowers today?"

Frau Steinhauer walked over to the garden gate and cordially shook hands with Rosa. "These last couple of days I've been so busy at the store that I haven't even had time to get out here and see what's ready to harvest. How are you, Frau Geyer? You're looking a little pale and drawn."

"Oh, you know how it goes. First, we have the lunch and dinner crowds, and then we have to clean up. There's always something. Did you hear that dog barking all night last night? I swear if that happens again tonight, I'll report it to the constable. Well, please say hello to your family for me. I'm off to dig up a few things and maybe cut some flowers for the dining room. I'll see you again soon."

Rosa walked on down the path to the garden that Wilhelm had had for years. *I hope Frau Steinhauer believes the stories about why I don't look well. I've always liked her, but I won't be able to talk to Franz if she is so close by.*

As Rosa entered the garden, she put her basket on the grass and retrieved a hoe from the garden shed. Before she left the shed, she peeped through the partially open door to see if Frau Steinhauer was still in the garden. *Oh, thank God, she has everything in her basket and she's leaving.*

I'll go out and start hoeing some of the weeds until Franz comes. In spite of the guilt, I honestly have to admit that I can't wait to see him again! God forgive me.

A few minutes later, Franz strolled slowly down the path and stopped to lean casually on the garden gate. Rosa's heart jumped at the sight of him.

"Good day, Herr Baumfeller.[13] How are you today?"

Rosa's lover

Rosa greeted him loudly in case anyone else was within earshot. Rosa examined Franz's appearance as she approached him. *Oh, why does he have to be so handsome? His kissable lips are irresistible!*

Franz watched Rosa walk toward him. "Well, you look nice today, Rosa," he said in a light tone of voice. To himself, though, he thought he should be projecting more seriousness.

But he continued to fantasize about her shapely body. Her sad expression only made her look more vulnerable and appealing.

Rosa's face showed signs that she had been crying. "Franz, we really do have to have a serious talk. What will become of us? I'm exhausted from worrying and I have no answers."

Franz looked at Rosa intensely. "Rosa, I've also been thinking and I've made a decision that may seem harsh to you, but it's the only way out. I have to stop seeing you and find a wife before I end up living alone. That would not be fair to me and it wouldn't help you. I know that sounds cruel, but your situation is not going to change and Anna has

---

13   Rosa's lover – the man in the photographs is an unknown contemporary from about 1910; *Zeitgenössisches Foto.*

always known you and Joseph as her parents. … Isn't there some chance that you and Joseph can still patch up your marriage?"

"Joseph!" Rosa whispered in disbelief at Franz's remark. "Franz, Joseph isn't attracted to me and he'll never be happy with me. His sex life is a mystery and so is his personality. We're strangers who happen to be sharing a marriage. I don't see him deserting the girls and me, but we'll never be in love. He knows about us, so he is humiliated and suffers as much as I do. There is no hope for our marriage, but for now, Franz, that does not matter. You still have a chance for happiness, so you must take it. I think I'll always love you, but I agree that we have to stop seeing each other and you have to find a wife." Rosa wept and dabbed her eyes with her apron. "It's bad enough that my own life is ruined, and I've destroyed Joseph. The pain of losing you and the shame caused by my mistakes is almost more than I can bear. I honestly don't see any way out of this agony."

Franz looked around him to see if anyone was nearby, and then he looked tenderly into Rosa's eyes. "No matter what happens, remember that I will always love you. We'll have to love each other from a distance, but it won't stop the way we feel."

"I know." Rosa inhaled a deep breath before speaking. "At least we agree that our relationship has to end, but it is so, so very painful. I will mourn for you as I have for my loved ones who have died."

"Yes. When we run into each other around Uberauen, we'll have to just greet each other like acquaintances," said Franz softly. "Rosa, I don't dare kiss you in public, even though I'm aching to grab you, but please know that I'm giving you a sincere lover's kiss right now. I won't say goodbye because as long as we live, we'll always share a special bond."

Franz turned and walked briskly back up the path to Forellenbacher Gate and toward the rest of his life.

Rosa quickly retreated to the garden shed before anyone could see her crying. After a few minutes, she snatched a few carrots and started back to the Golden Knight. *I'll have to start slicing onions as soon as I get back,* she planned, *to explain my tears, or Emma will be worried.*

As she walked home, Rosa continued grieving her loss of Franz and considered solutions that would help her survive that loss. *It will be so hard to see him in public and still try to treat him with indifference. I guess it's part of my punishment and a skill I'll have to learn.*

Even while Rosa believed that losing Franz was the worst that could happen in their relationship, she had no way of knowing that she had not solved all her problems.

PART TWO:
TEEN AND YOUNG ADULT YEARS

Gretel Geyer (front center) with friends and family

9. DOUBLE WEDDING

A few months went by and Maximilian had become a happy part of Wilhelm Rossfeld's business and home.

Everyone soon noticed that Emma and Max were "visiting" an awful lot when he brought meat to the butcher shop to sell to customers. Emma was a mature twenty-four-year-old woman who had worked hard all her life. But when she was around Max, she giggled like a young teenager.

Gretel chuckled to Rosa, and then said, "Can you believe how much Emma likes Max? And he seems to be clumsily flirting with her too."

"I'm so glad to see that she has found someone nice," Rosa said. "So many boys were killed in that awful war that I was afraid she wouldn't find anyone. He seems to be especially smart and he's very handsome."

"I know. He really looks too good for the hard work of being a butcher," added Gretel thoughtfully.

"Yes, but being a butcher brings in good money," Rosa answered.

Gretel and Rosa smiled and spied out the kitchen windows to watch Emma and Max talking and laughing in the courtyard of the Golden Knight. Sometimes Emma and Max sat under the grapevine at the kitchen window. Nobody said anything about them being away from their work. Wilhelm, Gretel, Rosa and everyone else watched and gratefully approved.

As the endless winter of 1919 began to thaw in Franconia, Max proposed to Emma.

"Yes, yes, a thousand times *yes*," said Emma as she lunged at Max and hugged him. "Oh, I'm so happy I could pop!"

Even though it wasn't a romantic place to share an engagement announcement, Emma and Max went quickly into the slaughter shed to tell Wilhelm.

"Really, you want to marry Max?" While smiling from ear to ear, Wilhelm hugged them both. "I suspected we'd be hearing this great news. Congratulations! I couldn't be happier!"

Gretel came innocently into the kitchen to tell Rosa all the news, without knowing the effect that it might have on her mama.

"Mama, Emma and Max are getting married! Isn't that great? And besides that, Aunt Frieda is marrying Franz Baumfeller on the same day. It's a double wedding. Everybody in Uberauen will be talking about this."

Rosa froze as if struck by lightning. *I have to keep chopping carrots as if nothing is different, even as my life is swirling out of control. Franz is marrying Frieda. He's marrying my own half-sister! My God, I hope she doesn't know about us. I can't bear this shame. And besides that, the pain of losing him is far worse than I ever thought it would be. I've got to get out of this kitchen right now!*

"Oh, Gretel, please help in the kitchen for a while. I'm going to lie down for a minute," Rosa explained as she quickly left the room.

"Are you all right, Mama? Should I make you some chamomile tea?" Gretel asked.

Wilhelm was so pleased with his covert plot to unite Emma and Max that he sprawled on the bench below the grapevine to enjoy an extra moment of silent retrospection. He lit his pipe and leaned back to absorb the pale, late winter sunshine. Wilhelm pondered life's mysteries as his pipe smoke swirled around him. *Life is so strange. It goes by very quickly and sometimes the sadness we have to endure is so intense that we think we can't go on.* He blew more smoke rings. *Then there are moments of such great joy that your heart is bursting. No, life is a mystery that I can't figure out.*

Although Wilhelm was a thoughtful and considerate man, he didn't realize the unbearable agony that Rosa had been experiencing just on the other side of the window behind him.

For a few minutes, Wilhelm happily celebrated the good news of Emma, Max, Frieda and Franz's double wedding. But then a tear ran slowly down his ruddy cheek as he again remembered Barbara, the love of his life, and Friedrich's recent death.

Wilhelm reflected as he blinked away more private tears. *Be happy, dear Barbara. Our wonderful Emma has found her handsome prince.*

On the first Saturday in May, Emma, Max, Frieda and Franz met at St. Severinus Church for their double wedding. Of course, practically the whole town of Uberauen was in attendance for the event. It was the place to be. The parishioners were all dressed up and sitting in the pews. Friends and neighbors greeted one another or occasionally gossiped about someone else.

Rosa, Joseph, Anna and Gretel sat in the pew together. Rosa looked cautiously around the church. Frau Luder whispered with Frau Pucher and looked at Rosa, causing her to wonder if she was gossiping about her again. Rosa hoped she didn't tell Frieda about Franz and her.

"Shh," Herr Blumentritt warned Frau Pucher. "The organ music is starting."

The organ began to play and the choir sang *"So Nimm Denn Meine Hände."*

Gretel sat quietly for a moment and remembered the funeral of Friedrich Rossfeld that had taken place such a short time ago right there in St. Severinus Church. She thought of her dear Friedrich, knowing he would love this day. Then her focus returned to the joy of the present.

Rosa's mind raced as she sat uneasily next to Gretel. *Franz is standing right in front of me. Do I wish I were the one marrying Franz today? I wonder how many people in church know that Franz was my lover? Now they're all watching and judging me. The shame of this moment is really so extreme that I feel like running for the door. I'm supposed to be happy for Emma and Frieda, but all I can really think about is how scared and ashamed I am.*

Wilhelm Rossfeld could hardly believe that two of his daughters were getting married on the same day. While he waited to give his daughters away, he was preoccupied with his own thoughts. Maybe now that Franz was marrying Frieda, Rosa and Joseph would find their way back together.

Wilhelm tugged to pull the stiff shirt collar away from his neck. He marveled that his little Emma and Frieda were getting married. He could remember so clearly when they were born. It seemed like only yesterday. He knew Barbara would have loved being there to see their daughters getting married.

While sitting with her family, cousin Rosine Kiefer and friend Fastnacht's Betti, Gretel looked around the church to see if any cute boys were there. So many young men had been tragically killed in the war, but the younger boys were growing up and looking interesting in their suits and ties. Ernst Waldberger and Gretel's cousin Fritz no longer stuck out their tongues at her, but pretended not to know she was there. Gretel wondered if she would end up marrying her distant relative by marriage, Ernst. He *was* nice-looking and funny.

Finally it was time for Wilhelm to walk down the aisle with his two daughters. When the organ music started, everyone stood up. The priest was already at the altar, awaiting the future brides and grooms. Heavenly music again filled St. Severinus Church.

After Emma, Max, Frieda and Franz had exchanged vows and put rings on their right hands, they took Holy Communion and received the priest's blessing: "In the name of the Father, and of the Son and of the Holy Spirit. Amen. I now pronounce you husbands and wives."

Everyone in the pews smiled and clapped. The husbands kissed their new brides and everyone clapped louder. Then they walked out the main aisle of the church while their neighbors, family and friends applauded and smiled. It was a moment they would remember for the rest of their lives.

In the pews many tears were shed and each person had his or her own private thoughts as the happy young people went out onto the marketplace to shake hands with everyone.

Rosa felt as if everyone was looking at her. *I wish I could sink through the floor of this church. The idea that I have to walk out and congratulate Frieda and Franz when the whole town may know about our sins, is so demeaning.* She tried to pull herself together for the gauntlet of friends and family that would be waiting outside on the marketplace.

Joseph felt equally ashamed and totally ill at ease as he and Rosa walked out of church together. He had to maintain some appearance of propriety. He told himself to just keep walking, smile a little and say hello.

In fact most people just wanted to celebrate the wedding. Gretel, aunts, uncles, cousins, nephews, nieces and grandparents hugged the two young women. Sometimes it was really wonderful to belong to such a big extended family.

Soon the young couples walked on across the marketplace and past city hall as they continued down the Brunnen Gasse to the Golden Knight for their wedding dinner. There would be no honeymoons. Young people still fell in love and got married, but times were tough in postwar Germany.

Upon reaching the safety of her room, Rosa hid away from the festivities that were under way in the dining room. No one said anything about her absence.

Franz sat next to his new bride, Frieda, as he experienced empathetic thoughts of Rosa. He felt so sorry for her because she had to bear all the public shame for their relationship. Yet he didn't know what to do.

Gretel went upstairs to change her clothes and hung everything back in the armoire. Alone in her own little world, Gretel touched the pretty pale-yellow bedroom wallpaper with the pink roses and green leaves and had no idea of her mother's suffering just down the hall. Gretel stood for a second to look out the window at the Brunnen Gasse. People were walking or riding in buggies and cars. Some were on their way up to the marketplace or turning right, past city hall. Gretel smiled. Life was so strange and constantly changing, but today, life in Uberauen was wonderful.

10. DOROTHEA

Gretel graduated from school in January of 1919, and she got a job at the general store. In the evening she helped serve the guests at the Golden Knight.

Gretel age 15 (on left) at the general store

A couple of weeks later, when Gretel came home from work she found Emma vomiting in the toilet next to the kitchen.

"Oh my God, what's happening? Are you okay?" she asked Emma.

"Yes, yes, there's nothing to worry about." Emma smiled and said, "I'm just pregnant."

"You're kidding. Really? That's wonderful!"

Gretel clapped her hands. "Does anybody know? Does Max know?"

"Yes, I told him as soon as I knew that I had missed my period. He's delighted." Emma's face beamed her happiness.

"What do Max and Grandfather think about you cooking while you're pregnant? Should I quit my job and cook until the baby is born?" asked Gretel, always looking ahead.

"I've never been pregnant before, but Elisabeth says that I should be able to work for a few more months and then be careful not to lift too much," answered Emma.

On the day that Emma went into labor, the local midwife came over to help and Emma's sister, Elisabeth, was there too. Max tried to continue butchering a hog with Wilhelm.

Max, concerned about Emma and the baby, said, "Wilhelm, I just can't stand to stay here and work when I can hear Emma screaming in labor."

"I'm glad you think so too. It's a good time to stop, so let's hurry and chill this hog and go see what's happening."

In 1919 a man did not normally take part in the birthing of a baby, unless he was a doctor or in an emergency. Wilhelm and Max did what men were expected to do. They sat, drank beer and pretended not to worry about their loved one who was in labor.

Max suddenly raised his hand. "Did you hear that? It's a baby crying!" He jumped up and ran upstairs, where he found a room full of women who were all smiling.

"Would you like to hold your new baby girl, Papa?" Emma smiled weakly.

Max quickly and cautiously took the baby. "Look how she moves her mouth all the time. Obviously a woman," he said, teasing. Then he bent down and kissed Emma.

"Are you okay, Emma?" he asks in a soft tone. Asked?

"Ha-ha, as well as can be expected." She smiled.

Max rushed back down to the Regulars' Table. "Grandfather, better get upstairs and check on your new granddaughter."

Wilhelm was grinning all over. He held up his beer stein and his friends all clinked them together. "To the baby!" Then everyone took a big gulp, and Wilhelm left to check on Emma.

As he climbed the stairs Wilhelm Rossfeld said a silent prayer. "Thank you, dear Lord, for bringing Emma safely through childbirth. And thank you for the wonderful gift of our new baby girl. Amen." Wilhelm finished his prayer as he came through the doorway, into the room with his daughters, step-granddaughter and a new baby granddaughter.

Wilhelm greeted each woman warmly and then went over and kissed Emma on the cheek. "How is our little Mama?"

Emma wanted to cry with joy, so she just held her father's hand and kissed him. Now it was Wilhelm's turn to hold the baby.

He asked, "So what are we going to name her?"

"I think Max and I agreed that if the baby was a girl, we'd name her Dorothea," Emma said.

"We'd better tell Father Weible, so the baby can be christened," suggested Elisabeth.

After a few days, the whole town gathered at St. Severinus Church for Mass and the christening of baby Dorothea Bergmeister.

Gretel walked into church with Wilhelm. "Grandfather, I'm so glad that we have a happy reason for special prayers today."

"Yes, there has been so much sadness that it's really wonderful to celebrate with Emma and Max." Wilhelm smiled at her.

Gretel and Wilhelm greeted parishioners as they took their seats. "Good morning, Frau Diehl. How are you, Herr Haferstroh?"

Gretel knelt and prayed: *Dear Lord, now that Friedrich is with you, thank you for sending us beautiful baby Dorothea. Amen.*

"I wonder who the father of this one is?" Gretel heard Frau Luder whisper to Edith. Both mother and daughter enjoyed the cruel, shared smile as they sit hypocritically a couple of rows behind Rosa, Gretel and Wilhelm. Sat?

Rosa also heard the cruel comments from Frau Luder and Edith, but she kept her head bowed and prayed fervently for the dear Lord to please grant her peace for the misery of her life.

Edith held up her fingers where Gretel could see them and pretended to count the months since Emma and Max were married.

Ooh, if I weren't in church, Gretel vowed to herself, *I'd stuff those fingers into Edith's mouth! Sorry, you stupid goose, Emma and Max have been married for ten months. So count all your fingers and toes.*

As 1920 arrived, Gretel was having fun working, wearing the new short dresses, nice shoes and the bobbed hairstyle of the times. Her sister Anna was now eight years old.

I'm worried about Mama, Gretel thought as she put a clip in her short hair. *She looks so pale and unhappy lately. I hope she's okay.*

Later on when Gretel was walking with Rosa to the drugstore, she noticed some neighbor ladies staring at them. *Why are the neighbors and friends acting so strangely? They keep looking at Mama until we see them staring and then they look away. That's odd,* thought Gretel. *Maybe they think Mama is sick. Oh, well, it's Uberauen. Everyone knows everyone and everyone else's business. But why are they avoiding us?*

Gretel could not imagine that passive bullying and shunning from neighbors and townspeople, along with her own feelings of guilt, were taking a heavy toll on Rosa. With each day Rosa's strength was ebbing away.

11. TRAGEDY

Rosa got up silently in the cold gray winter dawn in Uberauen. She paced around the bedroom, praying the rosary and crying while Joseph slept nearby. "Holy Mary, Mother of God, pray for us sinners at the hour of our death. I am at my wit's end. Franz is gone and has married Frieda. Joseph and I do not love each other. The neighbors all hate me because of Anna, and I can't show my face in town without somebody bullying me. Please pray for me and forgive me. I'm about to commit an unpardonable sin. Today I will end my pain and spare my family the shame of my life. Amen."

Without seeing anybody, Rosa walked across the misty, foggy courtyard from the entrance door of the Golden Knight, to the carriage house. Inside the stable, she found the harness reins for the horses and stood on a crate. She threw the strong leather strap over a beam and tied it securely around her neck.

Should I change my mind and not do this? Rosa tried to think while crying and praying. "Dear God, please receive my aching soul. Amen." Rosa abruptly stepped off the crate and ended her life.

Alone in a carriage house with only the snorting and stomping of the horses, Rosa Geyer's soul left her lifeless body.

Wilhelm came out of his bedroom next to the kitchen and found no breakfast coffee or oatmeal cooking on the stove. He knocked on her bedroom door and Joseph said he didn't know where Rosa was. Wilhelm went weak with alarm.

"Keep the girls in their room for a while, Joseph. I'll look for Rosa."

Wilhelm searched the cellar, butcher shop and smokehouse for Rosa, and then discovered her limp, lifeless body in the carriage house.

"Oh, dear God, no!" said Wilhelm in terror, at the sight of Rosa's body hanging from the rafter.

He quickly got a ladder and took her down in the hope of reviving her, but it was too late. Rosa was gone. With his mind still reeling from the catastrophic incident, he alerted Emma, Joseph and Max. At the kitchen table, the grieving group waited for the undertaker and the constable.

In his shock and sorrow, Joseph said, "My God, how can I tell the children that Rosa hanged herself? Their next question will be why? I can't tell them the complex reasons why she committed suicide."

Emma agreed sadly while patting him on the shoulder. "No, you're right, Joseph. We can't tell the children everything that probably led Rosa to this awful decision. I wish I had realized how serious her depression was getting."

"Maybe I'll just say that Rosa died of tuberculosis. Gretel and Anna don't really need to know everything that led Rosa to such a tragic choice," Joseph suggested.

Wilhelm said softly, "All I can think of is how devastated I am by another death in the family. I feel too weak to go out and work today. Joseph, I guess your explanation for the girls is better than telling them the complicated reasons, for now. Go ahead and do what you think is best. We'll tell Gretel and Anna and everyone else that Rosa died of consumption. Uberauen is a small town, so the real sorrowful truth is bound to come out at some time in their lives. At least we can spare them for now."

While the undertaker was downstairs removing Rosa's lifeless body, Joseph dragged himself up the stairs with an explanation for Gretel and Anna.

"What's happening, Papa? I'm going to be late for work and Anna's late for school," Gretel asked excitedly. "Who's that talking downstairs?"

All the shame, pain and sorrow of his life with Rosa was suddenly unleashed and Joseph started to sob uncontrollably while holding Anna and Gretel. The girls were puzzled by the unusual outpouring of emotion.

"Girls, your wonderful Mama has died," he whispered.

Both Anna and Gretel were stunned by the sudden announcement.

Gretel said, "How can she be dead? Just yesterday we were working together in the garden and today she's dead! This can't be happening!" Gretel held tightly to Joseph and Anna as her mind reeled.

Eight-year-old Anna was puzzled by the tragic news. "Papa, what happened to Mama? Has she gone to heaven?"

I know this is a lie, but it's for the best, Joseph told himself. "Your poor mother has been really sick lately and she died of consumption. Yes, Anna, Mama is now in heaven and she'll always watch over you."

Fortunately for Joseph, Gretel and Anna were so devastated by the announcement of their mother's death that they did not ask any more questions.

The police, coroner and undertaker were all convinced that Rosa's death was suicide. All three agreed to keep the details of Rosa's death a secret, especially from Father Weible, so that Rosa could have a Catholic funeral.

A few days later, there was a memorial Mass at St. Severinus Church. Everyone from Uberauen was there to grieve and pray for Rosa Geyer's soul and for her family. Herr Jorg played *"Dies Irae,"* but Gretel hardly noticed. Like everyone in her family, Gretel prayed while Father Weible spoke of Rosa's fine life as a good Catholic woman.

Then, Scripture from Genesis 3:19 was shared with the mourners:

"For as much as it hath pleased Almighty God of his great mercy to take unto himself the soul of our dear sister here departed, we therefore commit her body to the ground; earth to earth, ashes to ashes, dust to dust; in sure and certain hope of the Resurrection to eternal life, through our Lord Jesus Christ…"

"Holy Mary, Mother of God, pray for us. Dear God, please take the soul of my wonderful mother to be with you until we are all together again in paradise." Gretel prayed, wept and held hands with Joseph and Anna as the service was completed.

Men from the family and neighborhood carried Rosa's flower-draped casket down the aisle and out the main entrance. Out on the marketplace it was carefully placed on a horse-drawn hearse. As the driver jiggled the reins, the clip-clop of the horses' hooves set the unworldly rhythm as everyone followed the hearse across the marketplace and down the Gerstenfelder Strasse. Even the most insensitive of local gossips hung their head and prayed for Rosa's soul while they walked in her funeral procession.

Gretel walked with Joseph, Anna and the whole Rossfeld-Bergmeister family in the funeral procession behind the hearse and remembered. *Mama and I always walked down the streets of Uberauen together. I can't believe that now I'm walking behind her coffin and the pain is really too much to endure!*

The familiar half-timbered houses along the cobblestone street seemed almost to be in a painting and not at all real, as the family continued walking to the cemetery. The funeral procession, even with the friends and neighbors who had bullied, shamed and gossiped about Rosa, walked solemnly through the Gerstenfelder Gate and into the cemetery outside the medieval city walls. There, Rosa was laid to rest near her mother Barbara, Friedrich Rossfeld, and other family members who have gone before.

Standing with her loved ones, Gretel puzzled about her own mortality. *Is this really all there is to life? Are we destined to just live and then be suddenly dead?* Gretel was experiencing new and painful lessons of life. *We don't know the answers. Time goes by very quickly. Life can be short and also end suddenly or tragically.*

Dear God, please be with me as I try to make sense of this, Gretel prayed as she held Joseph and Anna tightly.

They all watched as flowers were put on Mama's grave. Emma and Wilhelm put hands full of soil into the grave, but Gretel couldn't bear to do that.

Franz Baumfeller stood silently next to his new bride, Frieda, and agonized about Rosa's death.[14] The pain of losing Rosa was like a knife slicing him. For Frieda's sake, he stayed dignified, but mourned his Rosa. His prayer asked the dear Lord to forgive him for the horrible consequences of his sins.

Next to Franz, other mourners prayed.

"Dear God, only you know how my heart is breaking," whispered Wilhelm. "Barbara is dead. I just had to bury Friedrich and now my Rosa is gone too. The pain of this life is really too much to bear. Please be with me, God. Give me strength as I try to go on."

Wilhelm, Gretel, Joseph, Anna and other family members held each other and cried in each other's arms. The pain and sadness from so many deaths in recent years had been wrenching. How would they themselves have the strength to go on with life?

Back at home in the Golden Knight, Gretel walked over and, through her tears, gazed out the window. Outside, the Brunnen Gasse looked the same. At city hall across the street, Frau Luder was probably already gossiping about Rosa's death.

Yes, Gretel thought, *Uberauen looks just the same, but I don't feel the same. Life seems suddenly sad and not funny. Is this what grown-up life is really like?*

Days and weeks went by. Gretel, Anna, Joseph and the extended family followed their daily routines and hoped that the grief of losing Rosa would fade away. Time heals all wounds, is what people say. Friends and neighbors all tried to be so nice now that Rosa had died.

---

14   Rosa's death: Gretel always said her mother died of tuberculosis, but family rumors revealed that Rosa Geyer committed suicide. What really happened will always be mere speculation. She might have hanged herself in the carriage house of the inn. See Notes, page 240 for additional information.

Gretel was a bit puzzled about her neighbors. *I'm thankful for everyone's kindness and grateful that they want to help Anna and me, but why are they so much nicer? Why have they all stopped whispering? Are they trying to make amends for something?*

12. INFLATION

Gretel's life in Uberauen stayed much the same in many ways after Rosa's sudden death. As difficult as it was, Gretel worked at the general store and continued to work in the evening at the Golden Knight.

Joseph became more and more aloof, and Gretel had only limited conversations with him.

During this portion of Gretel's life in the early 1920s, life for everyone was chaotic in Germany. As part of the Treaty of Versailles to end the Great War, Germany had to agree to pay and accept fault for the war. The money was to be paid to the Allies, who were victorious. Germany borrowed money and did not tax the populace to pay for the war reparations. Suddenly in 1923 the mark began plummeting in value.

One evening in 1923 the same group of guys met at the Regulars' Table in the Golden Knight for their dinner and beer. As usual, they were discussing their jobs, love lives, Uberauen gossip and politics.

Wilhelm was saying, "Since the Allies won the war, they've been making Germany pay them huge amounts of money as repayment for the war. Do they think we've really got that money lying around to pay them? It's not fair. Our money is getting more and more worthless!"

"I know," said Herr Jorg. "That's called inflation. I even saw a 50,000,000-mark bill this week. The money is worth less than the paper it's printed on! I don't know how we can continue like this."

"Georg Pucher says we need a leader who is strong enough to stand up to the English, Americans and French and tell them that we're not paying what they call 'reparations' for the war anymore," shouted Herr Meyer.

I don't care what Georg Pucher thinks. He's the biggest idiot in town, Max thought to himself. For the first time, however, he had the uneasy feeling that resisting a nationalistic political stand might cause him trouble.

The other guys agreed that the payments were driving Germany into bankruptcy.

"I know," said Herr Jorg. "Even donations at church are down to practically nothing even though the numbers say we're bringing in *millions.*"

"Lots of guys are trading extra work for food and clothing, but how do you pay the electric bill or pay taxes without money?" shouted Herr Meyer.

"I've been trading and bartering our meats for other groceries for weeks now," Wilhelm told his friends. "I don't see how things could get any worse."

In 1922, what would become the National Socialist Workers Party was already taking root in Germany, including up the road in Coburg.

By 1923 one U.S. dollar was worth four *trillion* marks! At this stage in the financial crisis, the mark was renamed the Rentenmark and twelve zeroes were dropped from the printed sum. The currency stabilized and the Roaring Twenties were off and running!

13. RUDOLF

Another party at the dance hall found Gretel already a pretty and popular twenty-year-old woman. Life had continued about the same in Uberauen since she and Anna had lost Rosa. Grandfather Wilhelm and Max ran the butcher shop and the Golden Knight. The family somehow managed to live through the devastating inflationary period of the early 1920s.

Gretel was glad to work at the general store and then at the Golden Knight in the evening. Anna's after-school job was to help Emma and sell meats at the butcher shop.

Emma's brother and Gretel's childhood friend, Fritz Bergmeister, married a woman named Maria Barbara, and moved to Schrumpfelbach.

And then there came another one of life's surprises. Emma and Max were expecting another baby!

The baby was born on December 30, 1923. "It's a boy!" shouted Max to the guys eating and drinking beer at the Regulars' Table in the Golden Knight.

All the men at the Regulars' Table clinked their beer steins together and laughed.

"That's great news," Herr Meyer said. "Now, you and Wilhelm will have a new guy to train as the next butcher."

"Max, Emma, what are you going to name him?" Gretel asked. "Are you going to name him Max Junior?"

"I think we'll name him Rudolf," answered Emma. "Is that still okay, Max?"

"Rudolf Bergmeister. Now, that's a fine name. He will grow up to be a great man ... like his father! Ha-ha." Max struck a muscleman pose.

A few days later Aunt Frieda and Franz Baumfeller, who now lived in Friedberg, Hessen, had their own baby, Christoph Baumfeller.

The news of baby Christoph Baumfeller made Wilhelm sadly remember the recent past. When he thinks about Franz and Frieda he could not help but remember his sweet Rosa and how she suffered from her affair with Franz. The way he found her hanging in the carriage house was an image that would always haunt him. But for the sake of his family, he kept that to himself.

After hearing about both babies being born safely, Gretel stopped by St. Severinus Church to pray for babies Rudolf Bergmeister and Christoph Baumfeller.

She sat alone and prayed in the church where so many family births, deaths and funerals had already taken place. *Mother Mary, St. Bernadette, please pray for me. Dear Lord, thank you for these two precious babies. Thank you too, that Emma and Frieda are both well. Amen.*

As she walked toward the Brunnen Gasse, Gretel walked over the spot where she and Friedrich had had their *Wurst* stand at the Christmas Market. She smiled, thinking of Friedrich Rossfeld. *I'll always remember you, Friedrich, and the fun we had here.*

A few days later, everyone in Uberauen was at St. Severinus Church for Rudolf's christening. The Rossfeld and Bergmeister families had grown to be so numerous that they occupied a big section of church pews.

"Just look at Gretel Geyer and her family," whispered Edith Luder to her friend. "The way she acts, you'd think she was royalty, and not the daughter of a woman who … whisper, whisper."

"Oh my goodness, Edith," gasped her friend while holding her hand to her mouth. "Stop saying those awful things about Gretel and her mother." The girl pretended shock.

After the christening, the family stood outside St. Severinus Church on the cobblestones of the marketplace while neighbors, friends and foes passed by to wish the family and baby Rudolf a long and happy life.

When Edith went through the greeting line she smiled and made small talk with Emma and Max. They both knew all too well that Edith was trouble.

"Congratulations on your new baby, Herr Bergmeister," Edith said. "I'm so happy for you and Emma." Edith wondered if this family member was legitimate, and she smiled coldly as she moved politely to the next person.

The whole Rossfeld and Bergmeister clan was in the greeting line, including Fritz Rossfeld. "Hey, Fritz, is this baby legitimate?" whispered Georg Pucher in Fritz's ear.

"You'd better get your sorry ass out of here before I knock your teeth out." Fritz glared at him. "And I'm just the guy who can do it!"

After scum like him taunted Rosa to her death, they still hunted for trouble. Well, he nearly said aloud, trouble was right there, *Arsch mit Ohren!*[15]

Georg knew he could not win a fistfight with Fritz, so he quickly moved on down the line and pretended to be polite while shaking hands with Max and Emma. He wasn't fooling anyone. Everyone knew everyone and everyone else's business in Uberauen. They all knew that Georg Pucher was a snake. After some time, the townspeople began to drift away from the marketplace and back toward their homes. The Rossfeld and Bergmeister family crammed into the Golden Knight for a dinner celebration for Rudolf, Emma, Dorothea and Max. Emma didn't even have to cook because Rosine, Gretel and Anna had done the cooking.

"I had to teach them everything about cooking," teased Fritz Rossfeld.

"Yes, Fritz and I had to tell Gretel and Rosine every move to make," Siegfried Kiefer said, teasing them.

"You little devil," Gretel said, laughing, as she pursued Fritz and tried to whack him with a dish towel—as they had as children.

---

15 *Arsch mit Ohren* – ass with ears

14. NEW STAR

Gretel was now old enough to join a theater group in Uberauen that did performances at the dance hall. She was so pretty and such a good actress that the local newspaper had these headlines: *"Ein Stern ging auf am Theaterhimmel"*[16]

Gretel was so proud of the newspaper article! After she had starred in some country folk–style plays, she allowed herself to dream. *I'll become a famous actress or film star, like the ones in the movies.*

Gretel and Fastnacht's Betti were both still single and really interested in the movies, so Grandfather decided to spoil them and paid train fare for the girls to see the movie, *Metropolis* in Wurzburg.

"I don't know when I've had so much fun," Fastnacht's Betti said as she and Gretel rode the train back to Uberauen.

"Me too. I love getting dressed up and seeing the romantic movies. Did you see some of those handsome boys sitting in front of us?"

Both girls giggled and enjoyed the ride.

As the train chugged closer to home, Gretel looked dreamily out the window and reflected. When the church steeple came into view, she thought, *I love Uberauen. I know it's just a small town and the people aren't all perfect, but I love it!*

As she and Betti stepped dramatically off the train, for an instant Gretel remembered her uncle Friedrich. *I'll never forget you, Friedrich.* She continued to laugh with her friend as they left the train station where Friedrich had departed for his fatal service in the Great War.

Being a movie star was fun to dream about, but the local dance hall was where boys and girls met to dance and have fun. She, her friends and her sister Anna went there to dance the Charleston or the Black Bottom.

While they were at one dance evening, they saw Waldberger's Ernst with his new Ford Model A. At least he flirted now, instead of just

---

16 *Ein Stern ging auf* ... There is a new rising star over the theater heavens.

pestering Gretel in school. His Ford wasn't exactly a Mercedes Benz, but it was fun to ride in.

"Hey, girls, come outside and see my new Ford," Ernst called out, waving to them.

"A Ford?" Rosine said. "Georg Pucher has a Mercedes."

"Yeah, well, he's rich. With that face of his, he needs a Mercedes! What can I say?" Ernst laughed.

The girls gathered eagerly around Ernst and his new Ford. They didn't actually care about Georg, anyway. One of Gretel's friends took their picture.

I know Georg is trouble, thought Gretel to herself. *I just can't resist teasing Ernst.*

Gretel, left, and Anna, third from left, 1926

"Come on, jump in," Ernst said.

The girls all tried to squeeze in at one time, but had to divide up into groups. Ernst drove with the girls down through the Gerstenfelder Gate, up to the marketplace and back.

"Next bunch," ordered Ernst, who was now dazzled by the attention of so many girls.

Ernst, Gretel and their friends were having fun riding in the car and waving at everybody. When Ernst came back to the dance hall with the last carload of girls, he saw Edith Luder coming out of the dance hall doorway and walking toward him.

Ernst decided that if she wanted a ride, he'd tell Edith he was just going in to dance.

But Edith knew every conniving trick. She spotted who she called that ignorant Gretel Geyer and her group of nobodies. Just because she'd been acting in plays and had her name in the paper, Gretel was thought of by Edith as acting like a celebrity. Edith calculated immediately that Ernst was avoiding her glance. She said to herself that she'd rather croak than ask that little shit for a ride in his stupid Ford. She turned back toward the dance hall to look for Georg Pucher and his friends. They're more fun than these country bumpkins, anyway. She swished past Ernst and his car full of girls while swinging her hips so that her short flapper skirt fringe swayed sexily from side to side with every step.

The group with Ernst enjoyed a good laugh at Edith's expense.

"Do you see Edith swinging her butt!" Anna exclaimed. "Does she really think any of the decent boys in Uberauen would want to date a floozy like her!"

Waldberger's Ernst and all the girls laughed in recognition of Anna's common-sense assessment of Edith's chances.

The next afternoon Gretel got teased as she cleared the dirty dishes at the Golden Knight. "Where were you yesterday evening,"—Emma gave her a knowing smile—"out with the boys?"

Anna and Emma both laughed and bantered remarks about Gretel being out with her friends, while little Dorothea listened with interest.

"What boys?" shouted Max from the Regulars' Table. "We'll lock Gretel up in the shed until she's at least fifty!"

All the men laughed and teased Gretel as she brought them their beer and the soup of the day: oxtail soup.

At this rate, I'll be fifty before you know it! Gretel thought ruefully.

15. OTTO

Church bells rang at St. Severinus Church, and Gretel joined her friends for yet another wedding. She couldn't help thinking, *I am so sick of going to other people's weddings. You have to get dressed up, find a way to give them a gift—and wish them luck. I want to wish myself luck!*

Yet again the bride was someone else, not Gretel. The bride marched sweetly down the aisle with her father. Everyone stood and beamed as the organ, now played by Herr Jorg's son, began to play *"So nimm den meine Hände."*[17]

The thing that was emotional was what came next. When the groom came out of the side chapel and waited at the altar for his new bride, it was Waldberger's Ernst!

I guess I have to be honest. I knew I didn't really want to marry Ernst and he didn't want to marry me. But if I don't marry Ernst, who will I marry? Will I end up being unmarried, like the Blumentritt sisters at their store? Will I just have to smile and watch other people fall in love and plan their lives? Gretel smiled a genuine smile at Ernst. Right now I'm really happy for him.

One afternoon after working at the store Gretel went back to the Golden Knight to help Anna sell meat in the butcher shop.

"I don't know what's wrong with me, Anna," Gretel confided to her sister. "All day today all I could think about was how I'm still not married and it's 1926! I'm twenty-two years old! Doesn't that make me an old maid?"

"It's not actually official until you're thirty-five," teased fourteen-year-old Anna.

"Girls who have been willing to have sex before marriage have all gotten men," Gretel said cautiously. "Maybe I shouldn't be such a prude."

"Oh, don't talk like that to my tender ears," Anna said while holding

---

17 "So Nimm denn meine Hände" – "So Take My Hands," a regional wedding march.

her hands over her ears and exhibiting melodramatic shock on her face. Then Anna added, "Seriously, you know a girl can't be too careful with sex. Aunt Emma and Grandfather pound me on the head all the time with warnings about romance before marriage."

"I know. Me too."

The taboo conversation ended as Edeltraudt came in to buy some kosher beef and sausages.

"Edeltraudt, Gretel is worried about being an old maid," Anna blurted out.

The girls laughed. Gretel, Anna and Edeltraudt gossiped, as usual, about Edith Luder. After they had enjoyed a good visit, Edeltraudt left and Gretel went to the kitchen to help Emma.

After a normal evening of waiting tables and cleaning up, Gretel climbed the stairs to her room. She went over to look out the window above the big entry gate to the courtyard at the Golden Knight. *I'm so tired from working at the store and then in the dining room, but I'm really glad that Anna and I are safe here with Grandfather, Emma, Max and this huge family,* she thought gratefully.

It was late, yet a few cars and pedestrians traveled between the Golden Knight and the city hall in the narrow Brunnen Gasse.

Yes, Uberauen is still the same. But here I am, twenty-two years old, looking at the world outside my window. I wonder, is this all that life has in store for me? Gretel felt unusually depressed and she did something rare for her. She sat hopelessly on the bed and cried.

As so often happens in life, when everything appears to be at rock bottom, something promising happens. Gretel came home to the Golden Knight from working at the store. As usual, she put on a nicely washed, starched and ironed apron that she had prepared. "Okay, Emma, what do you and Anna have for me to do?"

"There is a bunch of loud, rowdy men sitting in the dining room. I gave each of them a beer and I'll bet they're ready to order dinner by now," said Emma with a smile. "We can sure use the money, and they are all strangers." Emma winked.

Gretel smiled to herself too, as she hustled in to take orders. She quickly scanned the table full of unfamiliar young men who were drinking, laughing and smoking. Emma's three-year-old son Rudi was running around the dining room, to the delight of the workingmen.

"So, gentlemen, our special for today is boiled beef with vegetables, parsley potatoes and horseradish sauce. It's really good. You can also order anything from the menu."

The men sat silently and stared at her. Gretel was not afraid of them, but she suddenly felt ill at ease. Rudolf was bashfully hugging her around the leg and playing peekaboo with the men. Then, just as spontaneously, the men all burst out in loud boisterous laughter. Gretel smiled because she was no shrinking violet. She nonetheless still felt like a fool standing there in front of the young men with her order pad, and Rudi hugging her leg.

Finally, one handsome young man said, "I'll take the special and another beer when you get time."

All the other men thought the special sounded good, so Gretel thanked them and walked back into the kitchen. She could hear the men laughing loudly, but she wasn't frightened. In fact she surprised herself by feeling suddenly perky and kind of playful.

Gretel in traditional dress

Gretel and Anna served the men Emma's delicious dinners. Instantly, all talking stopped as the men dived into their food. After a few more minutes, Max and Wilhelm came in and sat down for dinner at the Regulars' Table. Both men looked tired, but they were in a good humor. Minutes later, more of the usual crowd came in to join Wilhelm and

Max at the Regulars' Table. After everyone was finished eating and they were back to their beers and smoking, conversation began to spread from one table to the other. Wilhelm and Max were always glad to have paying customers at the Golden Knight. Maybe some friendly joking would get the new customers to come again.

"So, what are you guys up to and what's happening?" asked Wilhelm with genuine interest.

"We've been working for a company that is stringing electrical power lines to all the towns and farms in this area," answered one guy.

"Really. That's good to hear. At least somebody is earning a paycheck."

All the beer drinkers enjoyed another loud and bawdy laugh.

Max asked, "How long will you guys be in town?"

In the kitchen, Gretel and Emma were listening to every word with Anna.

One of the men, named Wolfgang, answered, "Um, I'd say we'll be here for a few more months, maybe years. There are lots of houses in Forellenbach, Blauenbronn and Gerstenfeld that still don't have electricity."

Gretel, Anna and Emma did a little jig of glee despite the heat of the kitchen. "Can you imagine that!" Anna giggled. "Maybe we'll really make some money—and some of those guys are adorable!" The women brazenly giggled and eavesdropped again.

Wilhelm couldn't resist asking a money-making question. "Do you fellas already have a place to stay? We still have some vacant rooms." Actually, all the rooms were vacant except those used by the family.

"Oh my God, what if they want to stay! The money would be great, but I haven't put fresh linens on any of the beds," Emma told the women.

A man named Otto answered. "This is kind of complicated. We're all working for the Rural Electrification Administration. We buy old wood scraps and use it as a power source to produce electricity. After we get the power source up and working, we'll set up utility poles and string the wires for the power."

There was a moment of silence as Max and Wilhelm thought over what Otto was telling them.

"But where are you staying?" asked Max.

"We're staying in a barracks-type building that the company is leasing, down by the train station," answered Otto.

"Oh, I know right where that is," Wilhelm said, hiding his disappointment at losing paying customers.

The fortunate thing was that the workers enjoyed the delicious food at the Golden Knight and they came by every night. They got used to seeing Wilhelm, Gretel, Max, Anna and Emma.

One evening Otto Forner started bragging that his bunch of guys had formed a club that included some of the men from the Regulars' Table.

"Oh, great," said Gretel dryly, "so now we'll have all the worthless louts in one place."

"Yes," Otto announced as he jumped grandly to his feet, "we've named it the Mount of Olives Club."[18]

Mount of Olives Club

"You're kidding, right?" Max chuckled. "I don't see anything very holy about this bunch."

Everyone laughed again and had another drink of beer.

"Well, you know that oiling can also mean chugging beer," yelled Otto while holding his beer stein in the air and clinking it together with all the guys.

Otto gradually began to ask Gretel to go out for walks or to sit with him while he ate. Everyone watched with approval.

When nobody was looking, the new lovers held hands and exchanged kisses.

A few days later while Gretel was helping peel potatoes for the next batch of potato dumplings, she said casually, "Emma, what am I going to do about Otto? He's so handsome and smart and I really like him."

"Sounds like no problem to me," Emma said.

"I know. Sure, I'm so excited about him, but I wanted to talk to you about a couple of things." Privately, Gretel thought, *We always stay in public and I'm not giving him the idea that we can have sex. How long can we go on like we are now?*

Emma gasped with more melodramatic shock. "Wow! Where is this going?"

"Quit teasing." Gretel smiled. "You know how serious it is when you've fallen in love with someone. I was afraid I'd be an old maid and now I'm afraid of being too much in love!"

"Do you think you're the first girl who had to worry about when it's okay and when it isn't? Just don't forget about Rosa and my mama Barbara," Emma said.

"I don't want to talk about that," said Gretel, holding up her hands in a *halt* gesture. "Mama died of tuberculosis. I know I'm confused and I have to talk to you about it."

Both young women were tense while having a taboo discussion about sex, without really saying it directly.

"I'm glad you asked. You know what I think you should do?" Emma said calmly. "I think you should suggest to Otto that you become engaged and set a date to get married. That way, you'll know if he's serious about you, or just playing around, and he'll know that you're seriously interested in him."

Gretel was still skeptical about discussing marriage with Otto, but she was glad to discuss everything with Emma.

"Isn't the man supposed to ask the girl to marry him?" While scrubbing the big cooking pots, Gretel continued. "Otto is smart and educated and he's afraid we don't have the money to get married."

Emma turned from stirring her delicious beef gravy and concentrated on Gretel. "You're kidding, right? Can you remember the last time anybody could afford to be married? People just get married and make a go of it together. You discuss your future with Otto and see if I'm not right."

The next day Gretel worked at the store during the day. Edeltraudt stopped in, so Gretel tried to gossip with her a couple of times about Otto, but Edeltraudt seemed too distracted and worried to talk about love and marriage.

After work, Gretel helped Emma and Anna in the kitchen for a while, and then went out to the slaughter shed to ask Max and Wilhelm for a man's opinion of love. Of course, they teased her, as usual, until she asked them specifically.

"Grandfather, what do you think about Otto Forner?"

After a momentary silence to gather his thoughts, Wilhelm turned to Gretel and said, "I think he's a great guy. Are you interested in him?" Wilhelm already knew the obvious answer.

Before Gretel could say anything, Max blurted out, "I know you didn't ask me for my opinion yet, but I like him a lot."

"Do you think he is serious about me?" Gretel asked, while pretending to be interested in stacking sausages.

Wilhelm was finishing his long day's work, so he and Max took off their aprons. "I guess we're finished for today, Max. Gretel, you have to know for yourself whether Otto is in love with you. But I will tell you this. Men don't always make a decision unless they have to. It would not hurt to have a little grown-up talk with Otto. He's no fool. He knows you can't hold hands forever. You'll either have to get engaged or break up."

Again, Gretel couldn't believe that Grandfather was being so open and blunt with her.

He's treating me like a grown-up woman, she noticed.

"Thanks, you two. I'll go get your dinner ready." Then Gretel walked through the courtyard and under the big grapevine, to the entrance.

Back in the kitchen, Gretel announced, "Great news, Emma. We're all agreed that I have to ask Otto Forner to marry me!"

Emma, Gretel and Anna enjoyed another hearty laugh at the thought of the shy young country girl proposing to the man from "the big city" of Stuttgart.

When Gretel started the engagement discussion with Otto that evening, the wild young man suddenly became serious and mature. "Gretel, I've been planning to talk to you about marrying me, but I don't know if this is the right time. You know I don't have much money and my job will take me back to Stuttgart. Do you think you could leave Uberauen?"

"Otto, that's no problem," Gretel said, and giggled as she kissed him. "I thought you might want to live in Stuttgart, and that sounds really exciting. You know we'll be poor wherever we live, so I won't worry about money. You'll know what to do."

Otto and Gretel continued the serious discussion about their future together, and then Otto made an abrupt decision. "Well, we just can't get married until I get back to Stuttgart and have everything lined up for our life together." He seemed unusually upset and nervous about the discussion.

Gretel was so stunned at this sudden chill that she could only sit and look at him. *Is he serious? I believed we have been devoted enough to be married for weeks but he says let's wait!* Gretel got up from the table and gave Otto a quick kiss.

"We don't have to decide anything right now, Otto. Let's discuss this again tomorrow," Gretel suggested hopefully while holding his hand and moving away.

Emma had been listening to everything they said, as usual. She shook her head, sorry that when Gretel had finally met a nice man, now he was slipping away.

Back in the silence of her room, Gretel went to the window and looked out. *The world outside my window still looks the same. Everyone knows everyone else and everyone else's business in Uberauen. Tomorrow the big news will be whispered all over town. Otto may have broken up with Gretel!*

Again Gretel sat down on her bed and cried the heartbroken tears of a jilted lover. Then she vowed she'd never fall in love again. *Love hurts too much and I've suffered enough pain already,* she decided. *I'll be satisfied to work at the store and serve here at the Golden Knight. I'll have a nice enough life. All my friends will proudly talk about their husbands, children, and grandchildren, but all I'll have is memories of Otto. The man who got away.* Gretel continued to cry until it was so late that she just got undressed and went to bed.

Over the next few days Otto did not come to eat at the Golden Knight as Gretel had hoped. All the other men from the work crew pretended that they had only had a business relationship with Gretel and her family. It was so painful for Gretel to serve the men, but she didn't want them to think she had anything against them. Besides, she thought her family needed them as customers.

Then about a week later, Wolfgang from the work crew, told her, as the men were leaving, "Gretel, it has been a pleasure knowing you and your family. Our gang will be leaving tomorrow and heading back to Stuttgart."

"Thanks for telling me, Wolfgang." She held his hand an instant longer. "Please give Otto my regards, and have a safe trip home," said Gretel in a calm, mature manner.

When Wolfgang and the other men were gone, Gretel started gathering up the dirty dishes and beer mugs. *Life is so strange. I'd really like to sit down right here and cry! You keep looking for the right man who will make you happy for the rest of your life, but then he leaves. Does life ever make sense?* She carried the tray of dirty dishes to the kitchen, where she began washing them.

Gretel told Emma, "Wolfgang said they're leaving for Stuttgart tomorrow, so I told him to say goodbye to Otto for me. Do you think I was too forward?"

Emma thought about it for a minute and then answered, "No, I think it's much better to be honest. There is so much game playing in relationships that people don't know what is going on. I think it's better to just honestly show your feelings and see what happens. What's the point in being cool and then you never hear from Otto again!"

"I'm relieved to hear you say that. I don't know that I'll ever hear from Otto again anyway, but I feel better sending him a goodbye wish than to stay silent," Gretel said as she finished washing the beer mugs.

Anna had been listening patiently while she washed off the tables in the dining room. When she came back into the kitchen, she offered her opinion. "Don't worry, Gretel. You know what they always say ..."

Max had been silently listening to the women while he finished his beer. Before Anna could finish the quote of country wisdom, Max piped up, "If there is any way for things to screw up, they certainly will!"

Everyone was tired from a long day's work, and spent from worrying about Otto. Anna, Max, Gretel and Emma shared a long hearty laugh.

"No, no," Anna said. "I wanted to tell Gretel that there are a lot more fish in the sea."

Even though she continued to laugh out loud, Gretel was thinking to herself, *Yes, lots of fish in the sea, but not in Uberauen.*

Each day when Gretel came back from work, she'd put on her apron and then go in to check the kitchen counter that served as a desk. While Emma and Anna pretended not to notice, Gretel looked through all the mail to see if there was a letter for her. There never was one.

Days, weeks and months passed. Gretel continued trying to persuade herself to forget about Otto and move on with her life. Once the word got around that Gretel wasn't seeing Otto any more, single men who were interested in Gretel came to eat and drink beer at the Golden Knight. Gretel was no fool. She had had men flirting with her since long before they should have. She recognized their advances, and some of the men were actually catches. Nonetheless, Gretel politely pretended that the men were just being men, and kept her distance.

Anna watched as one attractive young man flirted with Gretel in the dining room. Back in the kitchen she commented on Gretel's behavior to Wilhelm. "Grandfather, why do you suppose Gretel isn't interested in that guy from the lumberyard? He seems nice enough."

"I know. He's a fine young man, but I'm afraid Gretel still can only think of Otto. Maybe in a few months she'll be ready to consider someone new," Wilhelm reasoned.

A couple of days later, Gretel asked Max a question while he was eating dinner at the Regulars' Table. "Max, do you think you could find out an address for Otto from the guy who rented out their rooms when the work crew was in Uberauen?"

Max was obviously ill at ease with the question.

"Sure, Gretel. I could easily find out what Otto's last address was, but do you really think that's what you should do? I mean, Otto has had plenty of time to write to you, but he hasn't. My guess is that he has left you and Uberauen far behind, without a second thought. I know it hurts, but I really think you need to find someone new. You'll eventually forget about him."

"I've considered all that too," answered Gretel. "It's just not the advice I want." She smiled thoughtfully and went back to work.

Gretel was already experienced enough to know that life has some strange twists and turns. *What will happen next?* she wondered.

In late 1928 Gretel came into the kitchen with her apron on and was ready to go into the dining room when Emma turned, smiling, from her cooking, and said, "Oh, by the way, Gretel, there's a letter for you over there on the counter."

Gretel immediately grabbed the letter and went out into the entrance hall to read it. It was from Otto!

Stuttgart
October 1928

Dear Gretel,

I hope all is well with you and your family. Things have been really busy here and my plans are constantly changing. Speaking of changes, have you started seeing someone else since I last saw you? If you have, I can certainly understand. I should have written to you months ago but I still didn't know what to do. To be really honest, I still don't know what I'm doing. Of course, if you're seeing someone else, that would be the end of the story.

After we had our serious talk about planning our lives together, I should have come back the next day and continued our discussion, but I was too confused. I didn't want to make promises that I couldn't keep, so I just stayed away. Thank you for sending me your kind goodbye with Wolfgang. I'm sorry I didn't say a fond farewell to you. That was cowardly on my part.

I find myself thinking about you all the time. I really miss you and I'm not interested in any of the girls I've met here. Please forgive my thoughtless treatment of you and let me hear from you.

Your Otto

—❦❦—

Of course Gretel immediately wrote back to Otto, and they started corresponding on a regular basis. Emma, Max, Anna and Wilhelm watched Gretel carefully to be sure she was okay. Otto and Gretel continued to write to each other and vaguely plan their future together, but with no firm plans. The year 1928 ended and Gretel spent another New Year's Eve at the dance hall without a date while everyone else celebrated the New Year of 1929.

Family and friends of Gretel Geyer, 1928 (Joseph is fourth from right, second row from top, with Gretel on his right and Anna on his left)

Who could imagine that the good times of the Roaring Twenties would not last forever? Then in October 1929, when Gretel was twenty-six, the New York stock market crashed and the world was plunged into the Great Depression. The Rossfeld-Bergmeister families struggled to keep the Golden Knight open and the customers coming back to the butcher shop. People lost their jobs and money was scarce. Everyone was scared. There seemed to be no end to bad economic news, and that spawned instability in the government.

Wilhelm, Emma and Max kept lowering prices for dinners in order to attract customers who were in desperate straits. The men who could afford to have dinner at the inn told wild stories about the high number of men who were unemployed. Gretel knew that some of her friends had lost their jobs in small factories, stores and on farms. The general store owner agreed to keep Gretel employed, at least for now. It was important extra money for the family.

As each month went by, social unrest began to build throughout Germany. The whole situation with government was complicated. It was serious business and tempers flared among the friends who met to eat and drink at the Regulars' Table. One guy might think that it would be best to bring back the old royal line to power, while the guy next to him blamed the banks or foreigners for the problems. Others were ready for more drastic change.

"We've got to help the Communists get in power in Germany. Then everybody will have a share of the money. Right now only the rich have everything," screamed one man at the Regulars' Table.

Everyone knew the Jewish German, Karl Marx, had made the theory of Communism popular. Communists had taken over Russia from the czar and changed the name to the Union of Soviet Socialist Republics.

"Are you nuts!" screamed Herr Meyer while he pounded his fists on the table. Beer steins jumped and his friends looked at him in amazement. "The only answer to our problems is to get a real man like Herr Hitler and the National Socialists into power!"

"I'm not sure about that," said Max. "Those guys have been beating up anybody that disagrees with them. Remember when that happened in Coburg?"

A determined Wilhelm Bergmeister glared at Herr Meyer. "I lost my boy Friedrich in the Great War, and Hitler is really aggressive. I don't trust him."

"What's not to trust," shouted Herr Meyer. "The new order is coming and you'd better join in, or things will not go well for you." As he made his threat, Herr Meyer's face was beet red. "That's what Georg Pucher says too."

"Georg Pucher, that loser and crook? Who gives a rat's ass what he thinks?" Max said as his own face rapidly reddened.

Herr Meyer jumped up so suddenly that he knocked his chair over.

He turned to all the men at the Regulars' Table and screamed, "The new way is coming, and you'd better watch your tongues! Our movement will not tolerate your stupid resistance. Remember that!"

The other men at the Regulars' Table sat as if they had been molded into iron statues. Herr Meyer's words about not resisting the National Socialists did not make everyone feel better and more secure. It made them instead feel angst, cautious and afraid. The only good thing from the arguing was that Herr Meyer never came to the Regulars' Table again. All the other guys were glad for a reprieve from his extremism.

Gretel, Anna and Emma had been listening from the kitchen and couldn't believe how the political situation had turned friends into enemies and upset the peace and quiet of Uberauen. But in spite of politics, everyday life continued normally.

Gretel and Otto had been writing to each other off and on for about a year since Otto left Uberauen. Now their plans for marriage seemed to have been dashed by the economic and political turmoil in Germany. By Christmas of 1929 it was clear to everyone in the Western world that a catastrophic economic depression was developing.

Otto wrote to Gretel.

Stuttgart
December 15, 1929

Dear Gretel,

As I'm sure you know, the economy is in a tailspin! I've managed to keep my job for now at the Rural Electrification Company, but I don't know how much longer I'll be working. I wish I had asked you to marry me last year, but I again have let you down. Now I really don't know what to do.

Let's wait and see what happens with jobs and the government for a few more months. I'm glad you're safe and cared for in Uberauen with Max, Wilhelm, Anna and Emma. I'd love for you to be here with me, but it is just too risky right now.

Please be patient with me, Gretel. I'm not going to leave you and I hope you don't lose faith in me.

With all my love,

Otto

Wonderful! Gretel smiled. *Otto is still planning to marry me. I mean, what else can I do? I'm too old for anybody else to be interested in me, anyway.*

She decided to share some of the news from her letter with Emma. "Emma, Otto still writes in his letter that he hopes to marry me when he is sure about the government and his job."

Siegfried Kiefer, Emma's sister Elisabeth's son, had started helping at the Golden Knight in order to earn a little extra money. As he brought in some coal for the cookstove, Emma turned and looked at Gretel.

While wiping her hands on her apron, Emma said seriously, "I don't know, Gretel. He's been saying things like that for two years. Do you still trust him? I'm beginning to think he's probably writing love letters to you and dating six other women in Stuttgart. Stranger things have happened, ya know."

Gretel was not shocked by Emma's analysis of the relationship with Otto. "I know, Emma. He could be just stringing me along, but what choice do I have? I love him."

Not to be outdone, young Siegfried offered his advice. "Hey, how about if you marry that old what's-his-name who owns the farm over in Forellenbach. He's nice."

Emma and Gretel laughed and sarcastically thanked him for suggesting a possible husband.

"No thanks, Siegfried. I'd really rather stay single than marry someone twice my age."

Little did Gretel suspect that she was not the only one who was gradually thinking about older men.

Within a few short months of the stock market crash in 1929, everyone in Uberauen was in a panic and wondering what would happen next. Not everyone was able to find some way to pay for their meat.

"If any of our customers and friends can't pay, let's just give them a few sausages. Is that okay, Max?" asked Wilhelm.

"Yes. And don't laugh, but a pig tail or sow's ear is better to have in the stew than nothing. We'll try to give people something if they're really desperate," Max said.

Gretel came in from work with some news. "Georg Pucher is leaving Uberauen," she announced with obvious *Schadenfreude.*[18]

"What? How are we getting rid of that jerk?" asked Max.

"This is just too delicious," Gretel said, and then giggled. "Do you remember that old Frau Luder retired from her job at city hall? When the new guy started to audit the books, he found that Georg Pucher had

---

18 *Schadenfreude* – malicious joy, gloating; glee at the misfortune of others

embezzled money while he worked with her there. There's no dirt on Frau Luder yet, but Georg got fired and has to pay everything back—with interest. The receptionist over there said that Georg screamed at the auditor and threatened to get even. The whole city hall is abuzz with gossip about him."

"Eww, that is too juicy." Anna giggled. "Maybe we'll be lucky and Georg will move away."

Gretel reported, "Oh, he's already moving to Munich and says he'll join the National Socialist Movement."

"Well, that's where he belongs. I don't care where he goes, as long as it's away," muttered Max. "I'm glad everyone finally found out what a crook that *Schweinehund* is."

Everyone present agreed that Georg really was a *Schweinehund*, and that they were lucky to be rid of him.

16. EDITH

The Great Depression struck everyone in Uberauen. Max and Wilhelm cared for their families, but things were different for Edith Luder and her mother. Because of their bitter personalities, the women had alienated almost everyone in town. The nicest boys and girls wanted nothing to do with Edith because she was basically a hateful bully. So now, at age twenty-six, she was still unmarried and had no means of supporting herself or her equally evil mother.

As the worldwide economic depression deepened, Uberauen was caught in the same wave of despair that was sweeping the industrialized world. Edith's father had died in the 1920s, and her mother had retired from city hall. Now the money was gone because of the period of inflation and Edith had wasted all the money they had left.

One evening Edith and her mother had yet another screaming match over the evening meal of boiled cabbage and stale bread.

"Edith, you have got to get a job," insisted Frau Luder. "All the money is gone and I've been trying to sell anything of value that's left in the house. I've sold my nice jewelry and now I'm down to thinking about what we can get for the furniture. You have to do something!"

"Well, I'm not going to work as a common shopgirl like that Gretel Geyer, and besides, nobody is hiring shopgirls. What do you suggest I do?" Edith asked in a snippy voice.

"Please don't remind me of that unruly Gretel Geyer," Frau Luder replied. "She has been rude to me since she stuck out her tongue at me when she was a child. And to think that she's the child of that Rosa!"

"Be glad that she just stuck out her tongue at you. She threw horse *Scheisse*[19] at me," she reminded her mother. Edith seethed at the memory.

Back on topic, Frau Luder said, "I always hoped you would marry a man with money so you'd be taken care of in a way that you deserve. It's

---

19 *Scheisse* – shit

too bad that Georg Pucher had to leave town. His family has money and he was smart."

"I never really liked him, but he did have money. Anyway, I heard that he moved to Munich and has joined the National Socialist Movement. The Brown Shirts will promote him, and I'll be left here stealing apples at night in Uberauen. I could just scream!"

Edith saw no connection between her behavior and the situation in which she now found herself.

"I heard that they're hiring cleaning ladies for the railroad cars at the train station. If you get down there early tomorrow, maybe you can at least get a day job," Frau Luder suggested in a soft tone.

"I'm not a *Putzfrau*,"[20] screamed Edith, "and I'm not cleaning train cars. Go clean them yourself!"

"You know, if you went from farm to farm you might be able to get a day job cleaning out stables. Maybe one of the farmers would pay you with eggs or some other food. We really need some food now."

Edith gave her mother a glare that would melt steel. "If I refuse to clean train cars, What makes you think I'll shovel shit!" Edith screamed. She left, slamming the door.

Her bitter mother could only sit and cry.

As night fell, Edith noticed that there was a small amount of light from the moon. *I know. I'll go get some vegetables from someone's garden. That way, I'll be able to get by until I meet some man.*

Edith calculated her every move. Ten at night would be a safe time. *I'll wear a long coat, and take some potatoes from Gretel Geyer's garden. I hate her and she's too stupid to miss vegetables, anyway.*

Edith's plan went well. She was able to find the garden by moonlight and then use a garden hoe that was leaning on the fence to dig up some potatoes. *It is just too easy getting food from these backward country bumpkins,* she thought. Edith smiled with satisfaction as she put the potatoes in her coat pockets and slipped back onto the path.

Edith got up at about 9:00 a.m. the next morning. Frau Luder had already found the six fresh potatoes on the kitchen sink.

"It's about time you got up, Edith. The men have already started cleaning the train cars at the station. But maybe you can go and try getting a job there tomorrow morning."

Edith yelled, "What's wrong with you? Are you stupid? I'm not going to clean train cars! And besides, I have found a way to get food until something else turns up."

---

20 *Putzfrau* – cleaning lady

"These potatoes are kind of small. Where did you get them?" asked Frau Luder.

"Where did I get them! They're too small! Did *you* find anything for us to eat? You make me sick!"

That afternoon after work Gretel went to tend the garden, where she had been so often with Rosa. "Look at that! Somebody stole some of our potatoes. If they need food, why can't they just ask? Well, this is serious, so I'd better tell everyone that our food is being stolen."

Gretel went straight home and into the slaughter shed. "Grandfather, Max, somebody got into the garden and dug up some of our potatoes."

"I've been waiting for this to start," said Max.

"Me too," added Wilhelm. "When people get desperate they'll do things that you'd never expect them to do. Why don't they ask for help?"

"That's what I thought too," answered Gretel. "The moon will be out again tonight, so maybe Siegfried and I should go out and hide in the garden shed to let them know we're on to them. The potatoes aren't really ready to dig up, and besides, thieves would just take something else."

Max said to her, "You be careful, Gretel. Anybody who would steal food might attack you."

After serving the few customers at the evening meal in the Golden Knight, Gretel and Siegfried Kiefer walked out through Forellenbach Gate.

This is so strange, thought Gretel as she walked under the big city gate in the moonlight. *Mama and I used to walk through here together when we went out to the garden with laundry or to bring back vegetables. Now she's gone and I still miss her terribly.*

"You're awfully quiet. There's no need to be quiet yet. It's only about eight," Siegfried teased.

"I'm thinking," Gretel said.

Siegfried knew by the tone of her voice that Gretel was contemplating something more serious, so he did not tease her again. Figuring out what girls were thinking was still a mystery to him.

After a few more minutes in silence, they reached the garden. Gretel and Siegfried walked through the garden gate where Rosa and Franz Baumfeller had reached their fateful decision to stop seeing each other.

"Did you say they dug up the potatoes? Let's put all the tools in the garden shed. We can hide inside and then if they don't come, we can at least lock the door when we leave," suggested Siegfried.

"Sounds good to me," Gretel agreed. She started pulling up a few carrots to take back home with her. "We'll have to be quiet in the shed—

and that won't be easy for either of us." She laughed.

Gretel and Siegfried quickly hid inside the shed and waited while seated on some crates.

Siegfried whispered, "How will we know how long to stay?"

"I don't know," answered Gretel, "but they'll ring the church bell until ten, and then we'll have to decide what to do next."

Time dragged.

Gretel said, "Edeltraudt told me that while she was working in the telephone office at the train station[21], she saw Edith Luder talking to old men, but she never leaves on the trains."

"Maybe Edith is working for the Salvation Army," Siegfried joked.

He and Gretel had a nice, long, muffled laugh while imagining Edith helping people.

Train Station

Gretel whispered, "Yes, as if that would ever happen."

"I'd tend to think she's planning to help men in some other way," Siegfried said, and he and Gretel muffled more delightful laughs and tried to keep their mouths clamped shut.

The time seemed to stand still over the next couple of hours, and then Gretel and Siegfried finally heard the church bells tolling 10:00 p.m.

"I'm not sleepy. Let's stay a little bit longer," he suggested.

Gretel thought for a moment and then said, "There's a train at ten fifteen. If nothing happens by then, we'll lock up and leave, okay?"

---

21 Train station photo taken at Eisenbahnmuseum Lehmann

"Sure. Speaking of trains, I wonder if Edith has started 'working' the train station? That's stupid. Everybody in Uberauen would hear about it."

There were more stifled giggles. The 10:15 train was coming into the station from Wurzburg and only stopped to pick up the mail.

"I guess we might as well go," said Gretel. "Nothing is happening tonight."

But as she got up and opened the shed door, Siegfried quickly jerked her back inside. Gretel immediately understood and suddenly felt frightened.

"Oh my God, a robber in Uberauen! What if he has a gun or a knife! What were we thinking?" Gretel froze and squinted to look through a crack in the door.

In the dim moonlight it soon became apparent to Gretel and Siegfried that the thief was not especially good at stealing. The figure was obviously a woman who was trying to teeter around on the soft ground while wearing high-heeled shoes. Then she searched in vain for a hoe or shovel.

Edith considered opening the shed door, but wondered if the door hinges would squeak. She muttered softly, "I'll dig up some of the potatoes by hand and get the hell out of here."

When the woman turned to totter over to the garden gate, Gretel and Siegfried rushed out.

"Who's there?" Gretel called out in an accusing tone.

The woman froze, and then started to run for the gate, but Siegfried was too fast for her.

"Not so fast, lady," he said firmly. "Let's see who has been digging up our stuff." He snatched the scarf off the thief's head.

There in the moonlight, Edith Luder stood and glared like a cornered animal. Both Gretel and Siegfried were, for once, speechless.

Finally, Gretel said, "Edith!"

"Get the hell out of my way!" said Edith as she tried to push past them.

"Oh no, you don't. You owe us a little apology for stealing our potatoes," Siegfried said while holding her back.

Arrogance and aggression couldn't hide the fact that she had been caught in the act, so Edith resorted to playacting, as she often did. After all, everyone knew everyone else in Uberauen and news travels fast. Better to nip any bad stories in the bud.

"Oh, I'm so ashamed. My poor mother and I have nothing to eat and we don't know what to do. Edith wept pretend tears as she held on to Siegfried. "Please don't tell anybody what I did."

While holding on to Siegfried's strong arm, she was thinking that if Siegfried wasn't such a clod she would put the moves on him.

Gretel said, "At least, I can believe the part about you wanting us to keep your theft a secret. Why didn't you just ask me for food?"

"Take your stupid potatoes. I'd never beg *you* for anything." Edith threw the potatoes to the ground and pushed past Gretel and Siegfried. The thief ran as fast as she could in the moonlight, wobbling in high heels and on cobblestones.

When she returned home, Edith ignored her mother's questions and headed straight up to her room.

"You know you can still try to work at the train station, Edith," shouted Frau Luder as Edith swept past her and up the stairs.

"Oh, I'll go look for work at the train station, all right, but it won't be cleaning railroad cars," Edith answered with a smirk. In her closet she looked through her now aging clothes for something attractive to wear.

A few months later, Uberauen was abuzz with the gossip that Edith Luder had married a very old man and had moved to Wurzburg.

"At least she found a way to avoid work," Emma said, and laughed while restraining Rudi from sticking his hand in the bowl of shredded potatoes.

Gretel laughed too. "What can you say? She was so determined not to take a lowly job and then she ended up being a whore!"

Both Gretel and Emma laughed at life's strange twists and turns.

17. MARRIAGE

The whispering about Edith Luder kept everyone busy in Uberauen for a few weeks, and then everything settled back into the daily routine.

As New Year's Eve came for 1930 to 1931, Gretel and Anna were with their friends at the dance hall to ring in the New Year. Gretel didn't feel much like celebrating.

"Oh, great, so now it's midnight and all the girls are getting kissed by their boyfriends, but I'm sitting here with you," she said, only half-jokingly, to Anna.

Anna quickly replied, "I wouldn't have chosen you to sit with now, either."

Then the sisters walked around the dance hall and talked with all their friends, both married and unmarried. Since people were a bit tipsy there was lots of boisterous laughter, and the music was blaring. After singing and dancing until about one, Gretel and Anna started walking home.

It was so cold that they walked quickly through the Gerstenfelder Gate, where they had driven with Waldberger's Ernst in the Ford, and then up to the Brunnen Gasse and back home to the Golden Knight.

The sisters said a quick good night and went to their rooms. Gretel was too tired to look out her window at the dark, cold, wee hours of January 1, 1931. She jumped into her bed and wriggled under her warm feather bedspread.

Before falling asleep, she prayed for 1931 to be a great year. "Dear Lord, thank You for the New Year and for all Your blessings. If it is in Your plan, please arrange for Otto to marry me. Amen." *I'm not sure that God is interested in me or my marriage, but it doesn't hurt to ask,* thought Gretel as she drifted off to sleep.

A few days later, Gretel received another letter from Otto. *He's probably telling me the big news about something that happened to him at work,* Gretel guessed. *Oh, well, I'll take what I can get.*

This time the news was a bit more interesting.

Stuttgart
January 10, 1931

Dear Gretel,

Happy New Year to you and all your wonderful family. I hope you had fun at the dance hall. I'll bet all of our old friends were there. Things were not very exciting for me in Stuttgart. The best days of my life are memories of Uberauen and you! I went to a dance hall with some of the guys from work that are still not married. It was okay. Honestly, sometimes girls flirted with me, but I just didn't feel like partying. All I could think of was how much I wished I was with you! My life is dull and boring. There is nothing to work for and nobody cares about me.

I know the economic situation is in even worse shape than it was when I left Uberauen. Who would have ever guessed that the world would start falling apart! As I sit and think about my life, all I can think about is marrying you! I know it's not very courteous to ask a life-changing question in a letter, but will you marry me? If you could just say "YES!" I'd be the happiest man in the world!

I'll wait impatiently for your reply. If you could decide to marry me, I'll arrange to come to Uberauen so we can get engaged and plan our wedding. Suddenly, I feel as if I can't waste another minute!

Your loving Otto

Gretel started jumping around the kitchen, waving the letter in the air. Dorothea and Rudi took it as an excuse to jump and dance too. Gretel grabbed their hands and danced around while Emma continued cooking.

"I really have no idea what could possibly be getting you so excited, but I guess that letter must be from that guy in Stuttgart ... what was his name? Grotto, grumpo, slobo?" Emma was so delighted that she finally stopped stirring and joined in the circle dance.

Siegfried came in with his mop and bucket just in time to be gathered up in the jumping and circling. Never one to pass up a chance at having fun, Siegfried immediately began circling with Gretel, Emma, Dorothea and Rudi. "What are we celebrating, anyway?" asked Siegfried. "Did Grandfather Wilhelm really have gold hidden behind his canopy bed?"

"No, silly," said Dorothea, "Gretel is getting married!"

This first vocal confirmation of the wedding proposal sent everyone into another circle dance around the crowded kitchen.

Emma was so happy for Gretel that she could hardly continue cooking. But she finally said, "Okay, everybody back to work."

Gretel grabbed Siegfried, Rudi and Dorothea, and said, "Come on. Let's go tell Grandfather and Max!"

Out in the slaughter shed, Max and Wilhelm were covered with blood and filth from butchering. "What's going on here?" asked Wilhelm. "Did you come to help me and Max hang up this hog?"

While Gretel was trying to tell Wilhelm and Max the big news, Rudi was already yanking on the hog's leg that was hanging closest to the ground.

"So, what's going on?" asked Max. "Does this have anything to do with that worthless guy from Stuttgart?"

"Yes, yes, yes," shouted Rudi and Dorothea, who were jumping and clapping.

Max and Wilhelm were delighted with the news and promised to give Gretel a big hug once they got cleaned up and were back in the dining room.

Of course Gretel wrote a letter to Otto that very night and accepted his marriage proposal. A couple of weeks later, Otto came steaming back to Uberauen on the train. That night he and Gretel announced their engagement to a group of their family and friends at the Golden Knight. There was lots of cheering and congratulating as torrents of beer, wine and champagne flowed. Then, as suddenly as he had arrived, Otto had to depart Uberauen and get back to work in Stuttgart.

Everything was arranged for Otto and Gretel to be married on April 5, 1931. It was a long-awaited ceremony, even with the busy Easter celebrations. There were so many plans to make.

"Gretel, I just can't bear to walk down the aisle with you at church," Joseph confided. "I'm so happy for you and Otto, but I want to hide and not be seen in public. I hope you understand. I'll bake you a beautiful wedding cake. Say, why don't you see if Wilhelm will give you away. He'd be perfect for that job."

"What, give you away? I'll pay somebody to take you," teased Wilhelm as he gave Gretel a bear hug. "Of course I'd be delighted to give you away, if that's what you and Joseph want."

Wilhelm and Max agreed that the family could pay for the wedding and buy Gretel a nice wedding dress. The Blumentritt sisters had no wedding gowns in their shop, so Wilhelm agreed to let Gretel go shopping in "the city." Fastnacht's Betti was now married to a railroad worker, but she was able to join Gretel and Anna on a shopping expedition to Wurzburg.

At the dress shop, Anna said, "Wow, that looks perfect on you, Gretel. Are you sure Grandfather didn't give you some money for your sister?"

"That would be great, wouldn't it? But I guess that you and the other girls can wear something pretty that you wear to church. You always look nice. At least, that guy from the city hall thinks you look good." Gretel giggled.

"Oh, you mean Eugen. Everybody knows that Anna has been goo-goo-eyed over Eugen," Fastnacht's Betti said, with a strutting walk like a fashion model's. All the women laughed.

Finally the big day arrived. Emma and Anna helped Gretel get dressed. Otto stayed in Max's old room down by the slaughter shed so he would have his clothes all ready. Otto's parents, Luise and Nikolaus Forner, had arrived from Stuttgart the day before and were now staying upstairs, next to Gretel, at the Golden Knight.

When it was finally time to go to the church everyone met downstairs and walked over to St. Severinus Church together. Gretel waited inside the front door with Wilhelm. Otto and Max went around to the other end of St. Severinus Church and went in the door of the sacristy under the bell tower.

Everyone from Uberauen came in and got ready for Gretel Geyer's wedding. There was lots of gossip because, after all, it was Uberauen and everyone knew everyone else's business. Since Edith Luder had left town in disgrace, her bitter mother sat next to old Frau Meyer and speculated as to whether Gretel was pregnant.

"You know what everyone says about Gretel's mother and grandmother," whispered old Frau Meyer.

"Of course. Everyone in Uberauen knows about those scandals. I hope that young man from Stuttgart knows what he's getting," wrinkled Frau Luder said.

Most people in Uberauen loved Gretel and admired her family. Wilhelm and Max had been feeding anybody who was starving. And besides, they all knew that Gretel was a smart and decent woman. They were here to be happy with her.

Herr Jorg's son struck up the organ while some teenager pumped the organ air pump handle behind the wall on the balcony. He played the Franconian wedding favorite, "So Take My Hands." Everyone stood and watched as Gretel and Wilhelm Rossfeld came down the aisle together. Gretel and Wilhelm passed row after row of people they had known all their lives. Many in the congregation were thinking of their own lives and how quickly time passes. But for now, the music was sweet and the walls vibrated.

As Wilhelm and Gretel approached the altar, Father Weible, Max and Otto came out. Wilhelm gave Gretel away. Max took a few steps to the side. The priest asked everyone to pray.

Then the priest said, "Otto Herman Forner, do you take this woman, Eva Margarethe Geyer, to be your wedded wife?"

"I do," vowed Otto, while watching Gretel.

"Eva Margarethe Geyer, do you take this man, Otto Herman Forner, to be your wedded husband?"

"I do," said Gretel.

"I now pronounce you man and wife. You may kiss the bride." And as the priest said those words, everyone applauded.

Herr Jorg began to play the organ as Otto and Gretel Forner walked back up the aisle to the church doors. Everyone on both sides was smiling and clapping loudly. Gretel and Otto tried to focus on a few friends, but it was all happening too quickly!

Fortunately, the weather cooperated and they went outside onto the marketplace to receive the good wishes of all their family members and friends.

I hope I get along with my new mother-in-law, thought Gretel as her she hugged Luise Forner.

"From now on, you have to call me Mother because you're my daughter now," said Otto's mother.

Otto's father, Nikolaus, gave Gretel a hug and kiss on the cheek. "We're so glad Otto found such a fine woman," he said seriously, yet with a twinkle in his eye.

All the neighbors and friends came by to shake hands and exchange hugs—even old Frau Luder. Then the whole family walked across the marketplace, past city hall and down the Brunnen Gasse to the Golden Knight.

While the large family took turns using the toilet downstairs, Gretel went upstairs to change clothes. After putting on an attractive dress, she came downstairs to celebrate with the family. Everything was happening so fast! Somehow Emma, Anna and the other relatives had managed to prepare a delicious meal *and* go to the wedding.

When all the celebrating was finally over and it was late in the evening, Gretel and Otto were anxious to retire to their wedding bed in Gretel's old bedroom.

"Pleasant dreams, Otto," shouted Max devilishly as Gretel and Otto left the dining room, smiling.

"I'll wake you early, Gretel, so you can help me cook," teased Emma.

That evening everyone in the Geyer, Rossfeld, Bergmeister and Forner families was very happy. Gretel and Otto had finally found each other. The wedding had gone off without a hitch and the world was in order.

The next morning the newlywed couple got up and started getting their things together. While Otto went downstairs for breakfast, Gretel welcomed a private moment at her window above the big gate. She patted the yellow wallpaper with the cute little pink flowers as if experiencing a momentous departure from her past life. Cars and pedestrians were already going by on the Brunnen Gasse, crossing the marketplace and mingling with pedestrians and horse carts. The windows in city hall were lighted and workers were busy.

This has been my window on the world during my whole life. Now I'm leaving and moving with Otto to Stuttgart. It's really exciting, but I must admit that I'll always love Uberauen and I'll really miss it. Gretel allowed herself a few tears. In this place she had grown up, enjoyed a wonderful childhood, suffered the losses of Friedrich and Mama, but now she was to leave with her delightful Otto. *I wonder what my life will be like from now on.*

Then Otto came back to her room and gave her a long passionate kiss. "So Gretel, are you ready to leave Uberauen for your honeymoon and move to Stuttgart?" It was a genuine question that he tried to ask in a lighthearted way.

"I'm ready. Let's get our stuff downstairs and I'll get something to eat. I'd follow you anywhere, but I only have to go to Stuttgart." Gretel laughed.

After breakfast with the large Uberauen family, the Forners and everybody else piled into cars and drove down the Bahnhofstrasse to the station.

As the car rattled over the cobblestone street, Gretel was thinking about life. *I've gone down this street so often. Sometimes I was with Mama to work in the garden. Then we walked down here to say goodbye to Friedrich Rossfeld when he left for the Great War. Waldberger's Ernst drove us through here with his Model A Ford. And now I'm leaving. Strange. Life is thrilling and really very strange.*

Otto and Gretel got on board the waiting train, along with Otto's parents, Luise and Nikolaus. They lowered the windows to wave and shout goodbyes to the family and friends who were at the platform.

Gretel's family on the railway platform

As the train was pulling away from the station in Uberauen, Otto snapped this touching picture of Anna looking up to say goodbye to her sister. Gretel saw some of her old friends. "I'm afraid I'm going to cry again. No, no, I can't cry. I'm happy!"

Anna's farewell to Gretel

Just as it had done when Friedrich Rossfeld left Uberauen to fight and die in the Great War and Edith Luder had left to marry a man twice her age, the engine began to slowly chug, chug. As the train gathered speed, Anna and the whole extended family waved goodbye. Many people were crying because of life's milestones and nobody knew when they would see Gretel again. Anna and Rosine Kiefer waited until the train had completely disappeared before returning to the Golden Knight.

On the train, Gretel tried to keep Uberauen in sight as long as she could. "I don't want to look melodramatic, but I do want to see Uberauen as long as possible," she told Otto. The last part of Uberauen that Gretel could see was the steeple of St. Severinus Church.

"Goodbye, Uberauen," Gretel whispered to herself. "Will I ever come back here?"

Otto was no fool. He gave Gretel a hug around her shoulders and all the Forners began a good visit on the train ride.

Life goes on and has its ups and downs. Today was a wonderful day for Gretel, Otto and her family. Everyone in Uberauen still knows everyone else and everyone else's business. Today, again, it was a chance to celebrate with a whole town full of well-wishers.

In Wurzburg, Otto and Gretel hugged Luise and Nikolaus a quick goodbye before the Forner families took separate trains. Otto and Gretel were off on their honeymoon, to Schliersee in the German Alps.

The next day, Gretel put on the new swimsuit that she had bought on her shopping spree in Wurzburg.

"Gretel, you'll freeze your ass off in that cold lake water," Otto said as he pushed her into the chilly lake.

Gretel on honeymoon at Schiersee, 1931

PART THREE:
STUTTGART YEARS

Christmas in Stuttgart, 1942.
Gretel, Hubert, Hans, and Helmut

18. WOLFGANG

After the long train ride from Schliersee, Otto and Gretel arrived at the Stuttgart Main Train Station.

"I have to admit that Stuttgart looks like a huge city compared to Uberauen. Oh, look, Otto, the *Schwaben*[22] even have paved streets," Gretel said, teasing him.

"You'd better be careful. The *Schwaben* are just as proud as the Franken in Uberauen. The neighbors will have you speaking *real* German in no time. *Woish?*"[23]

They walked the short distance to Otto's parents, Luise and Nikolaus's apartment in the Kriegsbergstrasse. After a polite visit, Gretel and Otto quickly left and walked over to their own apartment in Strohberg.

The second that they got into the door, Gretel and Otto ran playfully from room to room in their first apartment before ending up, romantically, in their secondhand bed.

Otto was fortunate for a young man getting married in the Great Depression. He had a new job with a Swiss publishing house, Concett and Huber. Since he was a little older and more experienced, he was promoted to general manager.

The first few days were fun and challenging for Gretel. Everyone tried to trick her by speaking in purely Schwäbian dialect. It was actually a fun way to break the ice and it gave all of Otto's relatives a chance to get to know her.

Luise worked as a cook, but on her day off she said, "So today, Gretel, I'll teach you how to make *Schwäbische Spätzle*[24] and tomorrow we'll make some *Maultaschen*[25]. No Schwab can be married to a woman who can't cook those two things," said Luise, only half joking.

---

22 *Schwaben* – traditional name for the folk group, and German dialect spoken in Stuttgart

23 *Woish?* – Ya know?

24 *Schwäbische Spätzle* – Schwabian egg noodles

25 *Maultaschen* – Schwäbische specialty similar to ravioli

"In that case, I'd better start learning. I've been cooking Franconian until now, but I'd love to learn something new," Gretel said as she eagerly tied her apron around her waist.

That evening Luise and Gretel presented dinner together for Otto and Nikolaus.

Luise said, "Okay, Otto, Gretel will dazzle you with her first batch of *Schwäbische Spätzle*."

Gretel's Strohberg kitchen

"I'm starving and everything looks really good," said Otto as he heaped his plate with the noodles, meat, vegetables and gravy that Gretel and Mama had made.

Gretel watched as Otto ate and savored every bite. "So," Gretel asked with genuine curiosity, "how did I do with my first batch of *Spätzle?*"

"If Mama wasn't here, I'd say they are the best I've ever had." Otto smiled at both his new wife and his doting mother.

The cooking trials went well. Luise and Gretel got along well with each other, and everybody was happy that Otto and Gretel had found each other.

Being newlyweds was wonderful. Some mornings Otto just had to pull Gretel back under the covers for more love before he left for work. Afterward, in a rush, Otto would eat some slices of bread and the hastily brewed coffee with Gretel. Then he'd say, "I've got to get going or I'll miss the next streetcar," as he dashed out the door.

Gretel went over and looked out the still-dirty windows. It was a new view from her window in Uberauen and she mentally examined the strange houses. There was more hustle and bustle in the Strohberg than on the Brunnen Gasse.

So this is my new life as Mrs. Otto Forner. I wonder what it will be like. I have to admit that I really miss Uberauen. When things settle down, I'll send Emma, Wilhelm, Anna and Max a letter with my new address. The first thing today is to wash these windows.

Within a couple of weeks Gretel and Otto were getting settled into their new neighborhood. Gretel had already noticed one really huge difference between the big city and Uberauen. There were daily news reports on the radio about street battles between Communists and the National Socialist Workers Party that would later be referred to as Nazis. There were banners on buildings all over Stuttgart supporting one party or another. Some were even advertising for a continuation of the Weimar Republic.

I'm not a fool and I do listen to the radio, but I can't decide what's best, thought Gretel as she read the banners.

"Stay in the neighborhood to shop and don't talk politics," Otto warned her. "The whole country is a powder keg, and we can't afford to make enemies. Nobody really knows us and we don't have a big family to protect us like you had in Uberauen. The Nazis are gaining favor by putting people to work, but some of Herr Hitler's fiery speeches worry me. We'll have to mind our own business, and see what happens in Berlin."

Gretel tried to discuss only church, children and cooking with the *Hausfrauen* that she began to recognize in their building or at the stores. Gretel found the nearby Marien Church, but Otto warned her about confessing or making friends.

While Gretel was still getting used to being in Stuttgart, she was pleasantly surprised in February to receive a telegram from Uberauen. It read:

BABY GUDRUN IS HERE WE ARE ALL FINE AND
VERY HAPPY

Gretel knew that Emma had been expecting her third child. When Otto got home that day, Gretel couldn't wait to share the happy news about the new baby. "Isn't it wonderful, Otto. I wish we could have a baby."

"Well, let's keep working on that right now," Otto said as he put his arms around her.

Gretel loved her new life with Otto—except that she mostly just cooked and cleaned. Then, in March of 1932, came the next shocker.

"Oh my God, I've missed my period! Could I really be pregnant already?"

At first Gretel felt the old fears of people questioning her decency, but quickly realized the advantage of not knowing everybody. There was nobody but family who cared about her pregnancy and, besides, she and Otto had agonizingly waited to have sex until after they were married.

That evening when Otto came home, Gretel said, "What would you think if I told you I was pregnant?"

Otto immediately knew what the question meant and hugged Gretel.

"No more sex for at least five minutes!" He laughed. "Okay, the five minutes are up!"

Gretel's pregnancy went on without a hitch. When she started having labor pains, Otto rushed her to the Hebammenschule that was right in the neighborhood. Before Luise and Nikolaus could get there, Gretel had already delivered a healthy son on November 22, 1932.

The next morning, Luise and Nikolaus came into the hospital room with Otto, to hold the new baby.

"What will you name him?" asked Luise. "How about Otto or Nikolaus?"

"Otto and I have decided to name him Wolfgang," answered Gretel. "I've always liked that name, and there is only one Wolfgang in my family. Otherwise it's full of Maximilians, Rudolfs and Friedrichs. I wanted to name him something new." Everyone agreed that Wolfgang was a wonderful name.

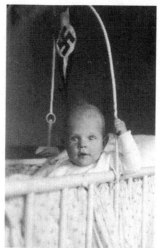

Baby Wolfgang Forner in his crib

At the time, the swastika seemed like nothing more than an interesting political party symbol and maybe progress out of the Great Depression, so Gretel and Otto hung one in Wolfgang's crib. The horror and devastation that followed under this symbol came later.

Otto sent a telegraph to the Golden Knight in Uberauen so everyone would find out that Gretel had a baby boy. The telegram delivery boy told everybody he met on the street and the marketplace the happy private news. Everyone was delighted.

That evening after the dishes were washed and put away, Anna and Emma sat down to write a letter to Gretel. Emma did the writing.

Uberauen

December 1932

Dear Gretel and Otto,

We're so overjoyed to hear that you have a new baby boy! What! You didn't name him Maximilian, Friedrich or Rudolf! Ha-ha.

My little Gudrun is already trying to focus on Max and me when we talk to her. She and Wolfgang will have a great time when we see each other!

Edeltraudt told me that her family is sending her to New York. There is more to that story and we'll tell you later.

Dorothea has turned twelve, so Herr Jorg is teaching her to play the organ at St. Severinus. Rudi is seven and is doing well in school, but he's really more happy when he can go with Wilhelm or Max out to the farms and pick up livestock to butcher.

Now that you're married and living in the big city, we're a little shorthanded in the Golden Knight and the butcher shop, so Frieda was nice enough to send us her Christoph.[26]

He's already peeling potatoes, cleaning out the slaughter shed and scrubbing the floors. I'm sure he hates it, but it's work we've all done. He's a very nice and funny boy. I love having him here.

Are you learning to cook Schwäbisch food? Now, don't forget to spoil Otto with some of your Franconian specialties!

---

26 Christoph – son of Rosa's lover, Franz Baumfeller, and her half-sister Frieda

Anna did not give me permission to tell you, but she is still flirting with Eugen Freitag. Hey, Anna, stop punching me!

Here are some hugs and kisses from me, Anna, Wilhelm, Max and Christoph Baumfeller. Kiss-kiss, hug-hug.

   Love,

   Emma

19. VISITING UBERAUEN

Things were going well for Gretel, Otto and Wolfgang in the summer of 1933, so Gretel decided to travel to Uberauen for a visit. Otto couldn't leave work, but he had enough money to pay for the train trip.

When the train arrived in Uberauen, Emma was there with Max and their children, Dorothea, Gudrun and Rudolf. Gretel rushed down the steps of the train, holding Wolfgang and dragging some carry-on baggage.

The conductor switched from being terribly official to being overjoyed at seeing Gretel and Wolfgang. "Is that you, Gretel? This can't be your son," said the conductor as he reached for Wolfgang's little hand.

Of course the child was frightened and turned to hug Gretel. Everyone laughed and visited.

"Emma, when I left Uberauen I couldn't know if I'd ever come back. It is so wonderful to be here!" Gretel squeezed Emma as she excitedly fussed over Wolfgang.

Christoph Baumfeller picked up Gretel's suitcase to carry it back to the Golden Knight.

"Christoph, no, that can't be you! Why, the last time I saw you in 1925, you were in kindergarten!" Gretel laughed again.

"Greetings Aunt Gretel. I'm glad to finally meet you," said Christoph politely.

Max, Emma, the children and Gretel walked with her old friend Fastnacht's Betti, back to the Golden Knight.

"It's so great seeing all of you and I love being back in Uberauen," said Gretel. "There is so much to tell about Stuttgart."

While the others talked and told stories, Gretel had a split-second memory of Friedrich and Mama. *The passage of time is so weird,* she thought.

As the crowd of family and friends entered the marketplace, neighbors came over to greet Gretel and fuss over Wolfgang.

"Oh, Gretel, he is so cute," gushed Frau Steinhauer.

Dorothea showed Wolfgang to everyone else who came by.

"Well, St. Severinus Church looks just like always." Gretel smiled while standing near city hall. "Emma, just imagine all the things that have happened in our church. It is such a long list of wonderful and terrible events. Our weddings took place right here. It seems like a thousand years ago."

"I know. We've had all of the kids christened, and soon Dorothea will be having her First Communion. Did I tell you that she's learning to play the organ?"

"Yes, I can't wait to hear it. Can I have a private recital, Dorothea?" Gretel asked.

"Yes, Aunt Gretel," Dorothea replied politely.

"Oh, my goodness. Dorothea, Gudrun and Rudi hardly know you. Soon enough, all three of them will stop being shy and they will talk constantly," Emma said, teasing.

Just a few more steps and they were walking down the Brunnen Gasse and Gretel could see the Golden Knight and the butcher shop. More neighbors and friends came by to greet Gretel and see Wolfgang.

"Is this your new little man?" asked Frau Blumentritt sweetly as she tried to hold Wolfgang.

"Oh my, can this handsome boy really be yours?" Anna's boyfriend, Eugen Freitag, said, laughing.

"Of course, he's handsome," said Anna, "with this beautiful mother."

Frau Steinhauer reached out her hands. "Here, Wolfgang, let me hold you too."

Wolfgang looked at all the admiring faces and certainly wondered what was happening.

In the courtyard Gretel could see the familiar buildings, the grapevine, Wilhelm's smoking bench and the entry door.

Max fetched Wilhelm from the slaughter shed.

"Grandfather!" Gretel yelled, "here is our sweet little Wolfgang."

"Gretel, it's so wonderful to see you, and now this cute little guy," said Wilhelm as he tried to hug her without getting her dirty. "I can't do as much work as I used to—just enough to get dirty."

"Grandfather, my heart has ached to see you and hold you," Gretel said lovingly. "I'll give you twice as many hugs this evening when you're washed."

Wilhelm and everyone laughed.

"Let me get Wolfgang upstairs. We'll nap for a short time and then I'll meet you in the kitchen," said Gretel as she started to climb the familiar stairs. *It is so wonderful to be back at the Golden Knight. I remember when Emma came tearing down these stairs to meet Max. Ha-ha. She was so excited. It was a wonderful day.*

"Oh, look, Wolfgang. This is Mama's old room. See this pretty faded yellow wallpaper with the roses? That wallpaper was put up by your grandmother and grandfather."

"Remembering you still hurts me, Mama, but the memories are also very dear and sweet," Gretel whispered aloud.

After putting Wolfgang down securely on the bed, Gretel drifted over to look out her window. People were walking and driving down the Brunnen Gasse, just like always. There were new people working at the courthouse and the German flag with the black swastika was hanging on the wall facing the Golden Knight. "Well, would you look at that. I wonder what that is all about, Wolfgang?" said Gretel in surprise.

The next morning after Gretel had eaten her breakfast, she took Wolfgang to show him off to her father.

"Hello, Papa. Look who I have here. This is Wolfgang," Gretel said as she handed him to Joseph.

"Oh my, just look at this big guy." Joseph smiled as Wolfgang reached for him. "He's beautiful! It's too bad your mama can't be here to see him."

Wolfgang was fascinated with Joseph's mustache and kept reaching up to pull on it.

"I know, Papa. There are so many memories in Uberauen that it is always a mixture of joy and sadness when I'm here. So, how are you doing?"

"It makes me feel great to see you and Wolfgang, but I actually haven't been feeling that well lately. I guess it must be old age." He laughed weakly.

Gretel stayed and visited with Papa until Wolfgang got fussy, and then she returned to the Golden Knight.

For Gretel, the rest of the day in Uberauen was like it had been when she was a girl—except that now, she was married and had Wolfgang to look after.

While Emma and Gretel worked and visited, they put Wolfgang out in the courtyard to play close to the kitchen window. He had a great time playing near the grapevine, where he found some empty bottles to put in and take out of a crate.

Wolfgang and friend playing under grapevine in Golden Ritter Courtyard

Wolfgang reading with friend

Later in the evening when everyone had visited, eaten, dishes were washed and everyone was off to bed, Emma whispered to Gretel: "What are the National Socialists like in Stuttgart?"

"I don't know. Okay, I guess. The Daimler, Bosch and Porsche factories are thriving. They've started building the Autobahn toward Munich and everybody has work. Otto just warns me not to discuss politics and to *never* say anything bad about the Brown Shirts," said Gretel confidentially. "What's it like here?"

"I told you that Edeltraudt left and went to New York," Emma said while she looked to see if anyone else could hear her.

"Yes, you told me in your letter. How exciting!"

Emma leaned in closer to Gretel and said, "It's more than just exciting. Edeltraudt's mother whispered to me that they're scared to death of the Nazis and wanted to get Edeltraudt out of the country until things calm down. I guess they figured it was better to let Edeltraudt look for a husband in New York and know that she's okay."

Gretel was embarrassed that she had not thought about politics very much. "What do you mean, calm down?" asked Gretel.

Emma looked shocked. "You're the big-city girl and you don't know! There are soldiers everywhere. Max says the factories all over the country are building tanks, planes and guns. Do you think they're planning to plant potatoes with them?"

"I'm glad you told me about the National Socialists. It's just what Otto tells me: 'Don't say anything against them.' He even tells me not to gossip with the people in our building, or go to confession," Gretel replied.

Emma said, "Let's hope that people will be satisfied with their new jobs and everything stays the same in Germany."

All too soon, Gretel, Wolfgang and the family made the walk back across the marketplace and down to the train station. Then Gretel and Wolfgang waved goodbye as the train left Uberauen again.

Gretel had no way of knowing that the most tragic loss of her life was drawing nearer.

All across Germany the political situation became more and more tense. Swastikas and solders were everywhere. The Fascist government began building military installations all around Stuttgart and across Germany. The economy continued to boom. Mercedes Benz was building trucks and tanks. Machine shops, the Bosch electrical company and chemical plants were working full shifts to make military equipment. Herr Porsche became part of the Nazi SS and his factories were building the Panzer tank. At the same time, Hitler ordered the building of the Autobahn to connect all the major cities of Germany without having to go through towns. There was no resistance because it had already become clear to everyone that nobody argued with the Nazis and lived to talk about it! Besides everyone was employed, fed, clothed and paid. It was easier to go along and keep quiet.

Even though she loved being back home in Uberauen, Gretel was delighted to see her Otto again. They dropped her luggage inside the front door, put Wolfgang in his crib and tenderly greeted each other.

After a couple of hours, things got back to the routine and Otto again warned Gretel: "Don't say anything about the government or Herr Hitler to *anybody*. The Nazis have spies in most apartment houses and businesses. If anybody is overhead criticizing the Nazis, they are hauled off and they never come back! We have Wolfgang and each other to take care of. It's bad enough that Papa Nikolaus is proud to be a Communist! He still wears his red carnation in public. Let's hope that he at least *tries* to keep still."

"Don't worry, Otto. I can keep my mouth shut. Women are supposed to be domestic. I'll just talk about making *Spätzle* and smile."

And so the Forners continued to watch while the political situation in Stuttgart grew more worrisome. Like almost everyone else, they tried to just live their personal lives while dangerous changes were taking place around them.

Gretel had only been back in Stuttgart a few months, when another sad telegram arrived from Uberauen.

JOSEPH GEYER HAS DIED WE'RE SO SORRY
GRETEL FUNERAL TOMORROW

When Otto came home from work, he found Gretel crying.

"What's wrong? Are you and Wolfgang okay?' Otto asked with genuine concern.

"Yes, Otto, we're fine, but I just heard that Papa died yesterday. I can't imagine that my poor sweet Papa can be dead. He had such a difficult life, and now it's ended already. It's so sad," said Gretel while dabbing her eyes. "Thank God I got to see him when I was in Uberauen. The funeral is there tomorrow, but it's too much for us to travel back there again so soon. Maybe we can go to my church and have our own private service for him when you get home from work tomorrow."

"Of course we'll go and remember him together. I'll get Mama and Papa to come over here to watch Wolfgang so we can pray for Joseph and light candles in his memory," Otto said. "I didn't know Joseph very well because he had a distant personality, but I think you're right. He seemed to have led a difficult and lonely life, and I really feel sorry for him."

At the private church service, the priest read some meaningful Bible verses and then prayed with the grieving couple. Both Gretel and Otto mentioned that it's hard to face life's great sorrows … but they had no way of knowing that the most devastating event of their lives was still to come.

20. SORROW

When Wolfgang was one and a half years old, Gretel noticed that he was fussy and had a temperature. When Otto came home from work, she quickly told him, "Otto, Wolfgang has a temperature and he's been crying all day. Can we take him to the doctor?"

Otto turned as white as a sheet. "I'll go over to the doctor's office right now and see if he will come over." Otto rushed out the door and down the stairs.

"Hurry, Otto!" Gretel yelled down the stairwell after him.

I'll run down the street to see if I can get to the office before it closes. If other people are disturbed by my running, so be it, thought Otto.

He arrived, panting, at the doctor's office but it was closed. Fortunately, in the depression year of 1934, the doctor lived in the apartment above his office. Otto ran quickly up the stairs.

While panting, Otto began pounding on the door and calling, "Herr Doctor, excuse me, but my baby has a terrible fever, and my wife and I are so worried about him. Can you please come and check him?"

The doctor was used to young couples who panicked at every spell of crying, but he agreed to come anyway.

"Could you please walk a little faster, *Herr Doktor,*" urged Otto.

Finally, after what seemed like an eternity to Gretel, Otto and the doctor arrived. The doctor began to examine Wolfgang and quickly determined that the illness was serious.

"Just wait in the living room for a few minutes, Herr Forner," ordered the doctor.

After about half an hour, the doctor came out and told Gretel and Otto, "I'm so sorry to tell you, but your baby has spinal meningitis. I'll do everything I can to treat him and get his temperature down. I'll have to take a sample of his spinal fluid to be tested. Herr and Frau Forner, please hold the baby down firmly on the mattress while I use a syringe to extract some spinal fluid."

Gretel and Otto reluctantly held baby Wolfgang down firmly on his stomach while he screamed at the top of his lungs.

"I'm so sorry, Wolfgang, Mama doesn't want to hurt you," Gretel said, weeping, while she and Otto continued to hold him still.

The doctor seemed to take forever, slowly drawing the sample of spinal fluid from the baby. Wolfgang screamed and cried in pain and terror.

Agonized over hurting his baby son, Otto said, "Gretel, I'm sorry we have to do this, but I'm afraid we have no choice."

"I know. I'm sure the doctor knows what he's doing," Gretel said hopefully.

Otto and Gretel watched as the doctor emptied the syringe into a chemist's glass beaker. Gretel observed something that she would remember all of her life.

"Otto," she said, "the liquid in the beaker looks like a crown."

"Herr Doktor, how could he have meningitis? I haven't had him outside the house except to go food shopping."

"It's really hard to say, because it's a very contagious disease," the doctor answered with cool professionalism.

In the next room, Otto did something he had not done in a long time: he prayed. "Dear Lord, I know I have not been a good Christian, but please hold and protect Wolfgang from this terrible disease. He's just a baby! Amen."

Otto and Gretel held each other, cried and prayed all evening and all night.

"I'll try to comfort Wolfgang while being sure that I don't get any of his body fluids on me," Gretel told Otto. "We can't risk all coming down with meningitis."

About eight thirty the next morning, the doctor came back and checked the liquid in the beaker.

"Frau Forner, you'll have to take the baby to the hospital each day for more spinal samples," the doctor said.

"Yes, Herr Doktor," Gretel replied, the gratitude obvious in her voice. *Dear God, give me strength to save Wolfgang. Amen,* she prayed.

As Gretel took Wolfgang to the hospital over the next few days for spinal fluid tests, baby Wolfgang quickly learned that the hospital was associated with extreme pain.

"Otto, it breaks my heart to take Wolfgang to the Olga Hospital! The poor boy already understands that he will be hurt and he screams so loudly that people on the street turn to see what is causing a child such agony. It's all I can do to make myself take him for treatment, even though I know it's for the best," Gretel confided.

The next time the doctor examined Wolfgang at home, the baby appeared to be sleeping in his crib.

"Herr Forner, why don't you both go into the other room and rest while I'm here," the doctor advised. "I'll come and get you if need be." He knew they would need all their strength when he had to tell them that their baby was dying.

About an hour later, the doctor motioned for Gretel and Otto to come into Wolfgang's room. They entered.

The doctor said gently, "I wanted you to be here now because I'm afraid the baby is about to die and I know you'd want to be here."

Gretel looked at the chemist's beaker where the crown-shaped spinal fluid was being tested. She exclaimed, "Dear Jesus, the crown seems to be covered with a veil of mourning!"

Otto and Gretel put their hands on the sheet that covered baby Wolfgang's tiny body. They stayed with him and cried until the doctor started easing them gently away from the silent crib. Wolfgang was dead.

Back in the living room, the doctor expressed his genuine sorrow at Wolfgang's death. "Herr Forner, do you have a funeral home that you'd like for me to call?"

"No," said Otto, "please pick one for us. We'll wait here with Wolfgang until they come."

After the doctor left, Otto turned to Gretel, who was still sitting near Wolfgang's bed. "Gretel, how will we ever live through this horrible day? Why did God take our wonderful Wolfgang?"

Otto and Gretel held each other and sobbed uncontrollably.

"It's really more agony than I can bear," confessed Otto.

After about another hour, Otto asked a neighbor if he'd be so kind and go over to tell Luise and Nikolaus that Wolfgang had died.

"Of course, Herr Forner. I'm so sorry to hear about your baby's death. I'll go right over and tell your parents."

Otto and Gretel grieved and cried together with Luise and Nikolaus. Later that day Otto and Nicklaus talked to the man who came from the funeral home. They then made arrangements for Wolfgang to be buried in the Forner family grave in the Häslach Cemetery.

Since Gretel had been going to the Marien Church, she and Luise went to see the priest about a funeral Mass. The priest was patient as both Protestant Luise and Catholic Gretel struggled in their grief.

They explained the sorrowful circumstances of Wolfgang's death and continued to painfully plan for the funeral.

Otto went to the train station and, crying over the tragic words, sent off a telegram to Uberauen.

The boy from the telegraph office in Uberauen did not stop to tell everybody the private news as he normally did. The death of Gretel Geyer's baby was just too sad and serious to blab all over Uberauen.

When he came into the Golden Knight, Emma and Christoph were cooking. Since he knew everybody, the boy went on into the kitchen.

"Frau Bergmeister, telegram," said the boy, handing it to her as he quickly left the Golden Knight to hide his own tears. Of course, he had read the telegram.

Both Emma and Christoph knew immediately that something was terribly wrong. The boy from the telegraph office was always bouncy and ready for a short chat, but not today.

Emma opened the telegram.

```
OUR PRECIOUS BABY WOLFGANG HAS DIED OUR
HEARTS ARE BROKEN GRETEL AND OTTO
```

⚜

Upon reading the terrible news, Emma felt weak. She sent Christoph to tell Wilhelm and Max. The two men were busy in the slaughter shed when Christoph came in.

"Oh, you're just in time. You can help us cut up this steer," teased Max.

There was an unusual silence, so the two older men turned to look at Christoph. "Gretel's baby died," he said softly.

Wilhelm and Max both stood frozen for some moments.

"Oh, no!" Wilhelm exclaimed. "That can't be true! Who told you that?"

"It was in a telegram that just came," Christoph managed to say.

Within minutes, all of Uberauen heard that Gretel Geyer's baby had died. Friends and neighbors came by the Golden Knight to express their shock and sadness.

"What can God be thinking?" said Wilhelm, while weeping. "Our family has suffered so much tragedy, and now this. Wolfgang was just an innocent baby!"

Anna, Emma, Christoph, Wilhelm and Max sat in the dining room and cried together. To give the family some privacy, one of the ladies from Steinhauer's Bakery came over and let the neighbors convey their condolences to her.

Gretel and Otto sent another telegram to urge their family and friends to have a funeral Mass for Wolfgang at St. Severinus Church on the same day and at the same time as the service at the Marien Church in Stuttgart.

Gretel, Otto, Luise and Nikolaus were joined by the Forner family, friends and neighbors for the funeral Mass.

As the priest prayed and others read the Holy Scriptures, Gretel, Otto and almost all of those present wept and prayed.

"Holy Mary, Mother of God, pray for us. This is too much agony to bear. I don't understand how God could take my precious Wolfgang. It feels as if a part of me has been ripped away! He was just a baby! Please hold my Wolfgang in Your arms for me until I can rejoin him," Gretel prayed as she held on to Otto and Luise.

The little white casket was kept closed, in accordance with Otto and Gretel's wishes. A spray of flowers lay on top.

After the funeral Mass, the family waited while Wolfgang's coffin was put into the hearse. Then the Forner family climbed into a car that was owned by Otto's cousin. The drive to Häslach Cemetery seemed endless even though it was only a few kilometers.

Gretel asked, without actually expecting an answer, "Luise, how could God take our baby?"

While looking at Gretel through her own tears, Luise said gently, "Gretel, I understand and my heart aches for you. As you may know, Otto had a sister, Hildegard, who died when she was only eight years old. I will never recover from the grief of her death and I know exactly how you feel. We don't have the answers for life and death, so all we can do is pray and trust that God has His purpose."

Otto was grieving and in no mood for philosophy or even religion. "All I know," he said, "is that Wolfgang is dead and I'm angry about it."

Everyone sat quietly and wept as the car moved along.

Gretel looked out the car window. *How can everything look so normal? Everyone is going about their business as if my precious Wolfgang had not died. Don't people understand that my heart is breaking!* Of course, Gretel knew that the world does not stop when a loved one dies. Life around us goes on even when we're in deep mourning.

At the cemetery everyone from the Forner family, plus some friends, moved slowly behind Otto as he carried Wolfgang's casket. Wind was blowing the beautiful flowers that bloomed on the immaculately kept graves. Wolfgang's grave was already dug, so the grieving family held each other and listened vaguely as the priest read the funeral rites. Then ropes were put under the child's casket and it was slowly lowered into the grave.

"How will I ever endure this, Otto? Why has God taken Wolfgang from us? Why?"

As Gretel cried and prayed, she felt something new that she had never been able to imagine before. It was the sensation that giving up on life was something to actually consider.

"Thank God I still have you, Otto, or I'd never be able to live through this pain," Gretel cried softly.

Otto held his mother and father while he cried and then held Gretel as all four grieved together. Gradually, family members and friends began to move the family away from the grave, and the men from the funeral home began to shovel dirt over the little white coffin.

Back home, alone in their apartment after the ordeal of losing and burying their little Wolfgang, Gretel and Otto held each other and mourned. Then they went to bed and wept until, from pure exhaustion and grief, they finally fell asleep.

The next day, Otto had to leave and go to work as if nothing had happened. He didn't dare miss a day. The Great Depression had left too many men looking for work and, besides that, he couldn't risk getting drafted.

When Otto had gone, Gretel walked into Wolfgang's room where his little bed was now empty and the room was painfully silent. It was a silence that was overwhelming. She sat alone crying and grieving most of the day. *When Friedrich Rossfeld had died in the Great War, I thought I would never feel such pain again as long as I lived. When Mama died and we walked behind the hearse to the cemetery in Uberauen, I thought I would never feel such deep sorrow. But by far the most agonizing event of my whole life will be this, Wolfgang's death.*

As she had at the cemetery, Gretel suddenly understood her mother's and her grandmother's deaths. *Now I understand how Grandmother could have been sad enough to take her own life. Up until now, it was an impossible idea. But after losing Wolfgang, I finally understand how deep sadness can take its toll.*

❈❈

While Gretel was mourning alone at home, Otto forced himself to go back to work. As he walked down the street, he kept thinking about Wolfgang's suffering. When he reached the spot where he could jump onto the streetcar, he suddenly felt overcome by grief. Otto wept softly and used his handkerchief to dab away the tears. Other passengers noticed and tried not to stare or take notice of the young man who was crying on the streetcar.

This pain is just too much to bear! I must be having a horrible dream. How can Wolfgang be dead? How will Gretel and I have the strength to go on when our hearts are broken!

After the ride to work on the streetcar, Otto had to go to work and be the tough manager without showing human emotion. He kept thinking, *How will I be able to function today? The other guys will think I'm crazy. I must stop this crying … at least in public.*

The other workers had already heard about Otto's terrible, tragic loss. They understood and silently left him alone to grieve.

As the next days, weeks and months went by, Gretel and Otto moved through life like grieving puppets. Nothing seemed real. The world went by almost without their noticing. One thing was clear for both of them: Wolfgang's death would mark one of the most horrible times of their lives.

The original photograph of Wolfgang and Anna was taken at the Golden Knight in Uberauen. It has a poem written on it from Otto, who kept this picture with the poem near his bed for the rest of his life. It is a heartbreaking description of his own pain and grief at losing Wolfgang. Here it is in the original German and in English.

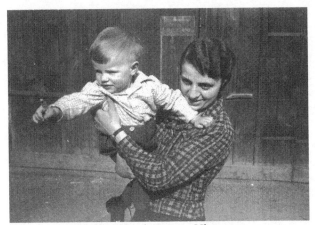

Wolfgang and Anna in Uberauen

Kleines Bild an meiner Wand,
wie oft nehm' ich dich noch zur Hand.
Abends vor dem Schlafengehen,
um dich noch einmal anzusehen.
Oft tu' ich's und immer wieder,
und du lächelst still hernieder.
Du bist so fern und ich bin hier
Nur dein Bild bringt dich noch zu mir

Little picture on my wall,
how often I still hold you in my hand,
evenings before I go to sleep,
So I can see you once again.
I do it often and every time,
you smile down at me.
You are so far away and I am here,
only your picture still brings you near.

21. BIRTH AND DEATH

The pain of Wolfgang's death was all Gretel and Otto could deal with for some time. While they attempted to continue on with life, Germany charged ahead on a war footing. Chancellor Adolf Hitler was suspected of having his forces set fire to the Reichstag, the Parliament Building in Berlin on February 27, 1933. Shortly after that, in March of 1933, in the midst of political turmoil, Hitler was given dictatorial powers. Since the Nazis were in complete control of the government by then, Hitler's selection as dictator was actually just a formality. The world watched and held its breath as Fascist regimes took power in Germany, Italy and Japan. At the same time, Joseph Stalin ruled the Communist Soviet Union with brutal force and was responsible for the deaths of millions of his own people.

In Stuttgart, Otto and Gretel were still living in Strohberg and worried about every word they spoke. "Remember now, Gretel, just talk about the weather and how you hate to do the wash. If someone talks about the government, they may be spies who are trying to entrap you. Don't say anything about politics! Just smile and act dumb."

"I understand, Otto. Everyone likes having a job and seeing people in nice clothes, but most people are afraid. Let's tune the radio to the German National Broadcasting Corporation this evening. I don't know if all we hear is true, but we can at least get some news," Gretel suggested.

The hold on Germany by the National Socialist Workers Party, led by Hitler, was total. Everyone had to keep quiet, or risk being shot or sent to concentration camps.

While the world continued to rush into militarist insanity, Gretel and Otto finally had some wonderful personal news to share.

"Otto, I have a little surprise for you," Gretel said, and smiled cautiously. "You're going to be a papa again!"

Otto smiled and hugged her. "That's wonderful news, Gretel," he said. "I'm so happy to hear that we can be parents again, after losing our little Wolfgang."

Gretel's pregnancy went well and she carried her baby full term. Otto and Gretel had prepared in advance.

"Otto, grab the bag of things I prepared," urged Gretel. "It's time. Let's walk over to the women's clinic while I still can."

Otto and Gretel arrived at the clinic in time for Gretel's routine delivery. Baby Hans was born on June 6, 1935. As soon as Gretel had recovered from delivering her baby, Otto sent a telegram to Uberauen.

```
BABY HANS FORNER IS HERE WE ARE
OVERJOYED
```

—⁂—

Otto, Gretel and Hans lived happily in their Strohberg District apartment as Hans grew strong and healthy. Two years later, they were able to move into a beautiful apartment house at 96 Schlossstrasse. Otto's former Swiss employers owned it, but they had had to leave the country under threat from the new Nazi government. The Swiss employer asked Otto and Gretel to move into their apartment, rent free, until it was safe for them to return to Germany. As soon as the move into the new apartment was almost finished, Gretel received a letter from Uberauen.

"Otto, I have to tell you the latest news from Uberauen," said Gretel as she showed him the letter. "Anna has been seeing Eugen Freitag from city hall and they're hoping to get married. Wouldn't that be sweet?"

Otto continued trying to tune in the radio. "Eugen? I guess she could do worse. What else is new in Uberauen?"

"Well, she wrote that if Dorothea marries that nice Johann Jessat, Max will have an apartment built for them above the smokehouse," Gretel reported.

"Above the smokehouse? How homey. At least they shouldn't get cold," Otto replied with his dry humor.

"It's free and you can't beat free." Gretel smiled at her husband.

Now that Hans was two years old and grown up enough to travel on the train, they decided that Gretel should take him to Uberauen for a family visit in the late summer of 1937.

All the planning went well for the trip and a few days later, Gretel and young Hans were arriving at the station in Uberauen. Gretel looked out her window at the church steeple and train station as the train pulled in.

Gretel spoke to little Hans although he couldn't understand everything. "This train station brings back so many memories. I was here with Wolfgang shortly before he died. We were all here to send Friedrich off to The War. And you know what else, Hans? When I was here with Wolfgang, I got to visit with Papa one last time before he died. But today it's all good news. Just look at all my family and friends waiting for us on the platform." Gretel waved wildly to Anna, Emma, Max, their children and Christoph Baumfeller. "Oh yes, Hans, everybody knows everybody in Uberauen, and all their business too, but today that's wonderful."

Little Hans had no idea what she was talking about, but he loved waving out the window and smelling smoke from the locomotive's smokestack.

As soon as the train slowed to a stop, Gretel rushed down the steps, holding Hans, and into her family's welcoming arms. Hug, hug, kiss, kiss, Gretel greeted each one. Emma and Max's daughter, Dorothea, quickly snatched up Hans before anyone else could get him. He did not cry as the big crowd of family and friends started to walk up to the marketplace.

Without outwardly showing her thoughts, Gretel remembered the sorrowful walks to the cemetery along these streets for Mama's funeral. She thought again about losing Papa and her precious Wolfgang … but today was a happy day.

"Emma, Max, I'm overwhelmed with joy to be back here with you in Uberauen," said Gretel as she walked arm in arm with Emma.

"We're happy to see you too, Gretel," said Max as he took Hans and held him up in the air. "And who is this guy? No, this can't be Hans. He's too big to be Hans!"

After giving Gretel a big bear hug, Max said, "Here, Gretel. Give me your suitcase to carry while you and Emma talk a mile a minute."

When the group entered the marketplace, Gretel thought to herself again, *Just look at the fountain, the tree and St. Severinus Church. I can remember all the wonderful and sad events that have taken place right here. Now I'm here with Hans.*

Then everyone walked past city hall that was now flying the red, white and black Nazi flag. Gretel looked at it for a second because that was a big change from her childhood. Hans was screaming and reaching for her as everyone started down the Brunnen Gasse, through the big gate and into the courtyard at the Golden Knight.

Hans was still crying and waving his arms as Anna tried to entertain him. Max handed Gretel's suitcase to Rudi, Emma's son, who carried it into the inn.

"Oh, look, Hans, there's Grandfather sitting on his bench, smoking, like always." Gretel rushed over, sat down, and gave Wilhelm a long, loving hug. "I've missed you so much, Grandfather," Gretel whispered to him.

Tears came to Wilhelm's eyes too, as he hugged her.

"So, we have some good news to celebrate today, huh? Little Hans is here and I'm so happy. Hans," said Wilhelm, "come over here and let me hold you on my lap."

"Grandfather, take Hans over to that spot in front of the beer garden and I'll take your photograph," Max suggested.

Hans with Grandfather

While Max was getting ready to take the photograph, Wilhelm thought again about his life. He smiled lovingly upon his Barbara's granddaughter, Gretel, and was holding Barbara's great-grandson, Hans. He loved Gretel so much and now she had matured into a wonderful young woman. First she had lost Friedrich, then Rosa and Joseph, and most recently, baby Wolfgang. Life had certainly been painful for her. At that moment, all he could do was to thank the Lord for Gretel's visit. "My cup runneth over," he whispered.

When the photograph was finished, there was lots of talking and commotion, but Wilhelm made sure that he shared his thoughts with Gretel.

While holding her hand, he said, "Gretel, I'm getting really old and I don't know how much time I have left." Gretel patted his hand and tried to indicate that he shouldn't talk that way. "No, seriously, my life has been wonderful and you've been a very important part of it. I love you as if you were my own daughter."

"I'll always love you too, Grandfather," said Gretel. "You've always been my knight in shining armor. That's why you live in a place called the Golden Knight." She laughed. "I'll cherish every minute we've shared together. Now, no more talk about growing old. Let's see what Emma cooked for dinner."

Gretel visited with Wilhelm and other family members all afternoon and evening.

Later that evening when everyone was heading off to bed, Emma handed Hans to Dorothea and asked if she would watch him for a while.

"Of course I'll watch the little devil!" Dorothea laughed as she rocked the young child and entertained him.

Then Emma took Gretel's arm and said, "Come on, Gretel, I need to work on some things in the laundry room."

Max joined the two as they quietly slipped through the narrow, dimly lit hallway that connected the kitchen with the slaughter shed. The hallway shelves were stuffed with metal spice boxes that emitted all the aromatic flavors of exotic Arabia. The passageway turned and led into the slaughter shed as they continued out into the courtyard. A few more steps brought them into the laundry room where they could finally huddle privately

"Well, this room never changes. It looks like it did when I used to help Mama wash the sheets." Gretel remembered those days with her mother fondly.

"I really asked you to come in here so we could finally talk without having to worry about being overheard. But still, don't talk too loudly," cautioned Emma.

Gretel was getting ever more puzzled. "What's this all about, Emma?"

Max explained. "There have been a lot of changes in Uberauen since you left and not all of them are good." He peeped out the window to be sure nobody could hear. "The National Socialist federal government is using city hall across the street as their headquarters for the *Sturmabteilung* [27] and all the city officials are expected to join the party. The troops moved in a few weeks ago."

"Okay," Gretel said, "so has it had any effect on you, Max?"

---

27 *Sturmabteilung*, SA – Security Detachment

"They opened up new membership in the Nazi Party in 1937 and they're always pressuring me to join them, but I'd rather not," answered Max.

"I keep telling him not to say anything," Emma chimed in. "You know how hard it is for me to keep my opinions to myself."

Emma and Gretel smiled knowingly at the thought of Emma or Max having no opinions.

"There is such a buildup of military everywhere that I'm afraid our Rudi and Christoph Baumfeller will get drafted. They don't want to go into the military. Rudi is already in the boys' government youth group, the *Hitler Jugend*. Dorothea joined the government-run girls' youth group, the *Bund Deutscher Mädel*. Everybody in town is expected to send their children to join these Nazi youth groups and there is really no choice. There are spies everywhere who spread rumors about people that the government doesn't like. Jews, anybody with mental illness, Communists, homosexuals and Gypsies are in great danger here," said Emma. "Is it that way in Stuttgart?"

Gretel wanted to share whatever news she had to offer. "Stuttgart is a big city, but I think the same things are happening there. You know that Otto was working for that Swiss company, Concett and Huber. They closed the business and left town in a matter of hours. We moved into their house as house-sitters. Otto tells me to be quiet, stay at home and only talk about cooking. I'm really sick of being quiet! Now we've got Hans, and Otto has been struggling to keep a job so I have to be cautious. It's not worth the risk of speaking out."

"Uberauen is not Stuttgart, but even here the Jews are especially scared. When he comes to buy meat at the butcher shop the rabbi tells me that everyone is afraid. It wouldn't surprise me to see Jewish families fleeing to Switzerland, England or America," said Max. "As you know, your friend Edeltraudt was sent to New York."

"I guess it's good that Edeltraudt is in New York until everything calms down. Max, how long will you be able to avoid joining the National Socialists?" asked Gretel.

Emma butted in. "He's avoided their insistence here locally since 1933 because the party was closed to new members. He had to be quiet, work and try not to get noticed. It's terrible! We always joke about everybody knowing everybody else's business in Uberauen, but in the past it has never been a matter of life and death as it is now!"

Then Max said, "The other thing is that it's just a matter of time before our Rudi, Christoph Baumfeller, Dorothea's Johann and Anna's Eugen get drafted. The world is really a frightening place."

Emma, Max and Gretel discussed the worrisome matter for about an hour, and then Gretel took Hans up to her old room.

"I'm so tired, Hans," she said as she laid her sleeping child on the bed. "Now the world is going crazy and I don't know what will happen next." She walked over to look out her window.

Gretel noticed how Papa's wallpaper had faded. It still brought back wonderful memories. Gretel was smiling as she reached the window and looked across the narrow street at city hall, with the big Nazi flag hanging down the side of the building. *If you are still alive, Frau Luder, you would love what has happened in your building. I'm not so sure,* thought Gretel.

On Sunday Gretel was glad to attend Mass again at St. Severinus, and slipped into the pew next to Emma. "My goodness, the whole church shakes when Dorothea plays the organ," Gretel said to her proud aunt, Emma. "I'm glad we don't have to worry about that nasty Edith Luder and her mother making rude comments as we did in the past!"

"I've heard Edith may be coming back," whispered Emma as they both rolled their eyes.

When the service ended, Dorothea came over to Gretel with a young man. "Aunt Gretel, I want you to meet Johann Jessat. Johann, this is my aunt Gretel."

While Gretel thought, *Dorothea has picked a handsome young man,* she said, "It's nice meeting you, Johann." She smiled. "I hear you two are getting serious."

Dorothea looked shocked and embarrassed by what Gretel might say next. "Oh, Aunt Gretel …" she said, and laughed shyly.

Emma was right, thought Gretel. *Johann is a very sweet and handsome boy. I hope everything will work out for them.*

All too soon, the days had gone by and it was time for Gretel and Hans to head back to Stuttgart. Everyone who could spare the time came down to see them off at the train station.

Gretel boarded the train with Hans and sat by the window so she could see her family and friends. The train started moving slowly away from the platform. *I remember leaving here with Wolfgang,* thought Gretel. *I pray that nothing happens to Hans.* Gretel waved goodbye as the engines revved up and made the familiar chugging sound.

"I will miss you, Uberauen," she said aloud.

The lady in the seat next to Gretel commented, "I don't see how anybody could miss a little nest like Uberauen."

"Oh, I'll never forget Uberauen. A big part of my heart is here, and it always will be," Gretel said. "It's home."

The fellow passenger could only reply with a polite, "Oh," and then continued with some small talk.

Gretel and Hans made it home safely to Stuttgart, where they found Otto and Nikolaus waiting for them at the train station.

"Otto, I'm so glad to see you," Gretel said as she hugged him.

"I've really missed you and I'm so glad you're home," Otto whispered in her ear.

"Hello, Nikolaus. Thanks for coming to meet us," said Gretel as she gave Nikolaus a hug.

"Come here, Hans, let Grandfather carry you," offered Nikolaus.

But Hans wanted to walk and kept jerking on Nikolaus's hand.

The little family strolled together up the Schlossstrasse, to Otto and Gretel's apartment house. After an afternoon coffee, Nikolaus left the young family alone.

Gretel settled back in and continued her routine, but she was not happy about being unable to speak her mind. "It is so difficult to never be able to talk honestly about what's happening in the world with anybody here except you, Otto. Oh, well, everything seems to be going fine for us, and Hans is healthy. I'll keep quiet, and hope the world doesn't get any crazier."

"Maybe we'll be lucky and the whole political and military thing will run its course," said Otto hopefully.

Then in November of 1937, Luise Forner suddenly became ill and died. It was a terrible blow for Nikolaus, Otto and Gretel. A funeral was planned at the Lutheran Church that Nikolaus and Luise attended. Sitting in church and praying for Luise's soul was heartbreaking. Not only were Nikolaus, Otto and Gretel grieving over losing Luise, but her death opened old wounds from the recent death of baby Wolfgang—a wound that would never heal.

After Luise's funeral service, the family followed the hearse to the cemetery where she was buried. Otto, Nikolaus, little Hans and Gretel put their arms around each other and listened to the minister's prayer. Everyone was crying and praying until the service ended and the family left.

When they got back to their neighborhood, Otto asked Nikolaus, "Papa, do you want to stay overnight with Gretel and me? It might be lonesome for you at home tonight."

Nikolaus was still in a blur from his grief. "No, thanks, Otto, you're my wonderful boy, but I'll be fine at home with my memories of Luise."

Gretel, Hans and Otto walked with Nikolaus to the streetcar and waved as he left. It was so sad for all of them.

Gretel said, "Don't worry, Otto. I'll take Hans over and check on Papa for the next several days. While I'm there I'll ask him to come and eat with us. I don't want him to grieve alone or get sick from sadness."

Otto gave Gretel a long hug and big kiss on the cheek. "You're a very kind and thoughtful woman, Gretel. I'm so lucky that you waited for me."

22. HELMUT

For several weeks toward the end of 1937 Gretel and Otto decided to see if she could get pregnant again. Then, early in January, she shared the news with Otto that she was expecting.

Otto was so excited that he picked Gretel up and swung her around. "That is such wonderful news! I hope we get a second son. Wouldn't that be great!"

Gretel laughed and said, "If you don't put me down, I may vomit on you."

"You always say things in such a romantic way," said Otto, as he held her in his arms.

Otto had recently changed jobs again, so he shared his thoughts with Gretel. "I hope that this job as the chief financial officer with Niethammer will last for a while. It seems as if I've changed jobs every few months for ten years. I'll have to wait and see what the company is like, but the factory seems to be busy."

Gretel said, "We now have an especially nice apartment, I'm expecting and your new job sounds wonderful. We'll keep our fingers crossed that our good fortune lasts."

One morning in the cold, dark German month of February 1938, Gretel heard a knock on her door. *Oh, no, who can that be?*

When she opened the door, a young man from the telegraph office was standing there. Gretel froze!

"Frau Forner?" the boy asked.

"Yes," said Gretel cautiously.

"Telegram," said the young man as he handed it to her. He tipped the brim of his hat, and started back down the stairs.

I just know this is bad news and I hate to find out what it is, but I have to know, she thought apprehensively. *No one is pregnant—except me, I don't know of anybody who is getting engaged or married, so I guess it's something tragic.* Then she read.

GRANDFATHER WILHELM IS DEAD FUNERAL ON
FRIDAY

"Oh, no!" she exclaimed aloud. "I knew Grandfather was getting old and he didn't feel well when I was last there, but I didn't expect to lose him so soon!"

While Gretel waited and sobbed at home, Hans kept asking her what was wrong.

"Don't worry. Mama just had some bad news," Gretel told him.

Hans laid his head on Gretel's lap to comfort her.

Wilhelm was such a loving and supporting part of my life, thought Gretel. *I can't imagine life without him. He cared for all the children he had with Grandmother Barbara. Then when my mama died, he looked after Anna and me when Papa was unable to do it. When I think about all those problems during the inflation and then the Great Depression, how did he ever get all of us through that?* Gretel continued to cry and reminisce. *I'll always remember him sitting on that bench in the courtyard under the kitchen window when he had a few minutes to rest. The weight of the world was on his shoulders, but he was always able to love all of us. He was a sweet, grumpy hero.* Gretel cried as she remembered times with her wonderful grandpa.

When Otto got home, he saw immediately that something was terribly wrong. "What happened?" he asked.

Gretel handed Otto the telegram and tried not to cry as she kissed him. "Grandfather Wilhelm has died," she said while beginning to cry again.

"Oh, no, I'm so sorry to hear that. It doesn't seem possible that Wilhelm could be gone. He was so strong physically and mentally, it seemed like he'd live forever."

"What will I do? I've got Hans and you. And I'm pregnant. I'm not sure I should make a trip to Uberauen in February. What do you think?" Gretel asked, trying to decide about how to honor Grandfather Wilhelm.

"I know. I'm glad you and Hans got to see Wilhelm last fall. I guess if you want me to decide, I'd say that you should go to Uberauen. Wilhelm was not only your grandfather, he was like a second father to you and Anna. We're not rich, but we can certainly afford a train ticket," Otto said while holding Gretel.

Little Hans watched and tried to figure out what was happening.

The next morning Gretel and Hans rode the streetcar down to the main train station in Stuttgart. Before boarding, Gretel went into a post office, where you could call on the phone with the help of an operator.

"Hello, Uberauen Operator? Is there some way you can send word to Maximilian Bergmeister that Gretel is coming home for Wilhelm's funeral?" Gretel managed to say before she began to cry again.

"Gretel? Is that you? Of course it's you. Who else would call from Stuttgart," said the familiar voice of the Uberauen operator. Gretel was relieved to speak with someone she knew. "Sure, I'll send the telegraph boy over to tell Emma and Maximilian. Don't you worry now, Gretel. I'm so sorry to hear that Wilhelm has died. Be sure to wave at me here in the telegraph office when you arrive. Have a safe trip."

There are some distinct advantages to small-town living, Gretel thought as she hung up the phone. *Knowing people personally at times like this is surely one of them.*

The ride to Uberauen seemed familiar by now. *Life is so strange,* Gretel mused while watching the German countryside sweep by. Hans was sleeping with his head on her lap. *We live through wonderful, high moments, only to be brought low by the next sad event. I can't believe that we're going to Uberauen to bury Grandfather.* Gretel wept, slept, cared for Hans and remembered her life with Wilhelm in Uberauen.

As the train chugged across the green rolling hills and through forests, Gretel noticed convoys of military trucks, flatbed trailers with tanks and large cannons. *What on earth is going on?* Gretel wondered.

When the train arrived in Uberauen, Gretel made sure to wave at the kind woman at the post office. *People do not have to be nice, so I want to be sure and recognize her efforts.* Gretel remembered the woman as she waved, but couldn't recall her name. *I've been away only a few years and already I can't remember everyone in Uberauen.*

Christoph Baumfeller was there to meet her, with Dorothea, Gudrun and Rudi. Emma was busy feeding the lunch crowd and Max was butchering.

"I'm so glad to see you, Aunt Gretel," said Dorothea while giving Gretel a hug.

Gretel noticed again that Rudi had grown into a tall young man and he was obviously a little ill at ease hugging his aunt. Gudrun hugged Dorothea around the waist while the women cried and talked about Grandfather Wilhelm.

The little group walked up to the marketplace, past the fountain and up to the church.

"Well, Christoph, the German flag on city hall looks even bigger than it did the last time I was here," said Gretel, but young Christoph made no reply.

Next they all turned down the Brunnen Gasse and passed the family butcher shop, where a young neighbor girl was selling meat.

"Look, Hans. See this door? Mama used to play hide-and-seek down there in the cellar," said Gretel. She had a quick mental image of the fun she had as a child.

"I want to play hide-and-seek too," said Hans. Everyone laughed.

Then the group walked under the big gate and into the courtyard of the Golden Knight. Gretel walked over to the bench under the grapevine and below the kitchen window, where Wilhelm had always sat to smoke his pipe when he had a free moment. Christoph and Rudi, being proud young men, did not want to remember anything that might make them cry, so they continued into the entry hall with Gretel's suitcase.

Emma came out and gave Gretel a long hug. Then the two women sat on the bench where Wilhelm smoked his pipe, and cried while they remembered him.

"Wilhelm was always larger than life for me. I can't believe he's gone," Gretel said between sobs.

"I know, Gretel," Emma said. "Papa was gruff and bossy sometimes, but he was so loving and caring. I'll always cherish his memory." She hugged Gretel.

Gretel and Hans spent the rest of the day with Max, Emma and the large group of relatives that had come to Uberauen for the funeral. "We let everyone stay here until all the rooms were full, and then some had to spend the night down at the Schwan and the Waldhorn," Max explained.

That evening the Golden Knight was closed to guests. The extended family had dinner together and shared fond memories of Wilhelm and years gone by.

"So, Grandfather and Grandma Barbara raised five children! That's amazing," said Rudi.

"It's even more amazing than that. Wilhelm also adopted all of Grandma Barbara's children from her first marriage and helped raise us grandchildren," Gretel said.

When it was late, Gretel and Hans went upstairs to her old room. There were so many people staying overnight that a couple of cots had been put in the room and some cousins were already sleeping. Gretel put Hans down on her bed since he was already asleep. She walked quietly over to look down from her window, onto the Brunnen Gasse.

Everything still looks strangely the same, thought Gretel, except for the big flag hanging from city hall. *There are some new streetlights,* she noticed. *Oh, my goodness! Will you look at that! Oh, no! The street has been renamed ADOLF HITLER STRASSE!* Then her thoughts drifted back to life as a young girl. *I have looked out this window to think and grieve over so many loved ones that it breaks my heart. But I somehow feel a connection to everyone who has gone before me, just by being here in the Golden Knight. It's very comforting.* Gretel said a private prayer for Wilhelm's soul, before falling asleep with young Hans in her old bed.

The next morning, after breakfast, the huge family with husbands, wives, children, uncles, aunts and cousins all met at the Golden Knight. It was a strange reunion of happiness at seeing one another again, combined with the sorrow of losing Wilhelm Rossfeld.

"Oh, is that Hans, and look at you, Gretel. You look wonderful!" Aunt Frieda laughed as she hugged Gretel. Little Hans enjoyed running around the dining room, as children had always done, with his newly found cousins.

Then Fritz came into the room. "Fritz Rossfeld, you devil," shouted Gretel as she ran over to hug her tall cousin.

"Remember when we got in trouble for playing hide-and-seek in the cellar?" said Gretel.

"What about my fuzzy spider adventure at school?" Fritz said, and then laughed.

Everyone was so eager to share stories of the past, but it was time to move the few yards to the marketplace and into St. Severinus Church. As the family filed in and found seats in the pews, they joined neighbors and old friends that they had known since childhood.

After a few minutes, everyone was seated and the holiday atmosphere quickly changed into the sorrowful celebration of Wilhelm Rossfeld's life.

Dorothea had asked Herr Jorg to come back and play the organ because she knew that she'd be grieving for Grandfather Wilhelm and unable to play. As the quiet organ music started to play "Jesu, Joy of Man's Desiring," hardly an eye remained dry in the church.

Gretel prayed: *Holy Mary, full of grace, have mercy on us. Dear Lord, please welcome Wilhelm's tender soul back into Your arms until we're all together with You again.*

Like most of those people present, Father Weible had known Wilhelm Rossfeld ever since he had been assigned to the parish at St. Severinus. "Please, dear Lord, help me to deliver a message of comfort to Wilhelm's family, and receive his soul to You. Amen," he prayed quietly during the organ music.

Everyone in the church experienced a shared feeling of deep sadness and loss at his passing. Wilhelm was such a formidable personality and community leader in Uberauen that everyone knew him, most people admired him and a few hated him. Father Weible delivered a moving eulogy of Wilhelm's achievements and contributions to his family, church and the city.

When the Mass was over, the family members and a large crowd of friends walked slowly back up the aisle and out into the cold, gray winter day on the marketplace. Everyone was still crying softly and not talking. Wilhelm's coffin was not carried in a hearse, but was instead carried by six men from the family. The mourners crossed the marketplace, moved on down the Gerstenfelder Strasse and passed under the city gate. Uberauen had not seen such a funeral procession in generations.

Gretel wept while she held Hans by the hand and walked arm in arm with Aunt Emma. *Sweet Friedrich Rossfeld,* thought Gretel, *now your wonderful father has joined you in paradise.* Behind Gretel and Emma the sad columns of mourners reached all the way back to St. Severinus Church.

At the grave, everyone was scattered around the paths among the winter grave greenery and alongside the gravestones. The church bell from St. Severinus Church was tolling in the distance. Wilhelm's children, adopted children and grandchildren held each other closely as Father Weible said the final Christian farewell to Wilhelm Rossfeld.

The graveside service was short and tasteful. A cold winter wind blew through the graveyard and dark gray clouds shrouded the funeral procession as everyone began to leave. The foreboding sky was like a warning of years to come for Uberauen.

Gretel and Hans walked with Max, Emma and their children. Young Christoph and Rudi looked grown up and manly in their new suits. Anna and Eugen walked behind them with Gretel's childhood friend, Ernst. Dorothea was holding onto the arm of her fiancé, Johann Jessat. Everyone walked and wept back up to the marketplace. After passing the fountain everyone noticed the huge black, red, and white German flag of the Third Reich hanging on city hall. The family members walked together down Adolf Hitler Strasse, formerly the Brunnen Gasse, and then back through the big arched gate and into the courtyard at the Golden Knight.

Once inside, everyone in the family was happy to get warm. As was the tradition in Uberauen, ladies from church and the neighborhood brought food and served lunch. Gretel, Fritz Rossfeld, Rosine Kiefer and others from Gretel's generation shared stories about Wilhelm, or mischievous tricks they had played as children. After a few hours of reminiscing and remembering Wilhelm Rossfeld, family members began to leave the Golden Knight. By evening, everyone had gone except Gretel and her little Hans.

The next morning, Gretel and Hans were already packed and after a hurried breakfast with Emma, Max and their children, it was time to meet the train.

"Take care of yourself," said Emma as she hugged Gretel. "I'll have to stay here and cook, so I can't walk you to the train. Please write to me again soon."

Max walked with Gretel and whispered some local news while he made sure nobody was listening. "Gretel, things are going to be rough in Uberauen from now on. I heard that the Security Detachment was bringing Georg Pucher and Edith Luder back to Uberauen to run the Nazi Party apparatus from city hall."

Shocked at the prospect of her old nemesis in Uberauen, Gretel said breathlessly, "Oh no, you're kidding! That awful woman and that criminal are coming back to be in charge of Uberauen? Is there no end to the insanity? How will you and Emma handle that?"

"Their spies are already everywhere," Max confided. "There are people watching everyone's movements from the train station, telephone/telegraph office, post office and at businesses. It's like an evil web that has everyone caught in it.

"We're almost at the train station. From now on, when we exchange letters, don't say anything that will get us in trouble. Believe me, the Nazis are capable of great cruelty. They can take our property and ship us off to a concentration camp. The rabbi has told me stories about what is happening to the Jews here that would scare you to death! Remember, don't write about anything controversial. We'll have to be satisfied knowing that we're all still safe, and wait to see what happens."

While Max and Gretel approached the train station, Gretel was thinking to herself, *We joke about everyone knowing everyone else and everyone else's business in Uberauen. Now the Nazis are using spies and gossip to control and terrorize us.*

As Gretel gave Max farewell hugs and kisses to share with Emma and their children, she looked around the platform. Then she and Hans got on board and sat near a window where they could look at Uberauen and wave at Max.

"Thank you, Max. Take care of yourself. I hope to see you again when my baby is born," shouted Gretel as the train pulled out of the station.

Gretel had done this departure so often, but it still had the same great significance. *I'm going to look at Uberauen as long as I can and I won't stop looking until the steeple of St. Severinus Church is out of sight.* Hans was squirming and her pregnant belly seemed to feel funny, but Gretel kept watching the church steeple get smaller and smaller ... until it finally disappeared.

"So, Hans, it won't be long until we get back to Papa in Stuttgart," Gretel said to herself as much as to Hans.

A month later, in March of 1938, Otto was busy with his new job, Gretel was still caring for Hans, keeping house, being cautious with her pregnancy and still thinking about losing Wilhelm.

There had been headlines in the newspaper, newsreels at the movie theater and reporting on the radio for weeks about how the people of Austria were natural members of the Third Reich.[28] It was only a matter of time before the Austrians demanded inclusion in the new German Reich. The newsreels showed throngs of people cheering for Hitler as he waved to the jubilant crowds.

On the evening of March 12, 1938, the Forners were listening to the National Radio Network. Suddenly there was cheering on the radio and a military band started playing the national anthem, *"Deutschland, Deutschland* Über Alles.*"*[29] Gretel and Otto listened intently to see what was happening.

After more cheering from the crowds, the reporter on the state-run radio announced that Austrians had eagerly demanded to be included in the new Germany. "Yeah, right," said Otto, "and you can call me Fritzle! No, I'd say that once Austria is securely part of Greater Germany, then will come the German-speaking Sudetenland in Czechoslovakia, and then more. The Allies have shown no stomach to resist Hitler so far, but if they lose patience with him, there could be a terrible war!"

"Now remember, Gretel. If someone says anything to you about the annexation of Austria, you are to say how wonderful that is. You're a pregnant wife and mother and you have to protect yourself."

"I know, and I understand that we can't do anything. I wouldn't know what to do anyway. I wonder what will happen next?"

---

28 *Reich* – nation, state
29 *"Deutschland, Deutschland Über Alles"* – "Germany, Germany above all"

In Germany during the month of September 1938, the Stuttgart newspaper was splashed each day with news of friction between Germany, France, England and the Soviet Union. Each evening after dinner, Gretel got some toys for Hans to play with and then she and Otto would sit and listen to the radio. On the government-controlled radio station, there were often reports about *Der Führer*[30], Adolf Hitler, and how he and the military were prepared to defend Germany from threats coming from all their neighbors. Sometimes famous government leaders would speak with great authority about how the German people were good and special, but they were always being threatened from outside.

Then on September 7, in the midst of all the political drumbeat and military buildup, Gretel woke up Otto. "Otto, it's time. Help me get to the women's clinic."

Otto and Gretel grabbed the clothes that they had prepared and jumped into them. Then they rushed the few blocks from their house to the women's clinic, where a second son was born.

The next day, Otto got some time off from work. He and Hans met his father at the women's clinic and together they got a look at the new son, brother and grandson. Hans was only about three years old. He looked skeptically at his new baby brother. "I don't like him," was all he kept on saying.

Otto held the baby boy for a while, and then handed him to Nikolaus. "So, little man, say hi to your grandpa."

"Gretel," asked Nikolaus, "what will you and Otto name him?"

"Otto, do you remember when we talked about naming him, you thought it might be fitting to name him Helmut? That's a nice distinguished name. What do you think?"

Taking the baby back from Nikolaus, Otto looked at the tiny, red-faced boy and could only smile and keep rocking him back and forth. "Helmut, Helmut? Sure, I think he looks like a red and wrinkled Helmut. And besides," he whispered, "none of the Nazi crazies are named Helmut."

Then it was Nikolaus's turn to hold the baby again. Gretel and Otto had warned him to "leave your Communist pins at home." With the number of military men at every government building, it was no time to test the anger of the local Nazi commander.

"Okay, young man," said Nikolaus, smiling, "can you wave your arms?"

---

30 *Der Führer* – the leader

Baby Helmut continued to make faces and wave his arms.

"See? He understands what I wanted him to do. He's imitating Herr Hitler."

Nikolaus laughed as Otto and Gretel nervously urged him, again, not to say anything political.

"Hans, would you like to hold your new brother?" asked Otto.

Hans looked at the baby with skepticism and clung to Nikolaus instead. Nikolaus patted him on the head.

Four days later, Otto and Gretel walked slowly back to their apartment with Hans and the baby. When they got to their stairwell, a neighbor lady passed by and said, "Oh, my goodness, is this the new baby? Congratulations! Is it a boy or a girl?"

"It's a boy," Otto answered proudly.

"Oh, he will make a great soldier for the fatherland," the lady answered with genuine enthusiasm.

"Yes, of course," said Gretel quickly, while she thought privately, *Over my dead body!*

When they were back safely in their own apartment and Gretel, Hans and baby Helmut were settled in, Otto said, "Gretel, steer clear of that neighbor woman. She's sure to be the Block Warden. If you can't avoid her, just go ahead talking about the children and don't let her trick you into saying anything political. She might be hoping to get a promotion by finding someone who is anti-Hitler. We have two boys to raise, so we have to be careful."

After dealing with childbirth and a long walk, Gretel was in no mood for an argument, so she simply replied, "Yes, Otto."

Otto and Gretel were pleased that Otto still had a job as the chief financial officer with Niethammer. They were able to house-sit in the Schlossstrasse home that was owned by Otto's earlier employer. Hans and Helmut were both happy, and the neighbors did not seem to pay much attention to them. After all, Gretel and Otto were both busy trying to work and care for their children. They were the picture of the perfect German couple.

Each evening while he was waiting for Gretel to feed the boys and serve him dinner, Otto would read the Stuttgart newspaper. On September 30 there were articles trumpeting the political victory of the National Socialist government and the German people over the threats from England and France.

There was a widely distributed photograph of British prime minister Neville Chamberlain, upon his return to England after giving his "Peace for Our Time," speech. Chamberlain believed that by giving in to Hitler's demands, war had been averted.

"Gretel, did you see this article and picture in today's paper about the English giving in? They have given up on trying to force Hitler to stay out of the Sudetenland. I guess that's good. The German-speaking minority in Czechoslovakia can be part of Germany again," Otto said, thinking out loud.

"If you say so," Gretel said. "Can you come and wash Hans's hands and mouth while I finish nursing Helmut?"

"Sure. I guess I should be glad you're not paying much attention to international politics. Maybe you'll stay out of trouble." Otto smiled as he helped Hans wash for dinner.

After the boys were put in bed at 8:00 p.m., Gretel and Otto listened to the Great German Radio Network in Stuttgart. The radio commentator spoke with very strong and aggressive language as he described how the German Nation had been able to include the poor, German-speaking minority from Czechoslovakia. The announcer also made very plain that Neville Chamberlain, the British prime minister, had given in to Hitler and National Socialists' demands.

"I wonder how this is all going to end? The Germans seem to be getting everything they want, so far. There is so much military talk in the newspapers and on the radio. Newsreels are full of films showing soldiers, tanks and military equipment. I even saw one of those huge cannons on a train that went through town the other day. Let's hope it's all bluff to get the Allies to deal, and that nothing further happens," said Otto.

"I have to admit that I don't understand all of it. Why are we arguing with the English and the French? What do they have to do with Germany and Czechoslovakia? Why don't they just mind their own business?" said Gretel.

"Well, it's not that simple. Every country has treaties and secret deals with other countries. They pledge to go to war against the enemies of their allies," explained Otto.

"Then which countries are allies of Germany?" asked Gretel.

"It seems like Hitler has made some arrangements with Italy and Japan," Otto answered. "There were even rumors whispered at work that Hitler has made secret deals with Joseph Stalin of the Soviet Union. Who knows?"

"Japan! Italy! What in the world are we doing making treaties with those people? They aren't even neighbors," Gretel said, being logical.

Otto laughed and pointed out that England had a huge empire, with men at arms from Australia to India. "It's not like Uberauen anymore, Gretel."

"Maybe we'd all be better off if it was like Uberauen," she replied. "Oh, yes, go ahead and talk about Uberauen, Otto. I remember very painfully how we lost Friedrich Rossfeld in the Great War, and I don't want to see any more young men sent to their death."

"I know," Otto confided. "I don't want to see our boys killed in a war, either. I just can't resist the temptation to tease you."

Gretel, Otto, Hans and baby Helmut continued living a quiet daily life for a few more weeks, until November 9 and 10, 1938, brought another incredible Nazi attack on the Jews. You could hear loudspeakers in the streets and there were Storm Detachment troops marching and shouting. Newspapers blared headlines about the Jews and how they were responsible for the wrongs against Germans.

Otto came home from work as early as he could on November 9th.

"Gretel turn the radio on," shouted Otto as soon as he was in the door.

Gretel rushed into the living room and turned on the radio. They listened to the Great German National Network for news of what was happening.

"Gretel, is the door locked? Be sure to keep the boys away from the windows. Who knows what is happening."

"Hans, get away from the window. Come and sit on my lap and we'll listen to the radio," Gretel called to him.

The radio announcer was shouting about how the German people were fed up with the Jews and the problems they were causing. Non–Jewish-Germans had been warned for months to shun Jews and not buy anything from them. The Nazi government had sanctioned the grab of Jewish money and property, while prominent Jews were dismissed from office. After recognizing the hostility from the German government, many Jews left Germany and went to settle in other countries, but others felt completely German and understandably didn't want to leave.

"Otto, just think about all the Jews in Uberauen who came to the butcher shop for kosher meat. We all got along fine with the rabbi. I swear, I don't understand it," said Gretel in frustration. "I'm sure glad that my friend Edeltraudt is in New York."

On the night of November 9–10, 1938 bands of brown-shirted thugs and common citizens who had been incited by Nazi propaganda, attacked Jewish businesses and synagogues. Jewish homes were ransacked, and men were hauled away to concentration camps. The frenzied destruction was cynically called the "Night of Broken Glass" or "Night of Broken Crystal."

The loud noise, marching and trucks with loudspeakers continued moving through the streets of Stuttgart until the wee hours of the morning. Gretel and Otto listened to the radio since they couldn't sleep, anyway. Hans and Helmut finally fell asleep, innocently oblivious to the brutal attacks that Jews were experiencing along the streets.

The next morning Otto left for work as usual. "Now Gretel, please stay in the apartment with the boys today and don't go out. There's no telling what will happen next. A woman and two little children do not belong in the middle of all this beating, breaking and burning. If you hear something happening in this building or on the street in front of the building, look out the window from the bottom, so shots from the street would go over your head. Do you understand?"

Gretel rose up to her full five feet four inches, and said, "You are not married to a fool, Otto! I know the world has gone crazy and it's happening all around us. I'll be fine." And then Gretel thought to herself, *I wish we were back in Uberauen.*

As if he were reading her mind, Otto said, "I don't want to burst your soap bubble, but I bet there is violence against the Jews we've known in Uberauen too. We can't do anything about it. Please stay inside the apartment. I've got to go," said Otto as he left.

"Be careful," Gretel shouted down the stairs.

PART FOUR:
WORLD WAR II, 1939–1945

Hitler's motorcade along roadway to the Fallersleben Volkswagen Works
Cornerstone Ceremony, Germany, 1938.
Photo by Hugo Jager, courtesy of Rare Historical Photos

23. ANOTHER WAR

As much as Otto and Gretel tried to get on with their private lives, the world continued to slip into war. Stuttgart was bristling with modern military machinery, and the installations in town and the suburbs had new construction. Everyone was happy to have a job, and Minister of Propaganda Goebbels's focused news machine was continuously telling everyone how wonderful it was to be German. Germans were told that they were the master race.

Otto and Gretel always read the newspaper and listened to the government radio broadcasts for the latest news.

Months and seasons came and went as tensions mounted. During the summer of 1939, behind-the-scenes plans were forming between Germany and what the Nazis considered inferior races in the Soviet Union. The agreement was to attack and divide Poland between them. Hitler hoped the plan would provide *Lebensraum* (living space). It was one of the Nazi's most notable pretexts for their aggression. The final agreement between Germany and the Soviet Union was signed and called the Molotov-Ribbentrop Pact.

On the morning of September 1, 1939, Gretel and Otto heard the Führer, with his shrill and dynamic speaking voice, making an impassioned speech on the radio. The Germans would no longer tolerate the provocations of Poland and therefore German forces had invaded Poland at 5:45 a.m. that morning.

In Uberauen on that fateful day, Emma, Max and all the Bergmeister family listened to the radio and read newspapers, as Otto and Gretel were reading and listening in Stuttgart.

Gretel trusted Otto's analysis of the situation, so she asked, "Do you think the Poles really were trying to be aggressive against Germany? The radio announcer has been saying all day that the brave German military is protecting the fatherland from aggression."

"It's never easy to tell, but I'm not so sure it's true. The only thing we know for sure is that the German army will make short work of the Polish forces and we will soon be at war with England and France," he said solemnly.

Gretel had good reason to trust Otto's opinion. He had bought a projector and had been showing commercially purchased home newsreels that depicted the wonderful German weapons as artillery was shooting; Panzers roared through the muddy streets of foreign villages; and onlookers cheered the victorious forces of the fatherland.

Otto was also right about the response of the Allies. As soon as the invasion of Poland was under way, the Allies declared war on Germany even though they were ill prepared. All during 1939 and 1940 the war raged across Holland, Belgium, France and England. The German blitzkrieg of fast-moving tank and infantry units swept across Luxembourg, Holland and Belgium, and then forced France to accept German occupation. All the while, German bombers were dropping tons of bombs on English cities including London and Coventry. Every night British citizens hid in their basements or the Tube and feared the next wave of German bombers.

Chancellor Churchill and the English Parliament kept hoping that the United States would join in on the side of England, but Americans were reluctant to get involved in another European war.

With each passing month, war news filled the radio reports and newspapers. In the fall Gretel and Otto received a cautiously worded letter from Uberauen.

Uberauen
November 12, 1940

Dear Otto, Gretel and Boys,

We hope all is well with you in Stuttgart. Did I understand correctly that Gretel is expecting again? That's wonderful! It's not too late to name one of your children Maximilian, Friedrich or Rudolf. Ha-ha. Oh, and if it's a girl, naturally you'll want to name her Gretel since we only have about five of them in the family already!

In other news, Max and Christoph Baumfeller have been using the horse and wagon to pick up hogs or steers to butcher. The last ones were from that farmer in Blauenbach.

This will probably be the last trip that Christoph can make to the farms. He got notice that he is to proudly serve the fatherland, so he will be reporting for duty in a few days. (Translation: We are all frightened by Christoph's induction into the army!)

Anna was hoping to marry Eugen before he left for duty, but they'll have to plan to marry later. Besides Christoph Baumfeller, Eugen Freitag and Johann Jessat have received their draft notices. Dorothea is crushed because she and Johann had planned to be married soon. (Nationalist comments are included to please the censors.) All of our brave young men will soon be wearing the proud uniform of the Third Reich!

This evening I'll be fixing one of your favorite dishes for dinner at the Golden Knight: potato dumplings with red cabbage. That is one of Max's favorite meals and my Rudi likes it too. Speaking of Rudi, can you imagine that he's sixteen already? (Translation: I'm horrified that he'll be drafted, maimed or killed!)

Hi, Gretel, it's me, Anna. I don't know if you've heard, but some old friends of yours have come home to Uberauen. Edith Luder (Schmidt) is now a widow. She has returned to work for the Security Detachment in city hall where her mother used to work. (Translation: That bully Edith is back in Uberauen with the Nazis. She hates us!)

Oh, and besides that, Georg Pucher has come back home to Uberauen. Didn't he go to school with you and Fritz Rossfeld? (Translation: That lying, bullying, thieving Georg hates all of us too!)

Well, I guess that's all the news from Uberauen, where everyone knows everyone else and everyone else's business.

Love,

Emma, Max, Rudi, Dorothea, Gudrun and Anna

When Gretel and Otto received Emma's letter, they were both stunned. "Otto, I know that we're in a war, but I'm scared to death for our boys. Anna's fiancé, Eugen, Christoph Baumfeller, and Dorothea's fiancé, Johann Jessat, have all been called up and soon it will be Rudi. Are all the men in the family going to be sent to this awful war? Oh dear, you could be next! If you're drafted, what will I do? I've got two boys and another child on the way!"

Otto understood that Gretel's compassion for her family and friends was genuine, but he also knew that her fears for him were well-founded. "I don't know, Gretel. I'm thirty-six, which is still young enough to get drafted. My boss did mention to me once that he was asking for a deferment for me because I'm the chief financial officer and nobody else can do that job. I know it's selfish, but I hope it works. The fatherland would be getting a poor soldier, and I can do a good job right where I am. I don't ask, but the electrical components that our factory makes are almost certainly used in ignition parts for tanks, torpedoes, planes and trucks."

Gretel completely understood how Otto felt about not serving in the military. "I know you've been worrying about your responsibility to serve your country, Otto, but you don't have to convince me. I'm glad that you're safe and here with the boys and me. Now that I'm pregnant again, I'd be lost without you."

Fall and winter came and went as the war was raging and Stuttgart bustled with military preparations. Each day the newspapers and radio were full of news about the war, but Gretel had to focus on her pregnancy.

Otto liked to tease her. He asked, "What were you thinking, getting pregnant during a war?"

"As if you had nothing to do with it." Gretel teased back.

In fact, both of them could not be as excited as in the past about expecting because of the danger and hardships. The war was causing rationing, men from their family were sent off to war and it seemed that danger was everywhere.

When Gretel's delivery pains started, she and Otto rushed to the hospital, which had also been transformed in part to a facility for nursing wounded soldiers. The nurses all seemed to be really busy and tired, but the director had said that Gretel could come there to have her baby.

Gretel had figured the delivery date correctly and, on May 27, 1941, she and Otto rushed to the women's clinic for the birth. She was attended by Dr. Pfleiderer, who had been the doctor for Hans and Helmut. All went well and baby Hubert was welcomed to the world.

The doctor made a joke with Otto. "The boy has all the parts he'll need,"—nudge, nudge. Both men enjoyed a relaxing laugh.

Otto and Gretel were so excited that Otto splurged and sent a telegram to Uberauen.

BABY HUBERT IS HERE NOW WE ARE FIVE BEST WISHES OTTO GRETEL

When Gretel was ready to be dismissed from the hospital the frazzled nurse gave her a form to fill out.

"What's this for?" asked Gretel suspiciously.

"Since you have given birth to four children, you'll be issued a Mother's Cross to honor your contribution to the fatherland," the nurse said as if reciting the message she had been ordered to say for each new mother who qualified.

Gretel turned and looked at Otto. He gave her that *Shut up and sign the damn form* look on his face. So Gretel signed the form and left the women's clinic with Otto, Hans, Helmut and baby Hubert.

A few weeks later Gretel and Otto attended a ceremony with other parents, as the women were presented with their *Mutterkreuz* (Mother's Cross), in recognition of the children they "had given to the fatherland."

Mother's Cross Ceremony, 1941. Gretel is front row in light suit

Mother's Cross

"Look, Hubert, see how pretty Stuttgart looks today," said Gretel as she pulled back the blanket that covered Hubert's blue eyes. He blinked and waved his little arms. "Isn't he cute," she said to Otto in a cooing tone.

Otto had to agree that Hubert was indeed a wonderful baby. "I'm glad you had sense enough not to ask questions about the Mother's Cross. I guess it's okay to take it. You certainly deserve to be recognized for being a good mother. We just always have to remember not to draw any attention to ourselves."

Gretel's and Otto's lives stayed as routine as possible during a world war. Then, by the middle of 1941, Hitler decided he had gotten enough from the "friendship" with Stalin and began to follow the footsteps of Napoleon by sending German forces to attack the Soviet Union. Among the troops was Anna's fiancé, Eugen Freitag, who marched all the way to Baku.

At the same time, U.S. president Franklin Roosevelt believed that the Axis powers of Germany, Italy and Japan would not halt their attempts to conquer the world without involving the United States. Nonetheless the U.S. remained neutral, at least formally, until the end of 1941.

Then on December 7, 1941, another horrible military action on the other side of the globe forced the United States to enter the war. The Imperial Japanese Navy and aircraft attacked Pearl Harbor, Hawaii. The surprise attack destroyed much of the U.S. Pacific Fleet and killed hundreds of American servicemen and civilians. When word of the attack reached Washington, President Roosevelt requested that Congress convene. At the joint session, President Roosevelt asked Congress to declare war on the Empire of Japan. It was Roosevelt's famous "A date that will live in infamy" speech. After a few days to consider the horrible chess game of war, Hitler declared war on the United States on December 11, 1941.

At the Regulars' Table of the Golden Knight, not just cigarettes, pipes and cigars smoked, but also the brains. The entry of the US in the war generated more questions for the men at the Regulars' Table, but they were aware that criticism of government action was out of the question. Discussion was confined to the facts they had been led to believe, plus an array of opinions.

Max asked cautiously, "So what do you think will happen now that the Americans are in the war?"

Herr Jorg's grandson answered just as cautiously, "I'm not sure. The Americans better think twice before doing combat with our military. Our troops and tanks are the best. I don't think the Americans can do much against them."

Herr Meyer's grandson was also convinced of German superiority. "The Americans didn't even want to be in this war. They only got in when they couldn't hide under the bed any longer. Their troops fought in France at the end of the Great War. They're a bunch of pansies! If they come over here, our boys will kick their asses!"

Rudi could not keep quiet any longer since he was the only one at the table who was young enough to be drafted and sent into battle. Max stared at his son to get his attention and then, without anyone noticing, shook his head *No!* Rudi thought he could word his question safely, so he said, "I'm seventeen. Do you think I'll get drafted?"

All the men knew what the question meant. Would Rudi be the next man sent to war and possibly to his death?

Nobody was willing to express any doubt that Germany was in the right, had the best military and would certainly be victorious.

Emma sat in the kitchen, as women were expected to do, but she heard what was being said. *I'd tell those idiots at the Regulars' Table the same thing I thought in 1917. You may think it's fun to march your young men off to war with flags flying and the bands playing, but many will be sent home in flag-draped coffins!*

Herr Meyer expressed the safe, pro-Nazi answer: "Rudi, you have the privilege of serving the fatherland. Do your duty and proudly protect our country."

Such fervent expressions of patriotism were being heard all over the world and in every country involved in WWII. All the men knew that Rudi had no choice but to serve when he was called up.

They didn't have long to wait. Just after his eighteenth birthday, he received notice that he was to report across the street at city hall, where he would be sworn in to serve the fatherland.

The night after receiving Rudi's draft notice, the family sat together at the Regulars' Table after everyone else had gone home.

"Rudi, I've been so worried about my Eugen, Christoph and Johann Jessat. Now you're being drafted too. It is so scary! Why doesn't somebody end the war? Couldn't Herr Hitler decide to stop it? Anna asked.

Max sat solemnly looking at his son. "I don't want you to go. None of us wanted the other guys to go, either. If I could, I'd send you out of the country where you'd be safe. The German border guards would never let you leave, and besides, in this world situation, where would a German go? Nobody will take us. Besides, you can't make yourself look like a coward."

Emma was terrified about her son going off to war, but she didn't want Rudi to leave with too much doubt and fear, so she said something similar to what all mothers were saying. "Don't worry, Rudi. You're a strong, intelligent, young man. Keep your head down and you'll be fine." But secretly, Emma was thinking, *I myself should be shot for telling my son such a disgusting lie!*

The next day, Max went with Rudi to city hall across the street, to be sworn in. They both dreaded going. It wasn't bad enough to be sent off to war. They also had to deal with the treacherous new Nazi overlords, Georg Pucher and Edith Luder, who both had despised their family for years.

"Well, well, look what the dogs dragged in. It's Herr Bergmeister and his wimpy son. Was this one legitimate?" asked Edith Luder, who could finally be openly surly and aggressive. Since she was in a position of extreme power, she could unleash all her venom without fear of retaliation.

"I'm here to be inducted into the forces of the fatherland," said Rudolf calmly. Max and Emma had prepared him for the hostile confrontation they knew would take place.

"Wait right here, Herr Bergmeister," answered Edith Luder in a condescending tone.

In a few minutes she came back with Georg Pucher, the local bully who was now the head Nazi in charge.

You scum of humanity! thought Max to himself as he gritted his teeth and looked at Georg. *They're sending Rudi off to fight a war while these two slimeballs are here safely at an office in Uberauen!*

Max decided that it was better if he waited outside to avoid conflict with the new Nazi bosses. Rudi was sworn in, and was careful not to be manipulated into saying anything to defend himself and his family against the verbal assaults from Edith and Georg. He knew that anything like resistance would have meant being thrown into a concentration camp or shot.

On the day that Rudi was to leave on the train, several young men from Uberauen and surrounding villages met on the front sidewalk of city hall, where Gretel had had her snowball fight in 1914. Then the group marched in rough columns down to the train station. Everyone walked behind the marching young men.

Emma had a terrifying déjà vu. *This is like a horrible nightmare, Max! We did the same crazy thing when Friedrich was sent to the Great War. Now I'm sending my own precious Rudi away and we may never see him alive again!*

At the train station, family members and girlfriends were hugging and kissing the young men goodbye. Georg Pucher stepped up to the top step of the train car closest to the platform and announced in a self-important voice: "Meine Damen und Herrn,[31] we're here today to give a hearty send-off to our group of local heroes who will be fighting for the fatherland!" He paused until there was some polite clapping. Georg made the Nazi salute and shouted, "Sieg Heil!"[32] Then the crowd responded as expected: "Sieg Heil! Sieg Heil!"

Rudi's family watched as the train pulled away from the platform in Uberauen.

"I hate this cursed train station," Emma muttered through quiet tears. "I've sent so many of my loved ones away from this spot. Friedrich never came home alive. And now we had to send my wonderful Rudi."

Max inwardly cursed the Nazi assholes and the horror they were spinning. He bit his tongue to keep quiet.

Rudi's family held each other's arms as they walked quietly back to the Golden Knight. At every step they had to be critically aware *not* to say anything that could be interpreted as resistance to the Nazi state. There were spies everywhere.

As the group turned down the Adof Hitler Strasse, they remembered better days when it had been called the Brunnen Gasse.

Finally, they were safely back at the Golden Knight. Nobody wanted to talk about what Rudi's leaving for action actually meant. They already knew they might have said goodbye to him forever.

German WW II Panzer crew. Propaganda photo by Friedrich Zschäckel, courtesy of German Federal Archives

---

31 *Meine Damen und Herrn* – ladies and gentlemen
32 *Sieg Heil!* – Hail Victory!

Uberauen,
September 10, 1942

Dear Gretel,

(Emma) We've been hearing about the terrible bombing of Stuttgart on the radio and in the newspaper. I hope you're all okay! We're managing to get by while we wait to hear from our boys Eugen Freitag, Christoph Baumfeller, our Rudi, and Johann Jessat.

Rudi wrote and told us that he was assigned to a Panzer Division that was serving the fatherland somewhere on the Eastern Front. I pray for all of them every day and light candles for them at St. Severinus Church. It seems so strange for Rudolf to be in a war, as I remember—and it seems like only yesterday—when he was christened at church. Now he's all grown up and serving his country.

Dorothea gets letters now and then from Johann Jessat. Of course it's mostly private declarations of love in the letters. Dorothea keeps them to herself, but she did tell us that Johann is stationed in Berlin. He's certainly lucky to be in the capital city, where there will be no action. I guess that's about all we know.

Frieda and I haven't heard from Christoph, but she told me that he's stationed in France, near the border with Germany.

(Max) Hi, Gretel and Otto, Things at the Regulars' Table remain the same. We try to solve all the world's problems or we at least argue about them. The latest discussion was about whether the Allies will invade Europe. Who knows!

(Anna) I get to write too because I have the most important news. Eugen and I are married! Yes, we finally found a chance to have our wedding. We got married on May 23, 1942, when Eugen came back from the Eastern Front. I'm so glad I was permitted to meet him for the ceremony. You must be shocked that we got married during the war, but we didn't want to wait any longer. Eugen has a very impressive rank, Oberkontrollassistent.[33] We had to write down what our profession was at the wedding ceremony, so I

---

33 *Oberkontrollassistent* – ranking toll keeper or tax collector

wrote that I am a Hausgehilfin.[34] I didn't know what else to say, since we all do everything at the Golden Knight. Anyway, we got married at a church in Gütersloh. It was very exciting but also scary to be married with all the troops around. I'm thankful that Eugen's officers let him have leave for us to be married. Of course, no matter when or where we had a ceremony, we're very happy and glad to be married at last.

With all our love,

Emma, Anna FREITAG, Max and the kids

---

34 *Hausgehilfin* – domestic help

24. FLEEING TO UBERAUEN

As the war in Europe continued to wreak death and destruction, Allied bombers began to bomb German cities on a regular basis. In Stuttgart the situation had become critical. Every few days Gretel, Otto and the boys hid in the cellar of the house on the Schlossstrasse in Stuttgart and prayed that their home would not receive a direct hit from the Allied bombing. Over the past few weeks, Nikolaus had joined the family for his own protection.

By November of 1942, the situation was getting horrendous. For several weeks there had been bombing raids on Stuttgart. Their targets were the Bosch, Mercedes and Porsche factories, among others, where war machinery was being built. The lead bomber dropped light-producing munitions called "Christmas trees" that marked the target. Then the heavy bombs and later the firebombs were released over the city.

"Oh no, Otto, the sirens are starting up again," yelled Gretel from the living room.

Otto answered quickly: "Just grab the bags of stuff by the door. Hans, you and Grandpa can carry the blankets and pillows. Helmut, bring the jar of water. Okay, Gretel, let's go!"

The family joined others on the stairs in their apartment house as they all fled to the cellar, where each family would pack into a routine basement spot for each attack.

In the meantime Gretel could hear the antiaircraft guns firing at the enemy planes. By this stage in the war, some were manned by boys who were only fifteen or sixteen years old.

Within minutes Otto and Gretel could hear bombs falling much closer to their home than usual.

"Hurry, Gretel! Helmut, let me carry you!" shouted Otto.

Gretel was carrying Hubert and trying to be sure she didn't fall down the stairs. Hans, Otto and Helmut were taking a little bit of food and water with them, along with some blankets, pillows and candles.

Otto thought of the possibility that if the building were bombed, the fire and debris would trap them in the cellar.

The whole world shook for a couple of hours as wave after wave of Allied bombers attacked Stuttgart. When the bombs exploded closer to their neighborhood, the building shook and debris sprinkled down from the walls and ceiling. Everyone tried to cover up with coats or blankets to protect themselves from the particles that filled the air. Flickering candlelight cast ghostly shadows on the walls and ceiling as the space in the basement filled with potatoes, apples, lumpy blankets, burning candles and most of all, fear.

Hans tried to be brave while Helmut hugged Otto and hid his face. Hubert was crying loudly while Gretel tried to reassure him.

I'm terrified myself, Gretel thought, *but I have to try to comfort the boys.*

"I have to pee, Mama," said Hans.

"Let's go look in the storage cage and we'll find an old can or glass jar. We'll see if you're able to pee in the jar. Do you want to try that?"

Helmut said, "I want to pee in the jar too, Mama."

"Me too," Hubert chimed in, and actually quit crying for a second.

Gretel took all three boys over to their basement storage area while the world outside was exploding and shaking. *How can kids think about having to pee when it sounds like the end of the world!*

Otto was trying to appear strong and in control too, so the boys would trust him to protect them. He hoped they would not get a direct hit. He identified a cellar window on one wall and two over on the other side next to the storage units. He figured the opening to the stairs had some extra support because that part was poured concrete. Since he couldn't actually do anything to protect his family, Otto kept his mind occupied with possible escape plans if the building collapsed on top of them.

The bombing raids seemed to last forever. Hubert's screams remarkably continued during the whole ordeal because he was too young to understand anything that was happening. He was just learning to talk and was able to say *"Böse Leut"* (bad people). Children from other families in the cellar were also screaming and crying, as were many of the adults. Family members held and tried to comfort each other like civilians had done when German planes bombed England and Stalingrad. Silent prayers for God's protection grew louder and faster as each family group dreaded the next intense wave of attack.

After what seemed like an eternity, the bombing stopped and the all-clear alarm was heard in the distance. Everyone gathered a few of their things and began climbing back out of the cellar and up the stairs to their apartments.

"The boys are exhausted," said Gretel to Otto. "Come on, boys. Let's see if we still have water, and I'll wash your faces."

Otto walked around the apartment, pushed back the blackout curtains and looked out the windows. Everything from the marketplace in Stuttgart, south to Unterturkheim and Bad Canstatt was dotted with huge blazes! There was also smoke and fire from the Bosch factory, which was closer to their house. Fire engine bells and sirens seemed to be moving in all directions.

"I can't believe this is happening," Otto told Gretel as she got the boys ready for bed. "The government says the Allies are too weak to keep attacking us and that final victory is imminent. How can that be true when Stuttgart is ablaze and we hide in the cellar like rats in fear for our lives!"

Then he and Nikolaus joined other men from the neighborhood who sought to put out fires, rescue anyone buried under the rubble or identify the corpses of those who had perished. He was out most of the night.

The death toll from the bombings in Stuttgart grew worse each day. Over the next few weeks Otto and Gretel decided that she and the boys should flee to safety in Uberauen. There were newspaper articles and radio broadcasts about other families who were seeking shelter for women and children in country towns.

Otto told Gretel, "I'll check with the authorities and see if there is an evacuation of children. If there is, I'll tell them that you can take the boys to safety in Uberauen. Then I'll send a telegram to Max and let him know that you're coming. If he can't take care of you, he'll help find somebody who can. It's plain that you can't stay here because we could all be killed."

Gretel cried softly while Hans and Helmut watched her in amazement and wonder.

"There's no bombing right now, Mama," said Hans.

That afternoon, Otto contacted the Civil Defense office in Stuttgart and asked about sending Gretel and the boys to Uberauen. The Civil Defense officer, a bitter, old, self-important Nazi, said that he could issue them free passage on a train to Uberauen. Otto scheduled the trip and then went to the crowded telegraph office.

```
GRETEL AND BOYS COMING TO YOU IN
UBERAUEN PLEASE HAVE MERCY AND TAKE THEM
IN GRETEL AND OTTO
```

—❊◦❊—

A few days later a letter arrived from Max, welcoming Gretel and the boys to stay in the apartment he had made in the Golden Ritter for Anna and Eugen. That same night the bombing in and around Stuttgart started again.

Otto shouted, "The sirens are starting! Gretel, get the boys and turn off the lights. I'll fill some pots and pans with water. Hans, go run water in the bathtub and cover the tub with a sheet so dirt doesn't get in it. Helmut, grab those pillows and blankets. Hurry."

"I've got the candles and bottles of water," said Nikolaus.

In no time the Forners joined their neighbors in the cellar again. As the bombs fell, the whole house shook and everyone could hear things falling or crashing in their building. Once again dust and particles of plaster and concrete sifted down onto the group of terrified people who huddled in the basement of Gretel and Otto's building. Hans and Helmut tried to be brave and Hubert screamed. Gretel rocked him on her lap to comfort him, but without any success. The Allied bombers came in wave after wave.

"I can hear the antiaircraft guns shooting at the planes," bragged Hans.

Helmut didn't want to look like a little boy, so he said, "I heard them first."

Little Hubert wondered if he should say that he had heard the flack too, but just then a loud bomb exploded nearby and he decided to go on screaming instead.

Otto and Gretel tried to get the boys to nap between bombing raids, but it was hopeless. The children were naturally too wound up to sleep.

Holding Hubert on her lap, Gretel prayed as she always did during the bombing raids. "Holy Mary, Mother of God, please protect me and my family during this terrible ordeal. Amen."

Women were praying similar prayers all over Europe and across the Pacific.

Finally, in the wee hours of the morning, the bombing raids stopped and the faint sound of the all-clear signal could be heard. When Otto tried to turn on the electric lights, he found that, not surprisingly, the power was off. Gretel allowed Hans, Helmut and Hubert to carry candles, which they now lit and then led everyone back upstairs to their apartment.

As soon as Gretel got inside their door, she went to see if there was water pressure. "Nope, no water. The bombing broke the water mains. Those bastards! Well, it's a good thing you and the boys filled some containers with water. I guess I should be glad we weren't all killed, burned to death or buried alive."

"Wow, buried alive!" Hans shouted. "That's like in a movie."

Everyone had to laugh in spite of the life-and-death event they had endured.

"Okay, you two, dampen a washcloth and wash your faces and hands," Gretel said to Hans and Helmut. "I'll wash Hubert, and then it's off to bed with you guys. With any luck, we'll be leaving for Uberauen tomorrow."

Helmut, Hubert and Hans, 1943

I'm glad to be able to take the boys to safety in Uberauen and it will be good to be home during a terrible crisis like this, but how will I live without Otto, thought Gretel privately. *What will I do if Otto is killed?*

While the Forners slept, the military commandant of Stuttgart ordered street clearing. He also ordered the commanders in charge of the water and electric lines to get busy and patch things together. Everyone secretly knew that the next bombing raids would undo all their efforts.

Patrols of prisoners, paid specialists, volunteers and military men began to run bulldozers and work by hand to open the streets for vehicles. Gasoline was strictly rationed so most civilian traffic had stopped weeks before. There were people picking up bricks and chunks of concrete and throwing it up on the sidewalk in piles. Groups of men were lifting out steel girders, wood and metal for reuse.

Otto and Gretel knew that their few moments of intimacy that morning would be their last, maybe ever, or at least for a long time. The gravity of the situation made them cling even closer to each other.

"I love you and I'll be lost without you, Otto," said Gretel. "Are you sure you can't go with us to Uberauen?"

"I don't dare change anything, or I'll be put in the army. You know that I love you too, Gretel. I hope this horrible war will end soon and that we will all live through it." He kissed her tenderly and then they made themselves get up and start preparing for her departure.

Otto had easily gotten permission to come to work late so he could get his family on the train to Uberauen. His employer was glad to have an intelligent, capable man who had not been drafted.

The refrigerator had stayed cold long enough to have some meat, bread, cheese and milk for everyone to eat. Since the power was still off and probably would not be back on, Gretel left the door open so it wouldn't get moldy inside.

Here I am worrying about the refrigerator getting moldy when the whole house could get blown off the map tonight! She made some tightly sealed packages of old newspaper to keep some bread and cheese for Otto. Hans, Helmut and Hubert drank the last of the milk, and Gretel made sandwiches for them to eat on the train.

"Otto, please start a fire in that old coal stove and we'll boil some water to drink while we're on the train," said Gretel while she looked for some clean bottles with stoppers to hold the water.

"I hope you have *me*, a refrigerator and a house to come home to when this insanity is finally over," Otto managed to say as he watched Gretel cleaning the fridge.

Finally at about nine, Gretel, Otto and the boys were ready to leave for the main train station. Nikolaus walked with them so he could enjoy his grandsons as long as possible. They all knew that in a horrible war like this, anything could happen and every moment together was precious.

His voice choked with emotion, Nikolaus said, "Gretel, I hope I'm still alive when you come back."

"Don't worry, Papa," Gretel said, "you and Otto can watch out for each other."

"Well, we're in luck about one thing," said Otto. "The Schlossstrasse is big and important enough that it was cleared of rubble during the night."

Hans and Helmut kept running ahead, climbing on the piles of rubble and chasing each other. They knew the bombing had been scary, but that was last night. Today, it was a new place to play. Several buildings on both sides of the street were heavily damaged, burned down or merely smoky, empty shells with no floors inside.

"Don't you boys go into those houses," Otto shouted. "They're ready to collapse."

Hans and Helmut did what he said without answering.

Gretel, Otto and the family noticed work gangs of prisoners clearing the rubble, but knew that they could not dare to have any contact or they'd be the next one in a concentration camp.

There were guys from the waterworks banging on the pipes to piece together water and sewer lines. Sometimes on poles and sometimes under the street, electricians were trying to patch up the electrical power wires. Otto wanted to ask if the lights would be back on, but wisely decided to keep his mouth shut. The Schlossstrasse actually ran all the way down near the main train station, so they made the walk in about a half hour.

When the Forner family stepped into the cavernous hall of the station, it was a total madhouse. The windows had been blown out by the bombing. Glass and rubble were still on the floor and nobody had had the manpower to clean it up. The sky was clearly visible through gaping holes in the roof. Crowds of people were bunched together, pushing, squeezing past each other and trying to reach the ticket counters. Everyone looked frightened and acted like they were trying to reach lifeboats on the sinking *Titanic*.

"Gretel, stand here, hold on to the boys and *don't let go of them*. Papa and I will push our way through to get the tickets," explained Otto calmly.

Then Otto and Nikolaus pushed, like everyone else was pushing, and squeezed past angry people until they reached the ticket counters that were marked WOMEN AND CHILDREN. Fortunately, women and children's tickets had been set aside and labeled so that they were sure to get seats on the next train out of Stuttgart.

Otto and Nikolaus had hardly struggled back through the crowd to Gretel and the boys when a Nazi officer with a megaphone shouted out across the crowd, "Silence!"

Immediately, everyone froze. All the hopeful passengers knew that to disobey would certainly keep them in Stuttgart or get them arrested.

Then the official shouted out, "Women and children traveling to Wurzburg, platform 7," Gretel quickly hugged and kissed Otto and

Nikolaus. Then she grabbed Helmut and carried Hubert. Hans was dragging their suitcase and lunch. Everything happened really quickly.

Otto led the way, followed by Hans, Helmut, Nikolaus and Gretel carrying Hubert. Each had food or luggage to carry.

"Quickly, Gretel," shouted Otto. "If you can't move faster, there won't be seats for you and the boys."

As she rushed past him to climb the steps, he gave Gretel a quick kiss and whispered to her, "I wish you didn't have to leave."

Gretel and the boys quickly climbed up the steps and into the waiting train. After thankfully finding a couple of seats, Gretel put the window down and tried to see Otto. "I can't see him. He was just here," she said to the boys. "Let's wave and maybe he'll see us."

Hans and Helmut waved and they shouted, "Papa, Papa," also not seeing Otto in the crowds. Almost instantly, other people began to pile into the train car. Gretel grabbed Hans to squeeze in next to her in a seat with Helmut by the window. She held Hubert on her lap. Hubert was, fortunately, so entranced by all the action that he was not crying but, instead, watching intently as more and more people crowded crazily onto the train. People were kissing, crying and calling out as the organized chaos continued. It soon became apparent that the authorities had decided to jam as many passengers as possible onto the train for evacuation. There were people of all ages and stations, but a few were well dressed. Some of the women were wearing expensive furs and jewelry. The men carried fashionable leather luggage and some had swastika pins on their suits. The majority, however, were women with screaming and crying children.

As the familiar chug-chug of the steam locomotive sounded and the train car couplings clunked under stress, the train began to slowly pull out of the Stuttgart Main Train Station. Gretel, Hans and Helmut kept looking out the window, trying to see Otto in the crowd, but it was useless.

The children stared at the other passengers in their compartment and tried to figure out what was happening. Nobody spoke and it seemed like everyone was happy to sit quietly and not talk.

I'm so glad nobody feels chatty. How can you make shallow small talk, thought Gretel, *when your whole life is in turmoil?*

Hubert kept reaching for the fluffy fur coat of the lady next to them, and the lady kept tactfully drawing the expensive fur away from his grubby little fingers while glaring at him.

For the moment, Gretel was occupied reading the city station signs and worried that she had boarded the wrong train. *Let's see now ... the route normally runs up to Heilbronn, where we change trains. Then we head for Wurzburg and get the train to Uberauen.* As she watched out the window, however, she saw a sign for Fellbach and Schwäbisch Hall. Gretel thought, *Can this be right?*

Hans and Helmut were already bored and asking, "Are we there yet?"

Oh my God, did I get on the wrong train? What is going on? thought Gretel in a calm panic. She waited and waited for the conductor to come and take their tickets. *The conductor will know what's happening. I'll ask him,* she decided.

After about half an hour, the boys were getting squirmy and fussy, but Gretel did not dare take them away from the compartment, or someone might grab their seat.

"Oh, look over there. Do you see the black-and-white spotted cow?" Gretel said, pointing.

Helmut looked and looked, but finally turned to Gretel and said, "Mama, I don't see the spotted cow."

"Well, you boys keep looking until you see one, and then I want you to tell me," she said.

The boys were kept occupied for short periods of time and then, naturally, they all had to go to the toilet. *What will I do?* thought Gretel. *I don't dare give up my seat. I know. I'll pretend to be the helpless Hausfrau.*

Seated a few spaces away was an old man dressed in worker's pants.

"Excuse me, sir. … Would you please take my boys to the toilet? I just don't know how to manage without my husband," said Gretel, the great actress from the Uberauen theater.

The old man agreed and even seemed happy for a change of scene himself. The boys were delighted that they could move down the aisles of the train and then pee in the train's toilet as the car moved from side to side. Hubert was running and laughing between the passengers standing in the aisles while Hans and Helmut chased him. The old man had seen it all before. He let the children play and have fun.

As the train drove out past the city and into the countryside, Gretel began to worry about something Otto had told her: "If fighter planes attack the train, get the boys down under the seats and try to lie down on the floor yourself. If somebody thinks you're nuts, just be glad to have a chance to live for another day."

When the boys came back from the toilet, Gretel whispered to Hans and Helmut that they should hide under the seats if fighter planes attacked the train.

The boys looked at her with big eyes and said, "Yes, Mama."

The conductor didn't come and didn't come, and Gretel was getting more agitated. *What will I do if I'm on the wrong train? What if we end up marooned in the Frankfurt station?* Finally, Gretel decided to break the nervous silence and ask the elegant, fur-clad passenger next to her about the route their train was taking.

"Excuse me, but do you happen to know why the train is heading to Schwäbisch Hall and not Pforzheim?"

The woman turned her steely gaze on Gretel and with a condescending tone, answered, "I don't work for the federal railway. If you didn't get the right ticket, it's your own fault." The woman again pulled her furs away from Gretel and the boys and ignored them.

Well, thought Gretel, *excuse me for breathing!* She decided that the next time Hubert began to scream or reach for the lady's furs, she'd let him. *That will serve the bitch right.* Gretel smiled to herself.

After what seemed like an eternity, the conductor came by to check their tickets. Gretel purposely waited until all the other passengers in the crowded compartment had finished getting their tickets punched.

Then she said to the conductor, "Can you please tell me if this is the correct train for me and my boys to reach Wurzburg?"

The poor, harried conductor looked as old as Wilhelm Rossfeld would have been. He looked at Gretel and answered in a routine, businesslike manner: "Change trains in Schwäbisch Hall. Use this same ticket. Change again in Wurzburg and take the train to Uberauen." Then he left the compartment as Gretel called "Thank you" after him.

We can do that, thought Gretel. *The boys are big enough to help me get all of our stuff on and off the trains while they're stopped. Now I can finally calm down and enjoy looking at the scenery, since I never took this route to Uberauen before.*

Gretel was about to learn that during a war to the death, there was little respite from danger. As she looked out over the forests, rolling hills and farms, she soon noticed a squadron of fighter planes approaching.

"Oh my God, Helmut, Hans, get down," Gretel shouted.

Fortunately, the boys immediately obeyed and squiggled under the seats. Other passengers looked at Gretel as if she had totally lost her mind. Then Gretel, still holding Hubert, also slipped carefully down onto the floor and crouched low and on top of Hubert.

The arrogant passengers exchanged knowing looks about how stupid the woman looked while she was flopped on the floor. The lady with the fur coat whispered to her husband, "That stupid woman. What is she, a cleaning lady? How did we have the luck of sharing a compartment with the lower classes? Those are just some *Luftwaffe*[35] fighter planes protecting the fatherland."

The mood in the compartment changed in a split second when the wave of fighter planes strafed the train cars with machine gun fire! Some of the bullets shattered the train windows and lodged in walls that separated the compartment from the hallway.

"Those pigs," shouted one of the well-dressed men with the Nazi lapel pin. "Those filthy pigs!"

Gretel kept low on the floor, where she was quickly joined by everyone else. All the passengers were suddenly in close proximity, literally lying on top of each other.

The fighter pilots must have understood that this was only a passenger train with no boxcars or flat cars transporting war machinery. The planes flew off to look for better military targets, and the haughty passengers became a bit more civil.

Every time Gretel and the boys had to change trains—in Schwäbisch Hall and Wurzburg—it got more difficult. They had to get off, carry their luggage, jackets and food, find the track to the next stop and then stand for long periods of time.

All the train stations had been bombed and some had hardly any roof left on the buildings. There were work crews filling deep bomb craters and making repairs where bombs had destroyed the tracks. Trains had to be switched around to the tracks that had been repaired. When Gretel's train arrived for boarding in Wurzburg, it stopped about one hundred meters down the track.

"That's funny," said Hans. "Mama, why is it stopping way down there?"

"The men are still trying to repair the tracks and the engineer is keeping the train from getting derailed," answered Gretel.

"What's derailed?" asked Helmut

"It means they don't want it to go off the tracks," Gretel explained.

Hubert was kicking and crying again. Gretel rocked him in her arms to get him to fall asleep, but there was way too much going on for him to go to sleep. Hans and Helmut were running and chasing other kids, while parents tried to balance letting them burn off some steam and also keep them from running wild. Gretel decided to keep an eye on the boys but to let Hubert run and scream as much as he could, with the other kids.

Finally a soldier came and told them to form a line of two by two so they could safely walk out to the waiting train. The boys still thought this was a great adventure and Gretel was glad that they weren't

---

35 *Luftwaffe* – literally, air weapon; German Air Force

frightened. Even Hubert seemed interested in watching people on each side as the crowd moved out to get aboard. Gretel and the boys found a compartment with two seats and quickly settled in.

"Mama, I'm hungry," said Hans.

"Me too," said Helmut, following suit.

"We'll be at Aunt Emma's house tonight. Then we can eat," answered Gretel. "There is still a little bit of bread in that pillowcase. Break it in two and share with each other."

Hubert was reaching for the bread too, but there really wasn't enough to share. In this compartment were other families. A nice woman from Gärtringen gave Hubert a cracker. It worked beautifully. He held up the cracker in triumph to tease Hans and Helmut.

After more exhausting hours, the last train pulled in to the station in Uberauen.

"Boys, we're here in Uberauen! It is so wonderful to be home," Gretel shouted with relief. She told the boys that they would probably have to walk up to the Golden Knight because Uncle Max would not know which train they were on.

Then Gretel saw Anna, Emma and Max waiting on the platform. "Wave, boys, wave," shouted Gretel.

Hans, Helmut and even Hubert waved at the relatives.

Once she and the boys were off the train Gretel gave each of her family a long hug that comforted her greatly. "It's so nice to be safely at home. Thank you for taking us in," Gretel said while daubing her eyes with a handkerchief.

"You know there's no reason to thank us. We're your family and we love you," said Emma as she and Gretel walked arm in arm to the marketplace.

Max did not want to frighten her, but the war had come to Uberauen too. For now, they were all glad to be alive and together as they walked up the dark Bahnhofstasse arm in arm, like in the good ol' days.

Hello, Mama, thought Gretel to herself as she walked along. *I'll never forget you.* They walked past the house where Edith Luder had watched Max when he was a young man coming for a job interview with Wilhelm Rossfeld.

Max whispered, "The stupid pig that used to live there is now one of the big Nazis in charge of Uberauen."

"Oh my God," Gretel answered, "I thought you had told me that, but I forgot. That's terrible! What is she doing here, anyway? I thought she married an old man and moved away."

As they continued walking and came into the marketplace, Emma whispered, "She has an office right over there in city hall, where her mother once worked. Her job is to spy on everybody and tell tales to the evil guy in charge. You know him too. Georg Pucher."

On the right was St. Severinus Church. As they passed city hall with the big red, white and black Nazi flag hanging down and facing the marketplace, Gretel was thinking to herself, *No place is completely safe. Even Uberauen hasn't been able to avoid what's happening in the world.*

They walked together down the former Brunnen Gasse, now Adolf Hitler Strasse.

"The butcher shop looks like it could use a coat of paint," said Gretel, trying to tease Max.

He laughed at her attempt to joke and have fun, but added, "Yes, it sure does. But these days I have a good excuse. There's no paint."

"You're a fast thinker," said Gretel cheerfully. "Oh, look up there, boys. That's my old room, up above the big gate." Hans and Helmut looked up. "See that low door over there? That goes down to the cellar, where I used to play hide-and-seek."

Gretel didn't realize that Edith Luder was already watching her from the same window at city hall where her nasty mother used to glare down at her twenty years before.

Once they were in the dark courtyard, Gretel saw that Emma and Anna had lit some candles in the windows so the Golden Knight would look welcoming in the dark.

After the long train ride, everyone helped Gretel and the boys carry their stuff up the stairs.

Emma told them, "Gretel, you and the boys get your old room that Max made into an apartment for Anna and Eugen. Anna can stay with Dorothea, and Max and I will sleep in Wilhelm's heavenly canopy bed. I have some hot oatmeal for you. I'll bet you're all starved."

The boys quickly slipped onto the chairs at the tables where silverware was set. Once they were all served, Helmut said, "Yum, Aunt Emma, this is so good."

Emma patted him on the shoulder as she felt relief to have Gretel and the boys safely at the Golden Knight.

It was getting late, but they stayed awake and talked while Dorothea put the boys to bed. Max turned to Gretel and continued telling her about the latest news in Uberauen.

"You know that we never got along with Georg Pucher. He has been a bully since we were kids. Pucher says that he has rid Uberauen of Jews, but we don't know what's happened to them.

"And of course, you and Siegfried Kiefer caught Edith Luder stealing our potatoes when she and her mother were starving, back in the '30s. Now they're two of the Nazi bigwigs in Uberauen. We have to be careful of everything we do. As much as possible, we don't even leave the Golden Knight and the butcher shop. We get news by listening to the radio or talking to customers while they're eating or buying meat."

"I could talk all night and try to get caught up, but I think I'd better go to bed. The boys will be up and rarin' to go at daybreak," said Gretel. "Max, you and Emma be sure and tell me how I can help. We appreciate you taking us in and I'll help you with the work as much as I can. I can wash dishes, do the laundry, help in the slaughter shed, sell meat in the butcher shop. Just let me know. Good night, now."

"Don't you worry," said Max, "we'll have a list as long as your arm ready for you."

Gretel took a candle and quietly climbed the stairs. She walked down the window-lined hall to her old room.

Hans and Helmut were sleeping on a cot with their heads at opposite ends. Dorothea had taken a drawer out of the chest and made a bed for Hubert next to Gretel's old bed.

As she had since childhood, Gretel walked over and peered out into the darkness of the Adolf Hitler Strasse. There were some lamplights in city hall for the officer on night duty.

I can't believe the Storm Detachment is in city hall. As time goes by, I hope Edith Luder doesn't see me over here. She'd like nothing better than to cause me big trouble, thought Gretel. *I know her little secrets and she won't like that. It's so quiet out here after Stuttgart. There is no one about so late at night in Uberauen.*

As usual, she touched the now faded and peeling yellow wallpaper with the pink flowers and green leaves. The thought of Mama and Papa caused her to smile. *Now that they've been gone so long, I don't try to stifle the pain of losing them anymore. I'm happy to cherish their memory.*

"Good night, Mama and Papa," she whispered softly to their memories. Then she got into bed while being careful not to step on Hubert.

For a few seconds Gretel said her prayers. As she was ready to fall asleep, she thought, *Edith Luder, that conniving Nazi bitch! Sorry, Lord. Everyone knows everyone and everyone else's business in Uberauen. Now she's in a position where she can do real harm to us. You can be sure she is carrying tales to her superiors about all of our family and friends. I'll have to watch out for her.*

25. SAFETY

The next morning, Gretel tried to get readjusted to life in Uberauen. *I love being back home safely with the boys, but I really miss Otto. I hope he's not playing around.* She had to laugh at herself because she had just managed to get herself and the boys to safety in Uberauen and now she was already jealous.

Max and Emma were wonderful and caring as always. They not only had their own immediate family of Dorothea and Gudrun to care for, but Anna and Gretel plus Hans, Helmut and Hubert were back in the Golden Knight.

Max was glad they were able to take in Gretel and the boys. He hoped he was clever enough to keep everyone busy, fed, clothed and out of trouble. When he was ready to grind some sausage he hoped that Anna would have some customers at the butcher shop. Everything was being rationed. His family's money was getting really low, and their neighbors were having money trouble too.

After breakfast, Gretel said, "Max, I'll walk Hans and Helmut over to our school and see if I can get them enrolled. After that I'll come back and go to work. Hubert will be happy to watch Emma and run around the Golden Knight."

When she knocked on the classroom door, she was shocked to see who opened it. "Geyer's Gretel? No, it can't be," said her old teacher, Herr Bästlein.

"Herr Bästlein, I thought you'd be retired by now," teased Gretel.

"Oh, you know how that goes. The young guys have all been drafted, so here I am," he answered. "Don't tell me these are your boys."

"Yes, these are the two older ones, and then I have another boy back at the Golden Knight with Emma. We were evacuated from Stuttgart because of the bombing."

"I'm glad you're all safely here in Uberauen. I'm so happy to see you," said Herr Bästlein.

"So, my boy, what's your name and what grade are you?" Herr Bästlein asked Hans. Then Herr Bästlein took him to his second-grade class as Helmut and Gretel thanked him and left for the kindergarten.

Hans was immediately the most popular boy in class. After all, he was from the big city of Stuttgart that had been right on the front lines of the war. He told the other kids how he had bravely endured the bombing, fought fires, rescued victims that were buried in the rubble and had gathered shrapnel from the bombardment. The local students from Uberauen stared at him with big eyes as he related his astounding adventures in the war. His story spinning had gone so well that he considered telling everyone that he had manned an antiaircraft position, but decided the other kids wouldn't swallow that story since his imagined brave deeds were already on the farthest edge of reality.

As Gretel prepared to leave, she smiled, looked around the classroom and had to laugh to herself about Fritz Rossfeld lowering the fuzzy spider down in front of Herr Bästlein's face all those years ago. *Now I can imagine my own kids driving the teacher nuts.*

As had been the case so often in the past, Gretel was thinking about Herr Bästlein spontaneously taking Hans into his classroom. *Yes, in Uberauen, everyone knows everyone and everyone else's business, but sometimes it's really wonderful!*

Back outside of the classroom and walking across the school playground, Gretel remembered her childhood dealings with Edith Luder and Georg Pucher, who had both been schoolyard bullies. Now they were back in Uberauen, to be very real threats to her family. *Those two are disgusting, and we have to be afraid of them,* thought Gretel as she walked with Helmut.

Finally, Gretel and Helmut came to the kindergarten. Catholic nuns were in charge, and Helmut was amazed by their huge white bonnets. Of course, here, too, the nuns immediately recognized Gretel and welcomed Helmut. They put him right into a circle of kids who were playing "Button, button, who's got the button."

Helmut hoped that the nuns in Uberauen were less strict than the National Socialist kindergarten teachers in Stuttgart, but that was not to be. He didn't tell Gretel the story about blabbing during naptime and the nuns putting tape on this mouth.

When Gretel returned to the Golden Knight, she asked Emma and Max what work needed to get done. She was thinking that they might need help cutting up the meat or mopping floors in the Golden Knight or even shoveling manure out of the animals' stalls.

While Gretel was discussing tasks that she would do, Hubert was already on his way to exploring the Golden Knight. He was everywhere at once and no room on the ground floor was safe from his curiosity. No work space around the courtyard escaped his inspection and every cellar was quickly examined. It didn't matter how remote and filthy, the farthest corners of his new domain were thoroughly explored and their mysteries uncovered. He peeped into the stalls where animals awaited slaughter, and then on to the massive barn filled with hay and straw. In the corner between the slaughter shed and the barn he could smell the pungent odor of animal hides that were stacked and waiting to be picked up by the tanner. In fact the whole courtyard teemed with a cacophony of aromas, dust, spiders, and creepy creatures of all kinds. Little Hubert liked playing in the garage because it was jammed with cars, trucks, trailers, old farm machinery and harnesses. In the truck he could bounce on the seats, turn the steering wheel or climb over the hood and fenders. Most thrilling of all was the veteran motorcycle with the magical brand name, "Wanderer." Hans, Helmut and Hubert loved crowding together onto the Wanderer to speed away in their fantasy to mysterious destinations.

By being alone to play by himself while the other family members were occupied, Hubert decided to make friends with the latest German shepherd watchdog named Hasso.

Hasso was chained securely to his doghouse because he was known to have a vicious streak. He had such a scary reputation that only Max dared come near him.

Emma stood at the kitchen window where she could cook and also try to keep track of Hubert, when she was horrified to see Hubert patting Hasso's head with his little hands. Since Hubert and Hasso were about the same height and were looking right into each other's face, it seemed that Hasso was puzzling over what type of creature Hubert could be. Gretel coaxed Hubert to come over to her and away from Hasso that day, but as time went by, Max let Hubert help feed Hasso until he completely trusted Hubert.

And so, as the outside world exploded in horror, Gretel's sons found themselves in a boy's paradise of country living, except for school. The Golden Ritter was for them an enchanted castle filled with secret corners, dungeons, wild beasts, creepy passageways, and remote tower rooms. They were as free as the birds to play, have fun and explore their new world in safety and wonder.

One day while everyone was working hard, as usual, Hubert ran out of the big gateway to the Golden Knight, up the Adolf Hitler Strasse to the marketplace and then down the Bahnhofstrasse, to the train station. Nobody noticed that he was missing. Once he reached the station, Hubert boarded a waiting train with the intention of visiting his papa. The train chugged away toward Nuremberg and Hubert kept busy looking out the window. The conductor saw Hubert sitting alone and asked where his mama was. Hubert answered that he was going to Stuttgart to visit his papa.

"Aha! I'll bet your mama is Geyer's Gretel," guessed the conductor.

So he kept Hubert busy until he was able to share his lunch with Hubert and then get him back to Uberauen on the next train. When the conductor brought Hubert safely back to the Golden Knight, Emma and Gretel were shocked because they hadn't even noticed he was missing!

For Emma, Max, Gretel and all the citizens of Germany, the war brought scarcities that the government sought to control by using rationing stamps. Every bit of food, animals for butchering, gasoline, flour, etc., were rationed. Periodically the rationing stamps from the Golden Knight were delivered to city hall for record keeping. Everyone dreaded having to face Edith Luder now that she was in charge. As a routine, the food products, sales and inventory were audited to be certain that everyone was following the rationing procedure. Since there was always room for fudging, strict punishments for breaking the rules were put in place and rigorously enforced.

Even though the rationing was strict, accidents did happen and misfortune struck. Maybe a sow ate her baby pig or a calf broke out and got lost in the forest. Max kept track of every squeal that was bought and sold, to avoid inspection by Edith and Georg in their new positions of authority. With all the bookkeeping, it still occasionally happened that sounds of normal livestock slaughter could be heard in an outlying village but nobody reported it. Sometimes a customer would get a gift under the table or a deal was made behind the barn, all without the bothersome rationing stamps.

Edith Luder stared across Adolf Hitler Strasse at the Golden Knight and fussed and fumed to herself. It was her patriotic duty to protect the German folk from law breakers. "Just wait," she swore, "I'll find out what you're doing with the rationing stamps over there at the Golden Knight, and then I can finally get even!"

26. FIREBOMBING

I'm glad Gretel and the boys are safe in Uberauen, but it sure is lonely here without them, Otto thought as he gazed out the window. The view of Stuttgart looked decidedly different than a few months ago because so many buildings were damaged by the bombing.

Otto sat and read the *Stuttgarter* newspaper to see what was happening in the war. On some nights there was even electricity and he eagerly listened to the Great German Radio Network for government-controlled news.

I know it isn't all true, but at least I can get the big picture, he thought.

Sometimes Adolf Hitler or Goebbels or some other government officials were speaking about the cruelties of the Allies or the invincibility of German forces.

"I hope you're right," said Otto to the radio, "but I'm not so sure."

Then on the night of October 8, 1943, Otto endured the most catastrophic night of his life since he and Gretel had lost Wolfgang. Otto heard the air raid sirens start up at about 8:00 p.m. As usual he and Nikolaus grabbed emergency supplies and some food before running down the stairs to the basement.

All the neighbors were there again for what seemed like an endless string of night attacks. Once again the house shook and you could hear the random thud, thud of the exploding bombs. Then suddenly, BOOM! BOOM! The bombs were falling very close by! The building shook as if it were in the clutches of an angry giant. Bigger pieces of masonry came down from the walls and debris sifted from between the boards of the floors overhead. To their horror, everyone in the cellar noticed that the bombs the Allies were dropping were firebombs. At every basement window, people could see the red-orange glow of huge conflagrations.

"I can hear people screaming and crying and troops shouting orders," reported the lady from across the hall.

No fire trucks could get past all the collapsed buildings, and blazes seemed to be everywhere.

Finally, a very old man who worked as a civil defense volunteer yelled down the cellar stairs, "Everybody out! The whole damn city is on fire!"

The neighbors, Nikolaus and Otto grabbed their things and rushed up the stairs and out onto the Schlossstrasse. The squadrons of Allied bombers were still flying over and dropping their deadly cargo on Stuttgart.

Otto could honestly not believe what he was seeing. The whole city was in flames! As more bombs dropped, the houses on all sides were burning, people were screaming and everyone was trying to find a way to avoid the extreme heat and flames. People who lived in the neighboring houses were screaming for help with fire. Otto and the others tried to find something to fight the fires, but it was literally an inferno. There was absolutely no way they could effectively fight the blazes.

A terrified man that Otto recognized as his neighbor across the tiny space between the buildings came up to him in a panic. "Herr Forner, *bitte*, our house is burning. Please let me put my piano in your apartment."

"Okay, we'll try. Is everyone safely out of your building?" asked Otto.

"Yes, yes, they're all out in the middle of the street to get away from the fire. Please hurry upstairs and let's move my piano," pleaded the man.

I think the deadly danger must have deranged the poor man's brain, Otto decided.

The two men ran up the stairs to Otto's apartment anyway. Again, Otto went to the window that faced the center of Stuttgart. "My God, there is nothing but fire in every direction. It's like hell on earth," he told the neighbor.

"Please, Herr Forner, please come and help me with the piano," the neighbor insisted.

Otto looked at the contraption of old boards that the neighbor had thrown together from window to window, across the alley. Hot embers and flaming debris swirled from the building as Otto walked cautiously across the wobbly boards and into the burning building with his neighbor.

Suddenly Otto's good sense took over. *What the hell am I doing here? I have a wife and three little boys and I'm here trying to save a piano that can't be saved. Forget it.*

Otto turned to the neighbor and said kindly, "It's no use. We can't possibly push an eight-hundred-pound piano up over the wall, through the narrow window and across some boards that can't carry its weight. You'll have to accept the idea that the piano is gone. Be glad you're still alive and let's get out of here, *now*." Otto gently urged the man back out and across the wobbly boards to Otto's building.

The extreme heat, thick smoke and showers of embers made breathing all but impossible, even on the street. Many people lay down on the smoky rubble to be as low as possible and used rags to cover their faces. Otto and his father joined his terrified neighbors. Injured and dying people were screaming. Burning buildings were collapsing all along the street.

Like most people in the fires along the Schlossstrasse that night, Otto lay on the debris and prayed, "Dear God, I know I have no right to ask You, but please save me from burning to death."

The screaming, roar of fires, unbearable heat and danger of being burned alive continued for hours. Remarkably, Otto's house did not catch fire. From time to time, he or other men went up to the roof and threw buckets of water from their bathtubs onto the fires that embers had started on the roof. They kept all the windows closed and hoped for the best.

By daybreak, the worst was over. Fires and thick smoke blanketed the city. The whole world looked charred. Fires and rubble filled the streets. Houses were burned out, with only the walls and vacant windows left standing.

Stuttgart after the bombing, April 15, 1943

Otto and Nikolaus helped their neighbors until they were both exhausted. "Come, Papa, we'd better go to bed and rest. Thank God we're still alive!"

While Otto was dealing with the disaster of the Allied bombing in Stuttgart, more news from the frontlines was reaching Uberauen.

Rudolf, like all soldiers during wartime, was not allowed to share specific information about his whereabouts or news concerning his mission. In his letters he could only write generalizations that let Emma and Max know that he was alive and well.

"Mama and Papa, our tank is a wonderful example of modern German machinery. We're fighting against the *Untermenschen*[36] on the Soviet front and having daily contact with the enemy. So far we are all well and doing our best to win this war for the fatherland."

"I wonder if this is really what Rudi wanted to write, or if the boys are given an outline of what a letter to their family should be like? Oh well, I guess it doesn't matter. I can't do anything to help him anyway. That does look like his signature, doesn't it, Emma?" Max asked.

"Sure, that's his signature. You're probably right that their letters are censored, so the boys write something neutral. At least, I guess he must be okay," she said.

Then came the morning that Max and Emma had dreaded. At about 6:00 p.m. a boy from the telegraph office came into the Golden Knight and asked to see Herr Bergmeister. Dorothea was the first person to see the boy.

"Oh my, no! No!" she shrieked.

Max came running from the dining room. "Oh, Emma, which one of our men is it?"

Gretel took the telegram into her shaky hands as if it were a poisonous snake.

"Please, dear God, don't let this be a death notice."

Then Gretel read out loud:

```
RUDOLF BERGMEISTER WOUNDED WILL BE
COMING TO FAMILY BY TRAIN
```

"Oh, thank God," said Max as he tipped the boy. "Rudi is alive!"

Everyone gathered around him to hug each other with great relief.

Each day after that, a family member went down to the train station to see when Rudi might be safely at home in Uberauen. Their acquaintances at the train station were very helpful and able to find out when he would be arriving.

---

36 *Untermenschen* – subhumans

All the Bergmeister extended family was there at the station to meet Rudi, but when they saw his condition, they were shocked. His tank had taken a direct hit and had exploded in a ball of fire. He was wrapped like a mummy, with gauze bandages that protected the severe burns. Some military medics carried him carefully off the train, and Max signed release papers indicating that Rudi had been returned to his family. He would still be allowed to get treatment at the nearest military hospital if the family could transport him there.

"Poor boy," whispered Dorothea as she wept. "I don't know how Rudi can live through such terrible burns."

"I know," Emma said. "Thank God he's alive and safely back home where I can doctor him. We'll take care of him and pray that he lives through this."

Using some of their rationed gasoline, Rudi was carefully taken back to the Golden Knight in the truck.

Gretel couldn't help thinking as she walked back arm in arm with Emma. *This has happened so often in my life. Sometimes it has been for wonderful events like my wedding day. But it has also been really sad, like when I came home for Grandfather's funeral. We walk to or from the train station and back to the Golden Knight. Today, thank God, Rudi is at least alive, and I pray that he will survive his horrible burns.*

27. NAZIS

The uneasiness between old enemies who were now with the National Socialists at city hall and Gretel's family at the Golden Knight continued over the first few weeks and months of 1944.

Max heard from the farmers who sold him their livestock that the government would no longer allow them to sell animals to private butchers. The military needed meat and everything was rationed. It was soon posted as government policy and inspectors were hired to keep track of all food sources and all transactions.

"I can understand that our men need to be fed. Rudi is safely at home with us after his horrible burns, but we've still got Johann Jessat, Anna's Eugen and Christoph Baumfeller who are serving, and don't forget all the other guys we know from Uberauen. The thing is, Emma, we also have our family and our neighbors who depend on us for food," Max confided. "I joined the National Socialist Party to keep us safe from being labeled Resistance, but that's all."

"Don't say anything," Emma said. "Those people! The people across the street hate us already for things that happened twenty years ago. We don't dare protest or show any resistance. Those people," Emma repeated while shaking her head.

"I already know that," admitted Max. "Those bastards across the street are watching us. Their people are happy to come here and have a good dinner and a beer, but their ears are perked up to anything that could cause us trouble. No, no, I'll have to be very clever and plan ways to feed everyone without their knowing it."

One evening Dorothea was gluing the used ration stamps onto the report form for city hall. They would be turned in and then purchasing stamps would be issued.

Emma said, "Now, you know, Dorothea, you can't make any mistakes with these forms, or Edith Luder and her crew will be over here threatening us again."

"Don't worry, Mama," Dorothea said, giving her mother's hand a squeeze, "I'll be careful. I don't want to see Edith's henchmen at the door, either."

"Okay. I've balanced the ration stamp usage with the amount of foodstuffs in the pantry and we actually have extra food left," Gretel reported to the family. "That's great!"

"Oh, I understand why," Emma explained. "I'm scared to death of the Nazis, but when I measure out amounts of flour, meat, broth, carrots and so on, there are always fewer grams of food than what I need. The food stamps may say fifty grams, but I only want forty, so that leaves ten extra." Emma laughed and said, "Those creeps from across the street sometimes pay with too many purchase stamps. Maybe they're trying to be nice or maybe they just can't be bothered. Anyway, we have enough. So now I'll try to make my new weekly menu with the meager food stores that we have, and hope to concoct something that tastes good."

"I know it won't be easy, but if anybody can make delicious dinners from very little, it's you," said Max as he gave Emma a pat on the shoulder.

"Emma," asked Max, "did you say you have some extra sugar, flour, syrup and baking powder after we've finished our quota? What can we do with that?"

"I know," Gretel said with excitement, "let's bake some of Papa's wonderful old cake recipes. We already have the makings."

"Yes, that sounds good," Max said. "I can use the cakes to do some creative marketing with the village farmers. Let's do it."

Everyone agreed to use the food supplies that they had obtained with ration stamps to make the cakes, and trade them for whatever was needed.

"Okay, that's settled. But Emma, can you bake anything that nice in the cookstove oven?" asked Max.

"Oh, no, the oven here is way too small for that. And besides, the great smell of baking cakes will cause the Nazis to get suspicious," she said.

Gretel had a suggestion. "How about if we take the prepared batter and forms next door to Herr Steinhauer so he can bake them in his baker's oven? We could give him a few to repay his kindness and still have plenty to trade."

"Great idea," said Max. "Gretel, you and Emma can take the dough over to him after we've fed everyone in the dining room this evening. Early tomorrow morning when he's up and doing his baking we can go over and pick it up."

And so it was decided and arranged to bake the cakes, but nothing ever goes as planned. As soon as he had enjoyed his evening meal of Emma's delicious cooking, a spy went immediately back across the street to city hall, where he reported to Edith Luder that he thought somebody was mixing cake batter at the Golden Knight.

"Aha! I knew that Emma and Max hadn't stayed within their flour ration. Now I've finally caught them in their scheme. I've gone over their records and ration stamp reports and can't find anything wrong, but now we'll catch them. Sergeant Schwarz, tonight you go wait outside the Golden Knight and see if there is something going on."

"Ja Wohl, Frau Luder,"[37] answered the young soldier, even though he hated the idea of standing out in the cold.

It was a really cold and frosty night as Emma and Gretel carried the big trays of prepared cake forms the few feet next door to *Bäkerei*[38] Steinhauer. The streetlights were out because of bombing raids, but the two women knew where to walk. Suddenly, they were blinded by the strong beam of a flashlight.

"Halt, or I'll shoot!" shouted a young man's voice.

Gretel's first thought was that the man must be kidding. He couldn't be seriously threatening to shoot them for delivering some cakes!

Emma and Gretel responded like the former theater stars they had been in Uberauen.

"May I ask who is there?" asked Emma sweetly. The quick-thinking question gave Gretel a split second to concoct a plausible answer.

"It's none of your business, lady, but I'm Sergeant Schwarz of the Storm Detachment in Uberauen. What the hell are you doing out at this time of night and what do you have on those trays?" demanded the soldier.

Thank God he didn't say 'Hands up,' Gretel thought.

"Oh, for pity's sake, you gave me such a fright, young man." Gretel gasped melodramatically. "Why, we're delivering these cakes to the cafe next door. We've been so busy with Kommandant Ertelt and his group of officers at dinner that we're just now getting around to it. Were you here for the roast pork this evening? In fact, we talked with him so long about our old chum, Frau Luder, that it made us late getting out. Do you happen to know Frau Luder? She's such an accomplished woman."

Gretel's playacting worked. As soon as the soldier heard that Gretel knew Kommandant Ertelt and the awful Frau Luder, his whole demeanor

---

37 *Ja Wohl, Frau Luder* – Yes, ma'am, Frau Luder.
38 *Bäkerei* – bakery

changed. "Heil Hitler," said the young soldier, and he abruptly turned to leave.

The young soldier was thinking to himself as he marched back to city hall, that he knew her all too well.

"That should keep him quiet," whispered Emma.

"That's right—unless Edith happens to hear of this. If she knows we're selling these cakes, she'd love to audit our books and accuse us of something," Gretel said. "Let's hope that young soldier doesn't try to ingratiate himself by talking about meeting us tonight."

A few days later, in January of 1944, Max talked with the women of the family while the children were busy "playing" the piano in the dining room. It was so out of tune that they couldn't do it any more harm.

"I think the war on the Eastern Front is going really badly, and I'm so worried about Eugen that I can't sleep at night. I wish I could do something to help him," Anna said while showing everyone pictures in the newspaper. "Of course, the newspaper says that our superior German troops will soon reverse course and defeat the *Untermenschen* in the Soviet Union, but I'm really getting very worried."

"In the meantime," Max said, "we have to prepare for the eventuality of having no electricity and no way to keep our meat from spoiling. It's hard enough to get any meat as it is, and we can't waste a single squeal. Tomorrow we'll go over to the pond where Grandma Barbara drowned, and cut some ice to put down in the cellar so we can preserve the meat. The thing is that we've been storing vegetables, kegs and lots of other stuff in the area where we need to put down fresh sawdust.

"Emma, after you get the children to school, you can run the Golden Knight, watch Hubert and sell meat. Just put a sign on the butcher shop door. Nobody in Uberauen is going to steal from you in broad daylight."

The next day Gretel and Anna went to work putting down fresh sawdust in the cellar. "I haven't been down here in years," Gretel said. She laughed while she spread the sawdust. "When I was a young girl, Mama and I used to bring vegetables from the garden down here to be stored. And of course I used to play hide-and-go-seek with Fritz Rossfeld and Rosine Kiefer. Fritz slid down that coal chute over there and got covered with coal dust and dirt. When we came out, Mama made him go change and take a bath before Grandather Wilhelm saw him, but Wilhelm saw us anyway." Gretel laughed heartily as she told Anna about the fun they had had as kids in the cellar.

When they were cleaned up from their work, Gretel and Dorothea cleaned Rudi's wounds and wrapped his burned limbs with fresh gauze.

Dorothea said, "Rudi, the doctor says you're recovering nicely, but how are you feeling today?"

"I feel weak, but I'm alive," answered Rudi. He couldn't suppress the moan that followed. He spent each day on a cot in Wilhelm's old bedroom next to the kitchen, so Emma could check on him now and then.

Gretel rode with Max to cut ice from the pond. "I don't know, Max. Do you think it's thick enough to cut ice blocks?"

Max used a hand-cranked brace and bit to drill a hole in the ice so they could tell how thick it was.

"I'd say it's about five inches (thirteen centimeters) thick. That's not the best and we'll have to be sure we don't fall in, but I think we can still get all we need. Just bring me that old two-man saw that Wilhelm used for cutting logs. I took the handle off one end so we can use it to cut the ice into blocks."

Max cut the ice into slippery blocks, and Gretel carried them gingerly up the bank to load them onto the big farm wagon.

"This is a lot heavier than I expected," shouted Gretel as she panted and grunted while handling the ice blocks.

Max continued to saw, and Gretel kept dragging and carrying until they were both worn out. They had loaded about twenty blocks of ice. The horse was stamping the ground impatiently.

"Let's take this load back to the Golden Knight and slide the ice down the chute, into the cellar. Then we'll see if we still have the strength to do a second load today," suggested Max.

Gretel quickly agreed. She was strong and healthy, but it was very heavy work for a one-hundred-forty-pound woman.

When they got back to the courtyard at the Golden Knight, they saw that Hans, Helmut and Gudrun were back from school.

"Hans, take Hubert into the kitchen to play while Emma is cooking. Then you three kids can help us slide these ice blocks down into the cellar," ordered Max.

The children were excited about helping with the adult work—until they started trying to move the blocks of ice.

"This is *heavy*, Papa," Gudrun said with surprise.

"I know. Now don't hurt yourselves. Look for the smallest ones and take your time. It isn't a race," Max told the children.

Sometimes Helmut helped Gretel and sometimes Gudrun helped Hans. Surprisingly, the eight- to eleven-year-old children were a big help.

Helmut asked, "When you go back to get more ice, can we go too?"

"Sure, why not. Then Gretel won't have to rock you savages to sleep tonight." Max laughed. He was worn out too, but he would not let the kids know that.

Rudi stood at the kitchen window with Emma and watched the activity in the courtyard. He told his mother, "I wish I could be more helpful."

"Oh, don't worry. We'll put you back to work when you're well again," Emma assured him with a pat on his shoulder.

Max thought he could feel the eyes of the Storm Detachment troops that were stationed at city hall watching as he, Anna and the children rode in the wagon to get more ice. "I wonder how long those *Schweinehunde* are going to be over there. They treat us like scum."

After a few more trips to get ice over the next couple of days, Max decided they had enough blocks and sawdust to chill meat in the cellar if necessary. Hubert helped Gretel pour the sawdust between and on top of the ice to insulate it and keep it frozen longer.

When everyone was relaxing after another day of hard work, all the guests who had eaten dinner had gone home and everything was cleaned up, Max began talking about his plans.

"It's a matter of life and death that we keep our stories straight about where I'm getting meat for the business. If the Storm Detachment suspects anything, they'd think nothing of torturing any one of us until we talk. We can't risk that. There has to be a story from the very beginning of questioning that is always the same from every one of us, and is such a good story that they won't question it. So, what do you think of this: 'Max always keeps some smoked meat as a reserve, until he gets another animal to butcher. I think he's been using the reserves lately.'

"That's all you women need to know. You're a room full of wonderful actresses. If they continue to question you at some time, just look blankly at them and say, 'I don't really know what Max does. He's the man of the house.' Every weak-wienie across the street will love that answer. One more thing, Gretel and Emma. It is absolutely vital that the children know that they *can't say anything*."

Gretel spoke up. "Hans and Helmut are old enough to understand the threat from across the street. I'll lecture them every day. I think the boys will remember to change the subject and talk about camping with the *Hitler Jugend*[39] to show that they have no interest in butchering. I think that will work."

---

39   *Hitler Jugend* – Hitler youth

Emma nodded her head and said, "I've said, '*Soch ner nix*[40] so often that the children mock me. Gudrun understands that the Storm Detachment is a threat to us. I'll tell her to just stare at them and tell them that she's staying with the babysitter and doesn't know anything about meat."

"I don't think they would dare question Rudi," mentioned Dorothea. "He's a genuine war hero."

"Well, I guess we've got our stories together and now we'll have to hope that we never need to recite them," said Max wearily.

Max really was using the smokehouse as butchers had for thousands of years, to preserve meat without refrigeration. Now the only problem was to find enough animals to butcher, when farmers were forbidden from selling them when the ration stamps ran out.

The next day, Max had a private conversation with the family at breakfast. "Now, don't tell the children and don't let them know, but I'm going out to try to get a hog to slaughter. We don't have any more animals to process for sale and the meat on hand will be gone in a couple of days. I went out and talked to that guy in Forellenbach where I've been buying livestock for years. After I talked around the idea for a while, he agreed to trade a hog for some money and smoked sausage. It's really dangerous for both of us, but I've known him since 1919. We have to trust somebody. What do you think?" Max looked at his son and family of adult women to see if any of them had any better ideas.

Dorothea and Anna probably decided they were too young to voice an opinion, but Emma trusted him to make the trade. Gretel was a daring woman, so she quickly urged him to try it, as did Rudolf.

It was a good thing that Max had been using the horse and wagon to carry ice over the last few days. People in Uberauen and the Nazis at city hall had grown accustomed to his driving away with the wagon and coming in with a load of some kind.

"What do you think I should put on the wagon to bring the hog back home if I get one?" Max asked Rudi and Dorothea.

By then the children were at school except for Hubert, so Gretel, Emma, Anna and Dorothea joined Max in trying to come up with a plan to fool the authorities.

"You know that Edith Luder, Georg Pucher and the other Nazis will be watching every move we make," said Gretel.

Max had one more idea. "I think we'd better stick with the sights that they have seen over the past few days. We really have enough ice, but let's

---

40 *Soch ner nix* – Don't say anything, in Franconian dialect

go get a couple more loads and this time we'll cover the wagon and ice with an old tarp. If there is a guard on duty at the corner of our street, I'll say hello to him. That way he'll remember seeing me with a wagon and load covered with a tarp. If he asks to look at the load, it will only be ice. Then we'll go get the hog and cover it with more ice. That way, they won't get suspicious."

Rudi and Max's harem of female relatives laughed and clapped to agree with his perfect scheme to hide the hog.

"Do you think the farmer will let you kill and hang the hog for a while before you load it on the wagon?" Emma wondered aloud. "A live hog would make all kinds of noise and grunts while you're on the wagon and you couldn't put it under the blocks of ice."

"I've thought of that too," said Max. "If the farmer is willing to sell me the hog, he won't object to start the slaughter process at his place."

Finally, on the third day after the plan was developed, Gretel and Hubert went with Max on the wagon to Forellenbach.

Emma didn't want anything to interfere with Rudi's recovery, but it wasn't impossible that the Storm Detachment troops would interrogate him anyway. "Rudi, if they come to question you, just moan and roll over. Don't answer them," suggested Emma. Then she smiled and said, "You can always look bleary-eyed and salute, 'Heil Hitler!'"

As they climbed onto the farm wagon, Max said, "There is nothing more disarming than a young mother and her child. Having you and Hubi on the wagon will make it look less suspicious, and Hubi will love looking at the animals at the farm again."

So the trio rode out to Forellenbach. The farmer had anticipated a visit from Max and the two old friends quickly agreed to sell the hog for some smoked sausage and twenty *Reichsmark*. He'll make his rationing records show that the sow had one less baby pig.

"Hubert, come over here and look at the chickens with me," Gretel said to tempt him. "After that, we'll hold the baby rabbits."

While Gretel and Hubert were safely out of sight, Max expertly killed the hog with a stun gun and then he and the farmer hung the carcass up to bleed out. The blood seeped into a small pit they dug in the ground, where it could be covered with fresh soil to hide any sign of the slaughter.

"Are you ready, Gretel?" Max called. "We can get back to town now."

He and the farmer had put down a layer of hay to absorb any blood that might seep out and then put the hog up on the hay-covered floor of the wagon. The adults put the tarp over the hog while Hubert watched with great interest.

"So far, so good," said Gretel hopefully as she, Max and Hubert enjoyed the slow ride back to town behind the draft horse.

It was already about three o'clock as they approached Uberauen. Gretel kept a close eye on Hubert while she and Max cut more ice blocks and carefully covered the hog with ice. Then they spread the tarp back over the ice and drove back through Forellenbacher Gate to the Golden Knight.

"We're in luck," whispered Gretel. "There's nobody outside city hall."

So they drove right on into the courtyard, where Anna and Dorothea were nervously waiting. They closed the big gates as soon as the wagon was inside.

"Don't let Hasso get out," spoke Dorothea loudly. If anybody was watching, that was a good reason to close the gates before dark.

"So far, so good," said Max with relief. "I'm really tired, but I'll work into the night skinning and cutting up the hog. Then we'd better hide it in the cellar. If anybody comes to inspect the smokehouse or slaughter shed, we can't leave the hog hanging there."

Everyone nodded with weary approval.

Then Emma turned to Hans, Helmut and Hubert and warned, "Those people, those people, *Soch ner nix!*"

The boys didn't understand who they were supposed to be quiet for, but they agreed not to say anything. It was much easier than trying to figure everything out.

—✳✦✳—

Gretel let Dorothea serve the dinner guests so she could help Max. After he had finished the hog, he slid the cut-up portions down the ice chute, with each piece wrapped in paper to keep it clean. Then he sent the children to go play hide-and-seek in the cellar. The kids loved the idea of playing hide-and-seek in the creepy cellar with Max, especially since it was already dark.

"Light a candle when you're ready to go down the steps. I'll come and play in a few minutes," Max said.

Gudrun, Hans and Helmut had never played hide-and-seek with Max, but they loved the idea. They went quickly through the low door on Adolf Hitler Strasse and disappeared down the steep stairs. After a minute, Max came out of the courtyard gate and opened the door to the cellar.

He shouted down the stairs from the open door on the street: "Are you kids down there in the cellar?" To spying eyes at city hall, it was supposed to look like he was searching for the children. Then he went down the stairs.

"I'm afraid we don't have time to play right now, but you kids can help me hide the hog parts. Would you like to do that?"

The children loved Max and quickly agreed to any plan. The first empty wooden barrel was open on one end.

"Hans, you and Helmut tilt the barrel over and hold it up while Gudrun and I put the hog meat under the open end. Now, are you going to tell anybody the hog is under this first barrel?" asked Max.

"Nooo," chanted the children's chorus.

"Soch ner nix!" said Helmut.

The children laughed as he mocked Aunt Emma's Franconian accent, but Max warned them that it was extremely important to keep their secret.

All went well for a couple of days. When anyone went down into the cellar to get vegetables, they'd put a few pieces of meat at the bottom of the basket. The Nazis paid no attention. Gradually, almost all of the meat had been processed, smoked or sold.

Then one evening while Gretel and Dorothea finished serving guests in the dining room of the Golden Knight, the door burst open and a Storm Detachment officer shouted, *"Achtung!"*[41]

The patrons immediately stopped eating and talking, and stared at the group of uniformed officers that paraded into the dining room.

"Everybody out. Now," shouted the officer.

The customers reluctantly dropped their knives, grabbed their coats and left within seconds. The room was empty except for the military officials.

"Proprietor, come in here," the commanding officer ordered.

In the meantime, Georg Pucher took the seat of authority at the head of the Regulars' Table. In a few seconds Max entered the room.

"Stand there," commanded the officer, indicating a spot in the middle of the room, next to the piano, where the children had once waited to be disciplined by Wilhelm. Max kept a calm expression on his face.

"Heil Hitler!" barked the officer.

Max responded, "Heil Hitler."

Georg enjoyed watching Max standing alone as if it was a courtroom. The atmosphere in the room was dangerously tense.

"It has come to our attention, Herr Bergmeister, that you are not a patriotic supporter of the fatherland. What would you say to that?" Georg glared with a hatred for Max that had been simmering for years.

---

41 *Achtung* – Attention!

"I'm actually quite surprised to hear that, Herr Kommandant," replied Max coolly. "You see, my niece's husband, Eugen Freitag, is serving on the Soviet front. Dorothea's fiancé, Johann Jessat, is stationed in Berlin. My nephew who used to work here, Christoph Baumfeller, my godson, is serving in France. Then too, you probably know, Herr Kommandant, that my son, Rudolf, is in a coma and recovering from severe burns that he received serving the fatherland in a Panzer explosion."

You Schleimscheisser![42] *While you're sitting here grilling me, in my pleasant inn, members of my family are out serving their country.*

For once, Georg couldn't think of a clever Fascist reply, so he just glared at Max and said calmly, "Search the entire property for fresh meat. If you happen to dig around in ladies' underwear while you're searching, just enjoy it."

All of the soldiers left the dining room and began to ransack the Golden Knight, including the living quarters and the butcher shop. Max stood calmly in the middle of the floor like a schoolboy in front of his master.

Emma suddenly appeared at the dining room door and Max gave her that *What in the hell are you doing?* look.

"Excuse me, Herr Kommandant, would you care for a beer?" Emma asked graciously.

Georg, who had openly speculated about the legitimacy of her children, looked at Emma in surprise. "Yes," he answered curtly.

Is she nuts? thought Max. *It's a miracle that Georg didn't begin questioning her on the spot!*

Max could hear the soldiers' bawdy laughter as they tossed the women's underwear around upstairs.

And the German National Radio Network warns German women about the dangers of American untermenschen, thought Max. *This is disgusting!*

He kept looking at a spot on the wall to the right of Georg's smug face.

He still has the same piggy face that he had as a schoolyard bully, Max observed, with a secret smile.

Hubert was crying upstairs, and Gretel was trying to quiet him while keeping Hans and Helmut calm. The soldiers were throwing her underwear around the room, but the boys were not shocked. They had always helped Gretel fold the laundry each week.

After what seemed like another eternity, the soldiers cautiously reentered the room and announced that they had not found any fresh meat.

---

42 *Schleimscheisser* – literally, slime-shitter. Swear word such as ass-kisser, or brown-noser..

Georg flew into a temper tantrum reminiscent of the screaming fits that had been made famous by the Führer, Adolf Hitler. "You idiots! A couple of Hitler *Jugend* would have found the illegal contraband by now, and you have nothing. Did you search the cellar, too?"

"Nein, Herr Kommandant," answered the Storm Detachment officer sheepishly.

"Idiots! Get out there and open the cellar door. I'll come and look myself. Bring Bergmeister with us," ordered Georg as he stomped out of the dining room.

A couple of the soldiers grabbed Max by the arms and manhandled him out of the room, out the entrance door, across the courtyard and out the big gate, onto Adolf Hitler Strasse. The soldiers had already opened the low cellar door, found the candles for the cellar and lit them.

"You two go first and we'll follow you," ordered Georg.

Oh no, how is this going to end? Please save us, dear Jesus! Max actually prayed sincerely for divine intervention. *If I'm found guilty and shot, the family will have to fend for themselves!(itself?)*

The soldiers, and even Georg, searched the room without finding anything but vegetables, ice and a pile of coal. Georg stood looking frustrated in the middle of the cold vaulted cellar. You could see his breath when he spoke. He started to walk toward the stairs and seemed ready to give up and leave the cellar, when he suddenly stopped and turned.

Max held his breath.

"What's under that barrel? No, not the first one, the second one." Georg pointed eagerly.

"Nothing, Herr Kommandant, just some potatoes," the soldier replied soothingly.

Georg shrieked, "*Scheisse!*[43] Out! Out! Everybody out."

The whole group climbed back up the steep, narrow stairs that the Rossfeld- Bergmeister families had used for generations.

Georg did not slow down or look back, thankfully, but continued stalking at a quick clip, up Adolf Hitler Strasse and around the corner, onto the marketplace. In just seconds the crisis was over and Max was standing alone at the cellar door, breathing a sigh of relief.

He felt weak, but walked normally back into the Golden Knight, where all the women were waiting to see if he would be arrested.

"Oh, Max, are they going to arrest you?" asked Emma, with a terrified look on her face.

---

43 *Scheisse* – Shit!

"No, I don't think so. They just, fortunately, looked under the wrong barrel and didn't find the cut-up hog under it. It was under the first barrel." Max chuckled. "So, who says that I'm not good at psychology? That Nazi bastard, Georg, I'd like to flatten that smug pig face. He orders everyone around and holds the power of life and death over us. I hope I live to see him get his due!"

"For now," said Dorothea, "I'm glad that another crisis seems to be past."

Gretel said, "I wonder who ratted on us."

"You know, I kind of have the feeling that they just got curious because the workers from their office come over here and eat every day. I'll bet they finally realized that people were eating and carrying meat from the butcher shop, but not enough animals were coming in. I'll have to think about that. I surely don't want them coming back in here," said Max. "Emma, please bring me a beer."

28. RESCUE

Dear Gretel and Bergmeisters,

I hope this letter finds all of you, the boys and our men in the war still alive and well. I know that Hubert's birthday is coming up. Give him a big hug from me.

As you can imagine, the city is about the same as when Gretel left. Papa and I even had to leave Stuttgart. Our house stood longer than the others, but now it's gone too.

Thankfully, Papa and I were able to move most of our furniture to Vaihingen before the bombers finally destroyed the house. We were even able to save your porcelain china set. Now I'm staying with Aunt Rikile, and Papa is staying at our new place.

The two Niethammers who ran the business, have been drafted, so now I'm in charge. They moved most of the factory out to the Schwäbisch Alps, where the Allies don't expect it to be.

How are you managing? Do you need money? I miss all of you terribly. There is so much to think about in the evening when I'm alone. I wonder if I'll ever get to see you and hold you again. Is life meant to be nothing but death and destruction? If I can get away for a few days, I'll try to come and see you.

Your Otto and Nikolaus

The war raged on endlessly. Boys as young as fourteen and up were drafted to serve in the military.

Max talked with Rudi about how he should survive the war. "Rudolf, we'll leave you wrapped in bandages even though you're mostly healed. I'm sorry that you have so many scars, but we're happy to have you alive and with us. If Georg or any of the Nazi *Schleimscheisser* come and want to check your wounds, say you're almost convinced that the trench fever you had is cured. That will keep them away. They're a bunch of snot-nosed cowards."

There were shortages of everything, and the mail only came sporadically. Trains came only occasionally and everyone had given up on a schedule. The citizens of Uberauen hunkered down and waited for the end of the war to come.

During the winter of 1945, Otto in Vaihingen and Gretel in Uberauen read the newspapers, listened to the government news reports and heard rumors of the war. The news for Germany was not good. The Allied forces from England, America, France and the Soviet Union were winning battles and their armies drew closer and closer to the German homeland. Everyone was scared, confused and wondering what would happen next.

Tragic news had been delivered to the Golden Knight. Dorothea's fiancé, Johann Jessat, was killed in action. Dorothea tried to be prepared for the worst, but it was still a shock when Johann's father let her read the telegram.

```
JOHANN JESSAT GAVE HIS LIFE DEFENDING
THE FATHERLAND OUR GRATEFUL NATION SENDS
ITS CONDOLENCES
```

"Oh, *no*, Aunt Gretel. I can't bear this. Really, I just can't live if Johann is dead." Dorothea sobbed as she walked to the kitchen.

"Dorothea, my sweet girl, I'm so sorry," said Emma softly, as she held her grief-stricken daughter.

Johann's father stood quietly with his head bowed as Dorothea and the Bergmeisters grieved together.

Gretel went out to the slaughter shed to tell Max. "Max, Johann Jessat was killed on the front lines. We just got the awful news."

"Oh, dear God, no, my poor Dorothea," Max said sadly. "How will she ever get over losing him? He was such a nice boy, and we all loved him. Can you finish cleaning up for me? I'll go in and try to comfort Dorothea." Then, as he took off his apron he said, "I swear, Gretel, who can explain life? When will all this death and destruction end?"

Gretel could only cry as she started cleaning the slaughter shed.

While Emma continued to cook as best she could, she was thinking about Dorothea's life and wondered how she would overcome her grief at losing Johann. She would do anything to bring back her girl's darling man. Emma likened life to one of the plays that Gretel used to perform in. Everything was moving so fast and they found ourselves in the middle of it, but often couldn't change what happened or how it ended. Emma dabbed at her tears while trying to cook.

A few days after Dorothea's tragic news about Johann Jessat, another telegram arrived.

Gretel opened the telegram while dreading the next horrible news. *Who will be killed this time? Eugen? Christoph Baumfeller? My Otto in Stuttgart? I'm so scared, but I have to read it.*

EUGEN FREITAG WOUNDED IN ACTION ARRIVING
IN UBERAUEN FOR RECOVERY

Thank God! Gretel screamed for Anna, who was working in the *Metzgerei.* "Anna, come in here quickly! There's a telegram about Eugen."

"A telegram. No. Has he been killed?" shouted Anna in terror.

"It's okay, Anna. Eugen is coming home because he was wounded," Gretel said while handing Anna the telegram.

A couple of days later Anna was working at the butcher shop, as usual. Between sales to customers, she thought about her life. *I'm so happy that Eugen survived battle on the Soviet front and was sent home for me to care for him. He's alive! I feel sorry for everyone who has lost a loved one, but I'm so happy that Eugen is coming home to me. I hope that's not a sin.*

Since Christoph Baumfeller had been working previously at the Golden Knight, the telegram concerning his death on the battlefield arrived there. As usual, Gretel opened it while dreading to read which of her loved ones was dead.

CHRISTOPH BAUMFELLER GAVE HIS LIFE
DEFENDING THE FATHERLAND OUR GRATEFUL
NATION SENDS ITS CONDOLENCES

Emma, Max, Gretel, Anna and Dorothea stood in the hallway outside the dining room of the Golden Knight and cried together for yet another family member who had been killed in the war.

"I'm sorry, but I keep asking myself, what can God be thinking, to allow so much tragedy?" Dorothea asked.

Families over much of the world were asking the same questions, but with different answers.

"I know, I know," said Gretel, while holding her. "As Otto's mother told me when Wolfgang died, we can't know the will of God, although it is hard to understand."

By the beginning of April, American forces were drawing closer to Uberauen and the surrounding areas. Gretel was worried that she and everyone else would be killed and that she might never see Otto again, so she wrote him a stirring letter.

Uberauen
April 8, 1945

My beloved Otto,

When you have this letter in your hands, you'll know that we are all alive and well. We have hard times behind us. When we're together again I'll tell you about it, but for now I'll tell you briefly what happened. On April 5 and 7, Uberauen was attacked by Allied bombers. The boys were never so quick getting into the cellar as they were on those days when the shooting and bombing began!

Eugen was still recovering from his wounds, yet he grabbed Hubert and started down the steep stairs into the cellar. Hubert kept saying that he lost his stocking. I had those long, warm stockings for him to wear, and when Eugen picked him up the stocking came half off. There was no time to worry about that when Eugen was worried about the artillery. Hubert is still talking about losing his stocking.

It was so strange to be down in the cellar for protection. While I was sitting on a crate and holding Hubert, all I could think of was the time we played hide-and-seek down there when we were kids.

During an artillery attack, masonry debris was sliding down the chute where Fritz Rossfeld slid down into the cellar and got dirty. What a memory. Then, too, I remembered not long ago when Georg Pucher, that

Schweinehund, tried to find Max's hog down here. We fooled the bastard that time.

From the 8th to the 10th of April we were almost always in the cellar. During one whole night while we stayed hidden, we could hear artillery fire. The two older boys slept as best they could on sacks wrapped in blankets, and I sat up the whole night holding Hubert in my arms while he slept. That awful experience was a cross for me to bear. For the most part, the only damage in Uberauen was to windows and roofs. That's the way it was here at the Golden Knight too. A few houses including the one owned by Haferstroh were more heavily damaged. When we were finally able to come out of the cellar, we straightened up the Golden Knight and cleaned the floors of debris and dirt. No sooner did we finish cleaning up our room than I got really sick. The cold, damp cellar, plus the fear and anxiety from the bombing gave me a terrible tonsillitis.

I won't try to count the many tears and worry I've shed for you. When I just allow myself to think that you're no longer in my life, how could I raise these boys? What kind of work could I do? I'm waiting in pain for news from you, even if it's just a few words.

So much has been happening here that I can't possibly tell it all. Dorothea is still grieving the loss of her wonderful Johann, who was killed in Berlin. As you know, Christoph Baumfeller was also killed in France. He was such a kind, handsome boy, who never got the chance to live out his life. How are we to bear this terrible sorrow? The grief and death are overwhelming.

Our distant cousins, Hugo and Sofie, arrived yesterday pulling a Leiterwagen all the way from Hammelburg. They were all safe including the two little girls. Max and Emma are giving everyone rooms as long as there is still space.

The brother of the neighbor guy, Hermas, named Alfons, walked all the way here with Max Schöneberger. They trekked for days to get here, so Max is letting them stay in the ironing room.

Frau Seher asks me every day if you happen to know her husband who is stationed at a barracks in Vaihingen. There are so many displaced people from all over, trudging across Germany. Family and friends are coming to stay with us. It's a houseful! We hear stories about refugees living in barns, basements and out in the woods.

Rudolf, Eugen and Werner Brücher are also here. They are no longer able to get treatment at the field hospital. The whole system is falling apart.

I still have some money left that you sent me, but I'm not able to get shoes for the boys. The stores are empty and I can't find anybody who knows how to make shoes. The boys don't care. It's finally warm enough outside and they're glad to run barefooted.

Be safe, my dear Otto, until I see you again.

Your Gretel, Hans, Helmut and Hubert

By April 9, 1945, Edith Luder, Georg Pucher and the other Nazis who were in charge of Uberauen had heard that American forces were drawing closer. Without Gretel knowing it, Helmut and his friends from school were on the sidewalk in front of city hall watching some action. It was beside the shed and garden where Gretel and Fastnacht's Betti had their snowball fight in 1914. Edith, Georg, the office workers and soldiers were busily burning secret documents. Helmut and his friends were intrigued by the big fire and excitement.

"Frau Luder, what about the lists of contacts who worked in the neighborhoods and arrested Jews. Should I burn those?" asked an older uniformed man who had recently started serving in Uberauen.

"Idiot! Of course you have to burn all the lists. Do you want those people to be hanged when the Americans get here?" shouted a flustered Edith Luder. "You there, Lieutenant, change into some inconspicuous civilian clothes and burn your uniforms. Then go get the other men to do the same."

Georg Pucher came out the front door with another group of elite soldiers. Georg's pudgy red face was covered with perspiration from exertion and he was obviously terrified. "Sergeant, you three go up to the second floor and bring all the files from the cabinets about party members. If you're not sure, just burn everything. Look for some civilian clothes to wear, and burn all your uniforms."

"Yes, sir, Herr Kommandant!" answered the men crisply and of one voice.

As the soldiers climbed the stairs to get another box of documents, their curiosity was piqued. "Schmidt, why do you think they're burning all the documents?" asked a private.

"You're joking, right? Haven't you figured it out already? Kommandant Pucher has gotten word that the Americans are getting close and he has to destroy all the evidence of who did what. That's what we're burning," Schmidt replied. "He wants to save his own fat ass!"

"Oh, now I understand. Do you have anything to change into? I'm not sure what I've got to put on. Maybe I can get some pants from one of the other guys. When do you think the Americans are supposed to be here?" the private asked.

"Who knows, but I hope we can get out of here before they bomb us out or shoot us on sight," Schmidt replied seriously.

Helmut and his friends watched the bonfire of documents with great interest. "I wonder why they're burning all the papers?" asked Helmut's best friend, Rudi.

Helmut answered, "I don't know, but it is a great fire." The boys continued watching. It was strange to watch spit-and-polish officers burning papers and folders.

"Great! Look," said another boy. "That officer is burning his clothes. He's even throwing his hat and winter coat onto the fire. Why are they burning their stuff?"

The boys continued to wonder and watch.

That evening Helmut returned to the Golden Knight. He had decided not to tell his mama what he was watching, afraid she'd spank him for being in a dangerous place and so close to Frau Luder. His mother had told him to keep away from her.

The night after Helmut watched Edith Luder, Georg Pucher and the other officials burning documents that told of their despicable deeds and Nazi sympathizers, Allied bombers again flew overhead. Everyone fled to the cellar where Gretel and Fritz Rossfeld had played as children and where Max hid the hog from the Nazis. It was cold and frightening, as Gretel had written in her letter to Otto, yet they were safe from the bombing.

The next morning, on April 10, 1945, Helmut walked up Adolf Hitler Strasse to the marketplace and then around the corner to the sidewalk and flower garden, where the officials had been burning their documents and clothes the evening before. Helmut figured he would dig around in the piles of ashes to see if there was anything interesting that didn't get burned up. Maybe he'd find a *Reichsmark*! After digging in the ashes for a while, lo and behold, he did find a treasure. It was a silver ring with a black stone that had lightning symbols on it—an SS rune ring.

The next few hours would prove to be some of the most dramatic in the history of Uberauen. Helmut watched Uncle Rudi walk up to the marketplace. Rudi hoped to find out if the Americans were getting close.

"Hey, Eberhardt, come with me and we'll climb up the church steeple and look for the Americans," Rudi Suggested to his buddy Eberhardt Haferstroh.

Once they had climbed up the tower of St. Severinus Church, Eberhardt looked through his field glasses. "Oh my God, the American tanks are parked at the sport center in Gerstenfeld!"

"Let me look," said Rudi as he grabbed for the binoculars. He turned in another direction and reported, "Oh, *Scheisse!* Three American tanks are already driving this way."

Before Rudi could tell everybody what was happening, he heard the Storm Detachment officer shouting orders on the marketplace below: "Go down to the Gerstenfelder Gate and build a barricade to stop the Americans from getting in."

Gerstenfelder Gate

Rudi could not control his temper any longer. He walked up and spoke to Georg Pucher. "Herr Kommandant, I've been in tank combat and I can tell you that the Americans would take five minutes to break through a barricade. The first three minutes they would stand around and smoke while they have a few laughs about how stupid we are. Then they'll spend two minutes blowing up the barricade. This resistance is really stupid!"

Georg, for once, was too shocked and frightened to answer Rudolf's insolent remarks.

Eberhardt and Rudi climbed back up the church tower and watched the tanks approach. People from all over Uberauen had heard by now that the Americans were coming and they began gathering in the marketplace.

Rudi shouted, "Oh, no. There's a woman getting out of one of the tanks and she's carrying a white flag."

Eberhardt and Rudi raced down the tower stairs and out onto the marketplace, where Nazis, family and friends were clustered, waving and babbling excitedly. What would happen next?

"Emma, Dorothea, what is Rudi doing and why is he running with Eberhardt Haferstroh? Where are Hans and Helmut?" Gretel wondered aloud while not expecting an answer in all the confusion. "Hubert, don't you dare try to get away from me."

The crowd on the marketplace had increased dramatically in size by now and really seemed to include everyone in Uberauen.

"Frau Bergmeister, what is happening with Rudolf and why are they running? Should we all run too?" Frau Steinhauer asked.

"I don't know. Everything is happening so fast that I can't be sure. Rudi wouldn't run away, so I guess he's looking to see if the Americans are here," Emma answered. "I wish he'd be careful. The poor guy is just getting able to move normally after those awful burns."

Rudi shouted above all the noise to Max, "The Americans are sending a woman to talk. We're going out the Gerstenfelder Gate to meet her."

Before anybody could interfere, Eberhardt and Rudi ran down the street and out to the property owned by the Kübler family. It was just across from the city gate.

The woman carrying the white flag was French, yet she could speak German well enough to tell them, "I want to speak to the mayor immediately."

Rudi and Eberhardt brought the French woman through the city gate and up the street to the marketplace, where everyone crowded around to hear and watch.

Gretel, Max, Emma and all their neighbors and friends were standing and straining to hear as the French woman spoke to Mayor Denkendorfer.

"In thirty minutes this town will be bombarded if you do not raise the white flag of surrender."

The mayor knew that all the townspeople and the Nazis were watching and listening. "I took an oath to never raise a white flag of surrender, but I will turn the town over to the Americans," the mayor announced with a show of being in charge.

The French translator looked calmly at Herr Denkendorfer and repeated, "There is no tolerance for refusing to fly a white flag of surrender." She then returned to get into the American tank.

Max squeezed past some of his friends until he reached Rudi. "Rudi, what's happening?" demanded Max.

"The Americans sent this woman to tell us to wave a white flag of surrender, or they'll blow up the town in thirty minutes. Herr Denkendorfer said that he would turn over the town, but is under oath to not surrender using a white flag, and the French woman left. The Americans don't give a shit about Nazi oaths. Will the Americans think he's surrendering without a white flag, or will they think he refused, and start bombarding Uberauen? I don't know!" Rudi shook his head in frustration. "This is not the way the Americans demanded that the surrender be handled. It's a huge risk."

Max started running back to the Golden Knight with Siglinde Schache, the lady who babysat Gudrun. "Siglinde, run upstairs and get a big white sheet from the laundry cabinet in the ironing room and bring it to me. *Run!*"

In the meantime Max grabbed a long pole that he used to hang *Wurst* while it was smoked and a handful of special twine that was also used on the *Wurst*. Just as he came running out of the smokehouse and into the courtyard, Siglinde came running out the entrance of the Golden Knight with the white sheet.

"Come on, there's no time to waste," Max shouted as he and Siglinde ran up Adolf Hitler Strasse and into the crowds gathered near St. Severinus Church.

Suddenly all hell broke loose. Georg Pucher, Edith Luder and the girls from the League of German Girls began screaming, "Traitor! Traitor!"

"Stop, or we'll shoot you down like the dog that you are," shouted Georg. "I'm under orders to shoot anyone who tries to surrender. Now stand still. This is your last warning, Bergmeister. Men, get your guns ready to shoot Herr Bergmeister if he moves."

Then to add to the confusion, the priest, Father Weible, said, "You can't put a surrender flag on the church because it's a public building."

Gretel was listening as the priest that she had known for years, started talking about the church as if it was a municipal building and nothing more. "Emma, what is that old fool talking about," whispered Gretel. "The town is in danger of being blasted off the map and he's talking about St. Severinus Church being a public building. Is he nuts?"

"That's easy to figure out," said Frau Steinhauer. "He's either a Nazi or they've scared him enough to make him do their bidding."

"Father, please go back into your parsonage," said Rudi firmly.

Thankfully, the priest turned and went inside.

On the marketplace there was a sudden and complete silence as everyone waited to see if Georg would really have Max shot, right in front of everybody.

The League of German Girls began shouting, "Traitor, Traitor," again.

Emma gasped. "Oh my God," she said, grabbing Gretel's arm, "are they really going to shoot Max?"

"Gentlemen, the war is lost," Max said calmly, yet loud enough for his neighbors to hear. "The Americans will begin bombarding Uberauen in a few minutes. All of us, our businesses, our wives and our children will be killed and the town reduced to rubble. Is that what you want? Yes, you can shoot me if you must, but I am walking away and hanging this white flag from the church tower." Max cautiously turned and started pacing briskly toward the tower door of St. Severinus Church.

Would Georg order him shot?

Emma and Gretel clung to each other and held their breath. The whole crowd froze and watched to see if Georg would shout the order to kill Max.

No shots were fired.

Tower steps.

Once he felt sure that Georg would not shoot him in the back, Max tore up the tower stairs, tied the sheet to the sausage-drying pole and waved it out the steeple window with broad, sweeping motions.

I hope to God the Americans are watching and can see that I'm surrendering. Hey! Over here! Look!

Church steeple

In the meantime, realizing that their reign of terror was coming to an end, the entire group of Nazi officials, including Edith Luder and Georg Pucher, disappeared down the narrow streets of Uberauen. They knew the day of reckoning was upon them.

Then Anton Schreiner, whose allegiances had been questioned in the past, started waving a huge old pistol that his family had kept hidden. "I'll shoot anybody who tries to hurt Max," he screamed over the crowd.

Remarkably, everyone accepted the decision that Max had made. All resistance stopped and the crowd on the marketplace began to calm down.

"What's happening, Mama?" Hans asked, with Helmut by his side.

"I think your uncle Max just saved Uberauen and all of us," said Gretel as she hugged her boys. "We have to wait and see."

"Uncle Max," Hubert said as he tried to get away from Gretel and run toward Max.

"Thank God," said Emma. "I'm a nervous wreck. All I could think of was that Georg Pucher, that bastard, would give the order to shoot Max. I don't know if my heart will ever slow down."

"Thank you so much, Herr Bergmeister, you saved all of us," said Siglinde Schache while shaking Max's hand vigorously.

"You didn't do so badly yourself." Max smiled. "I had no idea you could run like that. You know that you brought a perfectly good sheet, don't you?" he said.

While everyone was beginning to feel that the crisis had passed for the moment, Gudrun shouted, "Mama, listen, airplanes!"

"Oh my God, no," Gretel said.

"Look, Mama." Helmut was pointing proudly toward the planes. "There they are. It's Allied bombers!"

"Quick, run and get down in the cellar," screamed Dorothea as she started to run down Adolf Hitler Strasse.

After a few minutes of curious watching, the citizens of Uberauen noticed that the three bombers dipped their wings above the marketplace and flew off toward Forellenbach. No bombs were dropped. Uberauen was spared.

Everyone began to cheer and clap. No one knew at the time, but many of the bombs that could have been dropped on Uberauen were probably used instead to bomb Nuremberg and Schweinfurt.

Some individuals and families who had been strong Nazi supporters rushed home to destroy evidence in their own homes. There were lots of little trash fires burning in flower gardens that day.

Rudi and Eberhardt walked down to the Gerstenfelder Gate to watch the Americans enter Uberauen.

"This is really strange," said Rudi. "We fight the pigs for years and now we're here to watch them drive into Uberauen. I wonder what will happen next?"

"Look. Here comes the first American tank," Eberhardt said while pointing down the road. "I wonder why he doesn't drive on up to where the city walls have been removed at the Bahnhof Strasse."

The young men watched the American tank approach the eighteenth-century Gerstenfelder Gate, where so many Uberauen memories had taken place. The tank driver pulled levers to make the huge vehicle lurch left and right, until it was aligned with the city gate and it started to drive through.

"Oh my God," shouted Rudi. "Look, it's stuck!"

The young men and other neighbors and townspeople watched as the monstrous machine made loud scraping and banging noises. Black smoke poured out the exhaust while the driver attempted to force the tank through the narrow opening. Finally, the driver had to give up and back out. Suddenly, the inside second-story wall collapsed, and the apartment above the gate could be seen with all its furnishings, like a dollhouse.

Everyone watched and followed the convoy of Americans as they drove up the Bahnhof Strasse with Jeeps and with some soldiers on foot. Some of the residents of Uberauen decided to get on the good side of the new power brokers in town. Those who could speak English came up to shake hands with the Americans.

"I can't speak English and I don't feel like being that chummy with the Americans, but I'm sure glad this awful war is over for Uberauen," whispered Gretel to Emma.

Emma replied, "That's exactly the way I feel. We've lost Christoph Baumfeller and Johann Jessat in this terrible war, and I don't feel like being buddy-buddy with these guys." Gretel and her family watched to see what would happen next with the Americans.

Everyone observed as the Americans came into town and drove up to the marketplace. The trucks, Jeeps and soldiers began to survey the area. Then an American officer stood up on his Jeep and shouted above the crowd, "Who was the man who waved the white flag?"

"Oh my God," said Emma while clutching Gretel by the arm. "We got Max safely away from being shot by Georg Pucher, that *Schweinehund*, and now the Americans may want to shoot him."

Then someone spoke up: "That was Herr Bergmeister," and pointed toward Max, while others pointed toward the Golden Knight.

An American soldier came over to Max and, holding a pistol, motioned for him to approach the American officer's Jeep. A translator asked Max, "Are you the man who waved the flag of surrender?"

What could he say? "Yes, Herr Offizer," answered Max.

"Tell this man that I want to talk to him about setting up a new city government. Is there a place where we can talk?" the American commander asked coolly.

"Where can we speak privately?" asked the translator.

"My business is down there," Max said, pointing to the Golden Knight. "We can talk there privately."

The American officer agreed and sent some soldiers to search the whole property for snipers, booby traps and hidden soldiers. In the meantime, the citizens of Uberauen began to tell the Americans which of their neighbors had been working with the Nazis. The Americans had the suspects line up with their hands against the wall of St. Severinus Church, next to the Blumentritt sisters' old store.

When the sergeant came back and said that the Golden Knight was safe, the officer's driver drove the Jeep down Adolf Hitler Strasse, through the big gate and into the courtyard of the Golden Knight.

Hans shouted, "Look, Mama, the Americans are driving into the Golden Knight."

Everyone knows everyone else in Uberauen and everyone else's business, so a large crowd of people followed the American officer's two-vehicle convoy to the courtyard at the Golden Knight. Once the Americans were parked and all the extended Bergmeister family was inside, however, the officer ordered the big wooden gates to be closed so nobody could come in or see what would take place.

Max and Rudi led the Americans into the dining room of the Golden Knight and offered them seats at the Regulars' Table. In the meantime, everyone else in the family came inside and tried to listen while staying out of sight.

"Helmut, Hans, take Hubert and Gudrun and stay in Grandfather Wilhelm's bedroom," said Gretel.

"Oh, Mama, we want to watch," said Hans.

"I know, but we all have to stay away for now," Gretel told the boys.

Rudi held up a beer stein and asked the Americans, "Beer?"

The officer and those men present all accepted with blank looks on their faces.

"Should I offer to feed them?" Gretel asked Emma. Emma had been feeding people her whole life and it seemed like a logical thing to ask. "After all, they're sitting right here and they can take anything they want anyway. It might be better to just be ourselves and offer them some lunch."

Max and Rudi were trying to answer the Americans' questions with the aid of a translator. After it appeared that the planning was finished, Gretel came cautiously into the room and stood where she could be seen. When the American officer looked at her as if to say, "Yes, what is it?" Gretel made the motion of feeding herself and asked, *"Essen?"* (Food?)

"Well, Lieutenant, do you feel like taking the risk of tasting my food for poison?" the officer asked with a slight smile.

"Yes, sir," said the soldier. "It sure smells mighty good, sir."

While the men discussed who would be a suitable postwar mayor for Uberauen, Gretel brought in the food.

As Gretel put the plates of food in front of the Americans, she thought, *This is so strange and painful. The Americans killed Johann Jessat and our sweet Christoph Baumfeller. Now I'm serving them in the Golden Knight. Am I doing the right thing?*

During the discussions, Max told the Americans that he had joined the National Socialist Party in 1937 because the Storm Detachment workers at city hall had come to eat lunch each day at the Golden Knight. He told them that he was not a leader and that, in fact, Edith Luder and Georg Pucher would have loved to shoot him if they could have.

After a couple of hours of lunch and discussion, the Americans and their vehicles left the Golden Knight. The translator, who spoke an authentic southwest German dialect, asked if the officers could rent rooms at the Golden Knight. Since Gretel had learned to speak with perfect Schwäbian dialect in Stuttgart, she shocked the German American translator by speaking in his dialect. Everyone was pleased, and the German American postwar relationship could start.

Gretel took the boys upstairs to their room, where she hoped to get Hubert to take a nap. It had been an exciting and exhausting day. As she had done during her whole life, Gretel walked over to her window and looked down on the Brunnen Gasse. People were walking and driving by as usual. The Nazi flag had been removed from city hall. Gretel could see the Schwäbian American soldier sitting at Frau Luder's old window.

City hall from Gretel's window

"That is so strange, boys. The Americans are using Frau Luder's old office at city hall," Gretel said to her sleeping sons.

Suddenly the American, who Gretel recognized as the translator, threw the window open and yelled across the Brunnen Gasse in perfect

Schwäbisch, Otto's German dialect. He asked, "Hey, girlie, ya got a sewing machine? Our pants are all too big or too small."

Gretel gasped in shock. "Oh my God," she said, "what should I do? It's so strange to see that American who speaks *Schwäbisch*!" After a moment to gather her thoughts, Gretel opened her window and answered, "Yes, I can sew them for you. Just come over to the entrance gate."

As she stood frozen in that spot, Gretel looked down upon her suddenly changed world and wondered out loud, "Americans in Uberauen! Dear God, what will my life be like from now on?"

Epilogue

The town of Uberauen is based on a quaint Franconian walled village where the events from *Gretel's Cross* actually took place.

Gretel and the boys remained in Uberauen with Emma and Max until it was safe for them to return to Stuttgart in 1946. During the following years, Gretel and her family often spent summer vacations in Uberauen.

Anna and Eugen lived their whole lives in the neighborhoods of Uberauen. They are no longer living, but some of the family monuments are still in the town cemetery.

Gretel and Otto lived long and wonderful lives together in Stuttgart-Vaihingen until their deaths in the 1990s.

Their oldest living son, Hans, worked as a chief financial officer—like his father. Hans married and had two children and one granddaughter.

Second son Helmut became a doctor of engineering and worked as an influential executive for an international firm in France, Germany, and Belgium. Helmut and his wife, Barbara, now deceased, had two sons and three granddaughters.

Gretel and Otto's third son, Hubert, to whom this book is dedicated, trained in Paris and Stuttgart. For many years he worked as a talented professional display-designer in Stuttgart and later ran his own business in Florida. Hubert also has had an engaging and fulfilling life that includes a long, loving relationship.

Today Franconia is a vibrant, picturesque area and a delightful place to visit. It still has the same charm and positive aspects of small-town living that prepared and supported Gretel during times of challenge, upheaval and sacrifice. Sustained by love and loyalty, she lived to convey peace and promise into the next generations.

As for me, the writer, in the present, each trip I make to the town that is the inspiration for Uberauen is like returning home for me too. The family histories that I lovingly relate in this book have become my own cherished memories.

Notes

Footnote 3, continued from p. 20 – Barbara's death.

As a child, Gretel did not yet know the story of her grandmother's drowning death. It was always kept hush-hush. What really caused Barbara's depression will probably always remain a mystery. Was she clinically depressed? Were there problems with her husband and marriage? In 1906, she lived in a tightly knit small town of about one thousand inhabitants. Everyone knew everyone else and everyone's business. Family rumors indicate that Barbara's daughter Elizabeth had given birth to two children who were fathered by her fiancé, but no wedding had yet been planned. Speculation, scandal and gossip about the situation would surely have been rampant.

Barbara was a mother and wife of a prominent businessman. The shame, religious implications, and possible bullying or shunning may have finally been too much for her to bear. It is thought that she committed suicide by drowning herself in the pond used for cutting ice in the winter. Her daughter eventually married the father of their children. The true causes of Barbara's death may never be known.

Footnote 14, continued from p. 87 – Rosa's death.

Rosa and the character, Franz, had really been lovers, but we don't know how long the relationship lasted. Franz actually was Anna's biological father, not Joseph. As Anna reached age eight she looked so much like her biological father that the whole town noticed. Rosa almost certainly lived with great guilt and felt trapped in her unhappy marriage. It was suspected that the shunning, shame and bullying of her neighbors and the problems in her marriage, drove Rosa into a severe depression. The last straw could possibly have been her lover's marriage to Rosa's own half-sister, Frieda. That wedding had taken place a few months before Rosa, in shame and despair, tragically took her own life.

Glossary

Äpfel – apples
Bahnhof – train station
Bis später – until later, see ya later
Blauenbronn – town of Blue Fountain
Blockwart – combination of civil defense and spy
Bratkartoffeln – sliced, fried potatoes
Bratwurst – grilled or fried sausage
Brunnen Gasse – Fountain Lane
Bund – association
Das ist eine blöde Kuh – That is a stupid cow
Danke Schön – (thanks pretty); thank you
déjà vu – from French, meaning already seen
Deutschland – Germany
Du Abschaum der Menscheit – you scum of humanity
Dumme Sau – dumb sow (female pig), used as a swear word
Es tut mir leid – it does me pain, I'm sorry
Finanzamt – finance office, city hall
Forellenbach –Trout Stream, town of
Forellenbacher Strasse – trout stream street
Forellenbacher Gate – gate leading to town of Forellenbach (trout stream)
Franken – Franconia, region of Germany principally in Bavaria
Frankfurter Würstchen – pork sausages made in the Frankfurt region,
    similar to and the origin for frankfurters or hot dogs in the USA
Fränkisch – Franconian dialect
Frau – Mrs. or woman
Fräulein – Miss or unmarried young woman
Frikadellen – German hamburgers
Fünfzig Millionen Mark – fifty million marks (Germany currency
    before the euro)
Garten – garden
Gemischter Salat – mixed salad
Gerstenfeld – Barley Field, town of
Gretel – a nickname for Margaret (Gretel's full name is Eva Margarethe
    Geyer Forner)
Grossvater – grandfather

Grüss Gott – greet God, a way of saying hello in southern Germany
Guten Morgen – good morning
Haselnussbrötle – hazelnut cookies
Haus – house
Hausfrau – housewife
Hausgemacht – homemade
Herr – mister
Himmelbett – heavenly bed, canopy bed
Hof – courtyard, open area surrounded by walls or buildings
Hoppe, Hoppe Reiter, wenn er fällt dann schreit er – Hop, Hop rider,
   when he falls, then he screams
Ja – yes
Kaiser – emperor
Kappelle – brass band
Kartoffel – potato
Kartoffelsalat – potato salad
Kartoffelpuffer – potato pancakes
Kartoffelknödel – potato dumplings
Keller – cellar
Kekse – cookies
Kleiderschrank – clothes cabinet, wardrobe, freestanding clothes closet
Kerze – candle
Kerzlein – small candle
Kirchweih – consecration of a church, usually with a street fair
Knödel – potato or bread dumpling
Küche – kitchen
Lasst uns Erfreuen – let us rejoice
Leberwurst – liverwurst
Leiterwagen – ladder wagon
Lobet den Herrn – Praise ye the Lord
Luder – bitch, derogatory word for a woman
Mädchen – girl, maiden
Mädel – girl, maiden
Mama –Mother
Maultaschen – *lit.*: mouth pockets; savory ravioli-style meat-filled
   pastry (origin story: Monks in Baden Württemberg attempted to
   fool God during Lent by putting spinach in the ground meat and
   covering it with pasta)
Marktplatz – marketplace
Metzgerei – butcher shop

Mit – with
Nazis – National Socialist Workers Party, National Socialists
Ölberg Bund – mount of olives association (ölen: to oil; drink a lot to
  oil your throat)
Oma – grandma
Opa – grandpa
Onkel – uncle
Ordnung muss sein – order must be, we have to have order
Pass auf dich auf – take care of yourself
Pilzenpfad – mushroom or toadstool path
Pferdeäpfel – horse apples; horse manure
Putzen – to clean (Yiddish has a different, saucy meaning of the word)
Putzfrau – cleaning woman
Rathaus – city hall
Rindfleisch – beef flesh, meat
Rote Wurst – red sausage, a favorite bratwurst of the Swabian region
Schadenfreude – malicious joy, to feel joy at the misfortune of another
St. Severinus Kirche – Saint Severinus church
Schleimscheisser – slime-shitter, brown noser
Schwaben – Swabia; cultural, historic, and linguistic region in
  southwestern Germany, which includes the city of Stuttgart
Schwäbisch, Schwab – people from Schwaben
Schwäbisch – adjective to describe something from Schwaben or the
  Schwaben dialect
Schwein – pig or hog
Schweine – pigs or hogs
Schweinefleisch – pork meat
Schweinehund – pig dog, offensive swear word in German
Schweinsbratwurst – pork sausage
Soch ner Nix (Sag' nur nichts) – say just nothing; don't say anything
  (Franconian dialect)
So Nimm Denn Meine Hände – So take my hands
Spätzle – *lit.*: little sparrows; soft egg noodles from region around Stuttgart
Springerle – *lit.*: little runner; cookies with embossed designs
Stammtisch – Regulars' Table
Stille Nacht, Heilige Nacht –Silent Night, Holy Night
Strassenbahn – streetcar, trolley
Sturmabteilung – storm detachment, storm troopers, SA, original
  paramilitary wing of the Nazi Party
Tante – aunt

Thüringer Wurst – Thüringen style sausage

Tor – gate

Treulich geführt – truly led, "Bridal Chorus" by German composer Richard Wagner known in English speaking countries as the "Wedding March" or "Here Comes the Bride"

Uberauen – upper damp or soggy meadow, town of

Überlandwerk – an overland company for electricity, rural electrification project

Untermenschen – subhumans, inferior races

Vater – father

Verbrannt – burnt

Verdammt – damn it

Vielen Dank – many thanks, thanks a lot

Viel Spass – lots of fun, have fun

Wach auf! – wake up!

Was ist loss? – what's happening, what's up, what's going on, what's wrong?

Waschküche – wash kitchen, laundry room

Weihnachten – Christmas

Weihnachtsmarkt – Christmas market

Weihrauch – incense, frankincense

Weihnachtsstollen – Christmas fruit stollen

Wehrmacht – armed forces, military forces, defense forces

Weisswurst – white sausage, a traditional Bavarian sausage made from minced veal and pork back bacon

Wespennester – wasp nest, type of macaroon cookie

Wild – wild, venison, or deer

Wildschwein – wild boar

Wirtshaus zum Goldenen Ritter – Inn of the Golden Knight

Wurst – sausage

Würste – sausages

Zeppelin – a type of rigid airship or dirigible

Zimtsterne – cinnamon star, spiced Christmas cookie

Photo Credits

Made in the USA
Charleston, SC
21 July 2016